SOCIAL SECURITY LEGISLATION
SUPPLEMENT 2018/19

General Editor
Nick Wikeley, M.A. (Cantab)

Commentary by
Ian Hooker, LL.B.
Formerly Lecturer in Law, University of Nottingham
Formerly Chairman, Social Security Appeal Tribunals

John Mesher, B.A., B.C.L. (Oxon), LL.M. (Yale)

Edward Mitchell, LL.B.
Judge of the Upper Tribunal

Richard Poynter B.C.L., M.A. (Oxon)
Judge of the Upper Tribunal

Mark Rowland, LL.B.

Christopher Ward, M.A. (Cantab)
Judge of the Upper Tribunal

Nick Wikeley, M.A. (Cantab)
Judge of the Upper Tribunal,
Emeritus Professor of Law, University of Southampton

Consultant Editor
Child Poverty Action Group

GW00691236

SWEET & MAXWELL

THOMSON REUTERS

Published in 2019 by Thomson Reuters,
trading as Sweet & Maxwell.
Registered in England & Wales. Company No. 1679046.
Registered office 5 Canada Square, Canary Wharf, London E14 5AQ.

Typeset by Wright and Round Ltd., Gloucester
Printed and bound by CPI Group (UK) Ltd, Croydon, CR0 4YY

For further information on our products and services,
visit www.sweetandmaxwell.co.uk

No natural forests were destroyed to make this product.
Only farmed timber was used and re-planted.

A CIP catalogue record for this book is
available from the British Library

ISBN 978–0–414–07075-2

PREFACE

This is the Supplement to the 2018/19 edition of the five-volume work, *Social Security Legislation*, which was published in September 2018. Part I of this Supplement contains new legislation, presented in the same format as in the main volumes. Parts II, III, IV, V and VI contain the standard updating material—a separate Part for each volume of the main work–which amends the legislative text and key aspects of the commentary, drawing attention to important recent case law, so as to be up to date as at December 10, 2018. Part VII includes new primary and secondary legislation relating to social security matters, both substantive and procedural, as are currently devolved in Scotland. Finally, Part VIII gives some notice of changes forthcoming between December 2018 and the date to which the main work (2019/20 edition) will be up to date (mid-April 2019) along with the April 2019 benefit rates.

The many updating changes included in this Supplement describe and analyse important developments in the Upper Tribunal case law relating to the descriptors for both personal independence payment (PIP) and employment and support allowance (ESA). There has also been extensive significant case law in both the Upper Tribunal and the courts impacting on the right to reside. There are two further Commencement Orders relating to the controversial phased roll-out of universal credit.

As always, we welcome comments from those who use this Supplement. Please address these to the General Editor, Nick Wikeley, c/o School of Law, The University of Southampton, Highfield, Southampton SO17 1BJ (njw@soton.ac.uk).

Ian Hooker
John Mesher
Edward Mitchell   Mark Rowland
Richard Poynter   Christopher Ward
                                   Nick Wikeley

December 10, 2018

CONTENTS

CONTENTS

USING THE UPDATING MATERIAL IN THIS SUPPLEMENT

The amendments and updating material contained in Parts II–VI of this Supplement are keyed in to the page numbers of the relevant main volume of *Social Security Legislation 2018/19*. Where there have been a significant number of changes to a provision, the whole section, subsection, paragraph or regulation, as amended will tend to be reproduced. Other changes may be noted by an instruction to insert or substitute new material or to delete part of the existing text. The date the change takes effect is also noted. Where explanation is needed of the change, or there is updating relating to existing annotations but no change to the legislation, you will also find commentary in this Supplement. The updating material explains new statutory material, takes on board Upper Tribunal or court decisions, or gives prominence to points which now seem to warrant more detailed attention.

For the most part any relevant new legislation since the main volumes were published is contained in Part I, while amendments to existing legislative provisions are contained in Parts II–VI respectively, together with commentary on new case law. This Supplement amends the text of the main volumes of *Social Security Legislation 2018/19* to be up to date as at December 10, 2018.

Nick Wikeley
General Editor

PAGES OF MAIN VOLUMES AFFECTED
BY MATERIAL IN THIS SUPPLEMENT

Main volume page affected	Relevant paragraph in supplement
VOLUME I	
p.27	2.001
p.49	2.002
p.75	2.003
p.225	2.004
p.235	2.005
p.239	2.006
p.343	2.007
pp.396–397	2.008
p.424	2.009
p.430	2.010
p.462	2.011
p.464	2.012
p.572	2.013
p.761	2.014
p.764	2.015
p.767	2.016
p.776	2.017
p.777	2.018
p.797	2.019
p.802	2.020
p.804	2.021
p.807	2.022
p.810	2.023
p.812	2.024
p.813	2.025
p.814	2.026
p.817	2.027
p.822	2.028
p.830	2.029
p.832	2.030
p.864	2.031
p.865	2.032
p.921	2.032.1
p.1036	2.033
p.1072	2.034
p.1079	2.035
p.1079	2.036
p.1085	2.037
pp.1090–1100	2.038
p.1099	2.038.1
p.1140	2.038.2

VOLUME II

VOLUME IV

TABLE OF ABBREVIATIONS USED IN THIS SERIES

1978 Act	Employment Protection (Consolidation) Act 1978
1979 Act	Pneumoconiosis (Workers' Compensation) Act 1979
1995 Regulations	Social Security (Incapacity for Work) (General) Regulations 1995
1998 Act	Social Security Act 1998
1999 Regulations	Social Security and Child Support (Decisions and Appeals) Regulations 1999
2002 Act	Tax Credits Act 2002
2004 Act	Child Trust Funds Act 2004
AA	Attendance Allowance
AA Regulations	Social Security (Attendance Allowance) Regulations 1991
AAC	Administrative Appeal Chamber
AACR	Administrative Appeals Chamber Reports
AAW	Algemene Arbeidsongeschiktheidswet (Dutch General Act on Incapacity for Work)
A.C.	Law Reports Appeal Cases
A.C.D.	Administrative Court Digest
ADHD	Attention Deficit Hyperactivity Disorder
Admin	Administrative Court
Admin L.R.	Administrative Law Reports
Administration Act	Social Security Administration Act 1992
AIDS	Acquired Immune Deficiency Syndrome
AIIS	Analogous Industrial Injuries Scheme
AIP	assessed income period
All E.R.	All England Reports
All E.R. (E.C.)	All England Reports (European Cases)
AMA	American Medical Association
AO	Adjudication Officer
AO	Authorised Officer
AOG	*Adjudication Officers Guide*
art.	article
Art.	Article
ASD	Autistic Spectrum Disorder
ASP	Act of the Scottish Parliament
ASPP	Additional Statutory Paternity Pay

Table of Abbreviations used in this Series

A.T.C.	Annotated Tax Cases
Attendance Allowance Regulations	Social Security (Attendance Allowance) Regulations 1991
AWT	All Work Test
BA	Benefits Agency
BAMS	Benefits Agency Medical Service
B.C.L.C.	Butterworths Company Law Cases
B.H.R.C.	Butterworths Human Rights Cases
B.L.G.R.	Butterworths Local Government Reports
Blue Books	*The Law Relating to Social Security*, Vols 1–11
BMI	body mass index
B.M.L.R.	Butterworths Medico Legal Reports
B.P.I.R.	Bankruptcy and Personal Insolvency Reports
B.T.C.	British Tax Cases
BTEC	Business and Technology Education Council
B.V.C.	British Value Added Tax Reporter
B.W.C.C.	Butterworths Workmen's Compensation Cases
C	Commissioner's decision
c.	chapter
C&BA 1992	Social Security Contributions and Benefits Act 1992
CAA 2001	Capital Allowances Act 2001
CAB	Citizens Advice Bureau
CAO	Chief Adjudication Officer
CBA 1975	Child Benefit Act 1975
CBJSA	Contribution-Based Jobseeker's Allowance
C.C.L. Rep.	Community Care Law Reports
CCM	HMRC New Tax Credits Claimant Compliance Manual
CCN	New Tax Credits Claimant Compliance Manual
C.E.C.	European Community Cases
CERA	cortical evoked response audiogram
CESA	Contribution-based Employment and Support Allowance
CFS	chronic fatigue syndrome
Ch.	Chancery Division Law Reports
Child Benefit Regulations	Child Benefit (General) Regulations 2006
CIR	Commissioners of Inland Revenue
Citizenship Directive	Directive 2004/38

Table of Abbreviations used in this Series

CJEC	Court of Justice of the European Communities
CJEU	Court of Justice of the European Union
Claims and Payments Regulations	Social Security (Claims and Payments) Regulations 1987
Claims and Payments Regulations 1979	Social Security (Claims and Payments) Regulations 1979
CMA	Chief Medical Adviser
CMEC	Child Maintenance and Enforcement Commission
C.M.L.R.	Common Market Law Reports
C.O.D.	Crown Office Digest
Com. L.R.	Commercial Law Reports
Commissioners Procedure Regulations	Social Security Commissioners (Procedure) Regulations 1999
Community treaties	EU treaties
Community institution	EU institution
Community instrument	EU instrument
Community law	EU law
Community legislation	EU legislation
Community obligation	EU obligation
Community provision	EU provision
Computation of Earnings Regulations	Social Security Benefit (Computation of Earnings) Regulations 1978
Computation of Earnings Regulations 1996	Social Security Benefit (Computation of Earnings) Regulations 1996
Con. L.R.	Construction Law Reports
Consequential Provisions Act	Social Security (Consequential Provisions) Act 1992
Const. L.J.	Construction Law Journal
Contributions and Benefits Act	Social Security Contributions and Benefits Act 1992
COPD	chronic obstructive pulmonary disease
Council Tax Benefit Regulations	Council Tax Benefit (General) Regulations 1992 (SI 1992/1814)
CP	Carer Premium
CP	Chamber President
CPAG	Child Poverty Action Group
C.P.L.R.	Civil Practice Law Reports
CPR	Civil Procedure Rules
C.P. Rep.	Civil Procedure Reports
Cr. App. R.	Criminal Appeal Reports
Cr. App. R. (S.)	Criminal Appeal Reports (Sentencing)
CRCA 2005	Commissioners for Revenue and Customs Act 2005

Credits Regulations 1974	Social Security (Credits) Regulations 1974
Credits Regulations 1975	Social Security (Credits) Regulations 1975
Crim. L.R.	Criminal Law Review
CRU	Compensation Recovery Unit
CSA 1995	Child Support Act 1995
CSIH	Inner House of the Court of Session
CSOH	Outer House of the Court of Session
CS(NI)O	Child Support (Northern Ireland) Order 1995
CSO	Child Support Officer
CSPSSA 2000	Child Support, Pensions and Social Security Act 2000
CTA	Common Travel Area
CTB	Council Tax Benefit
CTC	Child Tax Credit
CTC Regulations	Child Tax Credit Regulations 2002
CTF	child trust fund
CTS	Carpal Tunnel Syndrome
CV	curriculum vitae
DCA	Department for Constitutional Affairs
DCP	Disabled Child Premium
Decisions and Appeals Regulations 1999	Social Security Contributions (Decisions and Appeals) Regulations 1999
Dependency Regulations	Social Security Benefit (Dependency) Regulations 1977
DfEE	Department for Education and Employment
DHSS	Department of Health and Social Security
DIY	do it yourself
Digital Service Regulations 2014	Universal Credit (Digital Service) Amendment Regulations 2014
Disability Living Allowance Regulations	Social Security (Disability Living Allowance) Regulations
DLA	Disability Living Allowance
DLA Regulations	Social Security (Disability Living Allowance) Regulations 1991
DLAAB Regs	Disability Living Allowance Advisory Board Regulations 1991
DLADWAA 1991	Disability Living Allowance and Disability Working Allowance Act 1991
DM	Decision Maker
DMA	Decision-making and Appeals
DMG	Decision Makers' Guidance
DMP	Delegated Medical Practitioner

Table of Abbreviations used in this Series

DP	Disability Premium
DPTC	Disabled Person's Tax Credit
D.R.	European Commission of Human Rights Decisions and Reports
DRO	Debt Relief Order
DSD	Department for Social Development (Northern Ireland)
DSDNI	Department for Social Development, Northern Ireland
DSS	Department of Social Security
DTI	Department of Trade and Industry
DWA	Disability Working Allowance
DWP	Department for Work and Pensions
DWPMS	Department for Work and Pensions Medical Service
EAA	Extrinsic Allergic Alveolitis
EAT	Employment Appeal Tribunal
EC	Treaty establishing the European Economic Community
ECHR	European Convention on Human Rights
ECJ	European Court of Justice
ECSMA Agreement	European Convention on Social and Medical Assistance
E.C.R.	European Court Report
ECtHR	European Court of Human Rights
Ed.C.R.	Education Case Reports
EEA	European Economic Area
EEA Regulations	Immigration (European Economic Area) Regulations 2006
EEC	European Economic Community
EESSI	Electronic Exchange of Social Security Information
E.G.	Estates Gazette
E.G.L.R.	Estates Gazette Law Reports
EHIC	European Health Insurance Card
E.H.R.L.R.	European Human Rights Law Review
E.H.R.R.	European Human Rights Reports
E.L.R.	Education Law Reports
EMA	Education Maintenance Allowance
EMO	Examining Medical Officer
EMP	Examining Medical Practitioner
Employment and Support Allowance Regulations	Employment and Support Allowance Regulations 2008
Enforceable Community right	Enforceable EU right

English Regulations (eligible children)	Care Planning, Placement and Case Review (England) Regulations 2010
English Regulations (relevant children)	Care Leavers (England) Regulations 2010
Eq. L.R.	Equality Law Reports
ERA	Employment, Retention and Advancement Scheme
ERA	Evoked Response Audiometry
ERA 1996	Employment Rights Act 1996
ER(NI)O	Employers Rights (Northern Ireland) Order 1996
ES	Employment Service
ESA	Employment and Support Allowance
ESA Regulations 2008	Employment and Support Allowance Regulations 2008
ESA WCAt	Employment and Support Allowance Work Capability Assessment
ESC	Employer Supported Childcare
ETA 1973	Employment and Training Act 1973
ETA(NI) 1950	Employment and Training Act (Northern Ireland) 1950
EU	European Union
Eu.L.R.	European Law Reports
European Coal and Steel Communities	European Union
EWCA Civ	Civil Division of the Court of Appeal in England and Wales
EWHC Admin	Administrative Court division of the High Court (England and Wales)
F(No.2)A 2005	Finance (No.2) Act 2005
FA 1990	Finance Act 1990
FA 1993	Finance Act 1993
FA 1996	Finance Act 1996
FA 2000	Finance Act 2000
FA 2004	Finance Act 2004
Fam. Law	Family Law
FAS	Financial Assistance Scheme
F.C.R.	Family Court Reporter
FIS	Family Income Supplement
FISMA 2000	Financial Services and Markets Act 2000
Fixing and Adjustment of Rates Regulations 1976	Child Benefit and Social Security (Fixing and Adjustment of Rates) Regulations 1976
F.L.R.	Family Law Reports
Former Regulations	Employment and Support Allowance (Transitional Provisions, Housing Benefit and Council Tax Benefit) (Existing Awards) Regulations 2010

FME	further medical evidence
FOTRA	Free of Tax to Residents Abroad
FRAA	flat rate accrual amount
FSCS	Financial Services Compensation Scheme
FSMA 2000	Financial Services and Markets Act 2000
FSVG	Bundesgestez über die Sozialversicherung freiberuflich selbständig Erwerbstätiger (Austrian Federal Act of 30 November 1978 on social insurance for the self-employed in the liberal professions)
FTT	First-tier Tribunal
GA	Guardian's Allowance
GA Regulations	Social Security (Guardian's Allowance) Regulations 1975
General Benefit Regulations 1982	Social Security (General Benefit) Regulations 1982
General Regulations	Statutory Maternity Pay (General) Regulations 1986
GMP	Guaranteed Minimum Pension
G.P.	General Practitioner
GPoW	genuine prospects of work
GRA	Gender Recognition Act
GRB	Graduated Retirement Benefit
GRP	Graduated Retirement Pension
G.W.D.	Greens Weekly Digest
HASSASSA	Health and Social Services and Social Security Adjudication Act 1983
HB	Housing Benefit
HCD	House of Commons Debates
HCP	health care professional
HCWA	House of Commons Written Answer
HESC	Health, Education and Social Care
HIV	Human Immunodeficiency Virus
H.L.R.	Housing Law Reports
HMIT	Her Majesty's Inspector of Taxes
HMRC	Her Majesty's Revenue and Customs
HMSO	Her Majesty's Stationery Office
HNCIP	(Housewives') Non-Contributory Invalidity Pension
Hospital In-Patients Regulations 1975	Social Security (Hospital In-Patients) Regulations 1975
Housing Benefit Regulations	Housing Benefit Regulations 2006
HPP	Higher Pensioner Premium
HRA 1998	Human Rights Act 1998
H.R.L.R.	Human Rights Law Reports–UK Cases

HRR	High Risk Renewal
HSE	Health and Safety Executive
IAC	Immigration and Asylum Chamber
IAP	Intensive Activity Period
IB	Invalidity Benefit
IB/IS/SDA	Incapacity Benefits' Regime
IBJSA	Income-Based Jobseeker's Allowance
IB PCA	Incapacity Benefit Personal Capability Assessment
IB Regs	Social Security (Incapacity Benefit) Regulations 1994
IB Regulations	Social Security (Incapacity Benefit) Regulations 1994
IBS	Irritable Bowel Syndrome
ICA	Invalid Care Allowance
ICA Regulations	Social Security (Invalid Care Allowance) Regulations 1976
ICA Unit	Invalid Care Allowance Unit
I.C.R.	Industrial Cases Reports
ICTA 1988	Income and Corporation Taxes Act 1988
I(EEA) Regulations	Immigration (European Economic Area) Regulations 2006
IFW Regulations	Incapacity for Work (General) Regulations 1995
I.I.	Industrial Injuries
IIAC	Industrial Injuries Advisory Council
IIDB	Industrial Injuries Disablement Benefit
ILO	International Labour Organization
ILO Convention	International Labour Organization Convention
ILR	indefinite leave to remain
Imm. A.R.	Immigration Appeal Reports
Immigration and Asylum Regulations	Social Security (Immigration and Asylum) Consequential Amendments Regulations 2000
Incapacity for Work Regulations	Social Security (Incapacity for Work) (General) Regulations 1995
Income Support General Regulations	Income Support (General) Regulations 1987
Income Support Regulations	Income Support (General) Regulations 1987
Increases for Dependants Regulations	Social Security Benefit (Dependency) Regulations 1977
IND	Immigration and Nationality Directorate of the Home Office

I.N.L.R.	Immigration and Nationality Law Reports
IO	Information Officer
I.O.	Insurance Officer
IPPR	Institute of Public Policy Research
IRC	Inland Revenue Commissioners
IRESA	Income-Related Employment and Support Allowance
I.R.L.R.	Industrial Relations Law Reports
IS Regs	Income Support Regulations
IS Regulations	Income Support (General) Regulations 1987
IS	Income Support
ISA	Individual Savings Account
ISA Regulations 1998	Individual Savings Account Regulations 1998
ITA 2007	Income Tax Act 2007
ITEPA	Income Tax (Earnings and Pensions) Act 2003
ITEPA 2003	Income Tax, Earnings and Pensions Act 2003
I.T.L. Rep.	International Tax Law Reports
ITS	Independent Tribunal Service
ITTOIA	Income Tax (Trading and Other Income) Act 2005
ITTOIA 2005	Income Tax (Trading and Other Income) Act 2005
IVB	Invalidity Benefit
IWA 1994	Social Security (Incapacity for Work) Act 1994
IW	Incapacity for Work
IW (Dependants) Regs	Social Security (Incapacity for Work) (Dependants) Regulations
IW (General) Regs	Social Security (Incapacity for Work) (General) Regulations 1995
IW (Transitional) Regs	Incapacity for Work (Transitional) Regulations
JD(NI)O 1995	Jobseekers (Northern Ireland) Order 1995
Jobseeker's Allowance Regulations	Jobseeker's Allowance Regulations 1996
Jobseeker's Regulations 1996	Jobseeker's Allowance Regulations 1996
J.P.	Justice of the Peace Reports
J.P.L.	Journal of Public Law
JSA	Jobseeker's Allowance
JSA 1995	Jobseekers Act 1995
JSA (NI) Regulations	Jobseeker's Allowance (Northern Ireland) Regulations 1996

Table of Abbreviations used in this Series

JSA (Transitional) Regulations	Jobseeker's Allowance (Transitional) Regulations 1996
JSA Regulations 1996	Jobseekers Allowance Regulations 1996
JSA Regulations	Jobseeker's Allowance Regulations 1996
JS(NI)O 1995	Jobseekers (Northern Ireland) Order 1995
J.S.S.L.	Journal of Social Security Law
J.S.W.F.L.	Journal of Social Welfare and Family Law
J.S.W.L.	Journal of Social Welfare Law
K.B.	Law Reports, King's Bench
K.I.R.	Knight's Industrial Law Reports
L.& T.R.	Landlord and Tenant Reports
LCW	limited capability for work
LCWA	Limited Capability for Work Assessment
LCWRA	Limited Capability for Work-Related Activity
LEA	local education authority
LEL	Lower Earnings Limit
LET	low earnings threshold
L.G.R.	Local Government Law Reports
L.G. Rev.	Local Government Review
L.J.R.	Law Journal Reports
Ll.L.Rep	Lloyd's List Law Report
Lloyd's Rep.	Lloyd's Law Reports
LRP	liable relative payment
L.S.G.	Law Society Gazette
LTAHAW	Living Together as Husband and Wife
Luxembourg Court	Court of Justice of the European Union (also referred to as CJEC and ECJ)
MA	Maternity Allowance
MAF	Medical Assessment Framework
MAT	Medical Appeal Tribunal
Maternity Allowance Regulations	Social Security (Maternity Allowance) Regulations 1987
Maternity Benefit Regulations	Social Security (Maternity Benefit) Regulations 1975
ME	myalgic encephalomyelitis
Medical Evidence Regulations	Social Security (Medical Evidence) Regulations 1976
M.H.L.R.	Mental Health Law Reports
MHP	mental health problems
MIG	minimum income guarantee
Migration Regulations	Employment and Support Allowance (Transitional Provisions, Housing Benefit and Council Tax Benefit (Existing Awards) (No.2) Regulations 2010

MIRAS	mortgage interest relief at source
MRI	Magnetic resonance imaging
MRSA	methicillin-resistant Staphylococcus aureus
MS	Medical Services
MWAS	Jobseeker's Allowance (Mandatory Work Activity Scheme) Regulations 2011
NACRO	National Association for the Care and Resettlement of Offenders
NCB	National Coal Board
NDPD	Notes on the Diagnosis of Prescribed Diseases
NHS	National Health Service
NI	National Insurance
N.I.	Northern Ireland Law Reports
NI Com	Northern Ireland Commissioner
NI	National Insurance
NICA	Northern Ireland Court of Appeal
NICs	National Insurance Contributions
NICom	Northern Ireland Commissioner
NINO	National Insurance Number
NIQB	Northern Ireland, Queen's Bench Division
NIRS 2	National Insurance Recording System
N.L.J.	New Law Journal
NMC	Nursing and Midwifery Council
Northern Ireland Contributions and Benefits Act	Social Security Contributions and Benefits (Northern Ireland) Act 1992
N.P.C.	New Property Cases
NS&I	National Savings and Investments
NTC Manual	Clerical procedures manual on tax credits
NUM	National Union of Mineworkers
OA	Osteoarthritis
OCD	Obsessive Compulsive Disorder
OGA	Agricultural Insurance Organisation
Ogus, Barendt and Wikeley	A. Ogus, E. Barendt and N. Wikeley, *The Law of Social Security* (4th edn, Butterworths, 1995)
O.J.	Official Journal
Old Cases Act	Industrial Injuries and Diseases (Old Cases) Act 1975
OPA	Overseas Pensions Act 1973
OPB	One Parent Benefit
O.P.L.R.	Occupational Pensions Law Reports

Table of Abbreviations used in this Series

OPSSAT	Office of the President of Social Security Appeal Tribunals
Overlapping Benefits Regulations	Social Security (Overlapping Benefits) Regulations 1979
Overpayments Regulations	Social Security (Payments on account, Overpayments and Recovery) Regulations
P. & C.R.	Property and Compensation Reports
pa	per annum
para.	paragraph
PAYE	Pay As You Earn
Payments on Account Regulations	Social Security (Payments on account, Overpayments and Recovery) Regulations
PCA	Personal Capability Assessment
PD	prescribed disease
P.D.	Practice Direction
Pens. L.R.	Pensions Law Reports
Persons Abroad Regulations	Social Security Benefit (Persons Abroad) Regulations 1975
Persons Residing Together Regulations	Social Security Benefit (Persons Residing Together) Regulations 1977
PIE	Period of Interruption of Employment
PILON	pay in lieu of notice
PIP	personal independence payment
P.I.Q.R.	Personal Injuries and Quantum Reports
PIW	Period of Incapacity for Work
P.I.W.R.	Personal Injury and Quantum Reports
P.L.R.	Estates Gazette Planning Law Reports
Polygamous Marriages Regulations	Social Security and Family Allowances (Polygamous Marriages) Regulations 1975
PPF	Pension Protection Fund
Prescribed Diseases Regulations	Social Security (Industrial Injuries) (Prescribed Diseases) Regulations 1985
Present Regulations	Employment and Support Allowance (Transitional Provisions, Housing Benefit and Council Tax Benefit) (Existing Awards) (No.2) Regulations 2010
PSCS	Pension Service Computer System
Pt	Part
PTA	pure tone audiometry
P.T.S.R.	Public and Third Sector Law Reports
PTWR 2000	Part-time Workers (Prevention of Less Favourable Treatment) Regulations 2000
PVS	private or voluntary sectors
pw	per week
Q.B.	Queen's Bench Law Reports

QBD (NI)	Queen's Bench Division (Northern Ireland)
QEF	qualifying earnings factor
QYP	qualifying young person
R	Reported Decision
r.	rule
RC	Rules of the Court of Session
REA	Reduced Earnings Allowance
Recoupment Regulations	Social Security (Recoupment) Regulations 1990
reg.	regulation
RIPA	Regulation of Investigatory Powers Act 2000
RMO	Responsible Medical Officer
rr.	rules
R.T.R.	Road Traffic Reports
S	Scottish Decision
s.	section
SAP	Statutory Adoption Pay
SAPOE	Schemes for Assisting Persons to Obtain Employment
SAYE	Save As You Earn
SB	Supplementary Benefit
SBAT	Supplementary Benefit Appeal Tribunal
SBC	Supplementary Benefits Commission
S.C.	Session Cases
S.C. (H.L.)	Session Cases (House of Lords)
S.C. (P.C.)	Session Cases (Privy Council)
S.C.C.R.	Scottish Criminal Case Reports
S.C.L.R.	Scottish Civil Law Reports
Sch.	Schedule
SDA	Severe Disablement Allowance
SDP	Severe Disability Premium
SEC	Social Entitlement Chamber
SERPS	State Earnings Related Pension Scheme
Severe Disablement Allowance Regulations	Social Security (Severe Disablement Regulations Allowance) Regulations 1984
SI	Statutory Instrument
SIP	Share Incentive Plan
S.J.	Solicitors Journal
S.J.L.B.	Solicitors Journal Law Brief
SLAN	Statement Like an Award Notice
S.L.T.	Scots Law Times
SMP	Statutory Maternity Pay

SMP (General) Regulations 1986	Statutory Maternity Pay (General) Regulations 1986
SP	Senior President
SPC	State Pension Credit
SPC Regulations	State Pension Credit Regulations 2002
SPCA	State Pension Credit Act 2002
SPCA 2002	State Pension Credit Act 2002
SPCA(NI) 2002	State Pension Credit Act (Northern Ireland) 2002
SPP	Statutory Paternity Pay
SPP and SAP (Administration) Regs 2002	Statutory Paternity Pay and Statutory Adoption Pay (Administration) Regulations 2002
SPP and SAP (General) Regulations 2002	Statutory Paternity Pay and Statutory Adoption Pay (General) Regulations 2002
SPP and SAP (National Health Service)	Statutory Paternity Pay and Statutory Adoption Pay (National Health Service Employees) Regulations 2002
SPP and SAP (Weekly Rates) Regulations	Statutory Paternity Pay and Statutory Adoption Pay (Weekly Rates) Regulations 2002
SS(MP)A 1977	Social Security (Miscellaneous Provisions) Act 1977
ss.	sections
SSA 1975	Social Security Act 1975
SSA 1977	Social Security Act 1977
SSA 1978	Social Security Act 1978
SSA 1979	Social Security Act 1979
SSA 1981	Social Security Act 1981
SSA 1986	Social Security Act 1986
SSA 1988	Social Security Act 1988
SSA 1989	Social Security Act 1989
SSA 1990	Social Security Act 1990
SSA 1998	Social Security Act 1998
SSAA 1992	Social Security Administration Act 1992★
SSAC	Social Security Advisory Committee
SSAT	Social Security Appeal Tribunal
SSCB(NI)A	Social Security Contributions and Benefits (Northern Ireland) Act 1992
SSCBA 1992	Social Security Contributions and Benefits Act 1992★
SSCPA 1992	Social Security (Consequential Provisions) Act 1992
SSHBA 1982	Social Security and Housing Benefits Act 1982
SSHD	Secretary of State for the Home Department

SS(MP) A 1977	Social Security (Miscellaneous Provisions) Act 1977
SS (No.2) A 1980	Social Security (No.2) Act 1980
SSPP	statutory shared parental pay
SSP	Statutory Sick Pay
SSP (General) Regulations	Statutory Sick Pay (General) Regulations 1982
SSPA 1975	Social Security Pensions Act 1975
SSWP	Secretary of State for Work and Pensions
State Pension Credit Regulations	State Pension Credit Regulations 2002
S.T.C.	Simon's Tax Cases
S.T.C. (S.C.D.)	Simon's Tax Cases: Special Commissioners Decisions
S.T.I.	Simon's Tax Intelligence
STIB	Short-Term Incapacity Benefit
Strasbourg Court	European Court of Human Rights
Students Directive	Directive 93/96/EEC
subpara.	subparagraph
subs.	subsection
T	Tribunal of Commissioners' Decision
Taxes Act	Income and Corporation Taxes Act 1988
(TC)	Tax and Chancery
T.C.	Tax Cases
TC (Claims and Notifications) Regs 2002	Tax Credits (Claims and Notifications) Regulations 2002
TCA	Tax Credits Act
TCA 1999	Tax Credits Act 1999
TCA 2002	Tax Credits Act 2002
TCEA 2007	Tribunals, Courts and Enforcement Act 2007
TCGA	Taxation of Chargeable Gains Act 1992
TCGA 1992	Taxation of Chargeable Gains Act 2002
TCTM	Tax Credits Technical Manual
TEC	Treaty Establishing the European Community
TENS	transutaneous electrical nerve stimulation
TEU	Treaty on European Union
TFC	Tax-Free Childcare
TFEU	Treaty on the Functioning of the European Union
The Board	Commissioners for Revenue and Customs
TIOPA 2010	Taxation (International and Other Provisions) Act 2010
TMA 1970	Taxes Management Act 1970

Table of Abbreviations used in this Series

T.R.	Taxation Reports
Transfer of Functions Act	Social Security Contributions (Transfer of Functions etc.) Act 1999
Transitional Provisions Regulations	Employment and Support Allowance (Transitional Provisions Regulations 2008
Treaty	Rome Treaty
Tribunal Procedure Rules	Tribunal Procedure (First-tier Tribunal)(Social Entitlement Chamber) Rules 2008
UB	Unemployment Benefit
UC	Universal Credit
UCITS	Undertakings for Collective Investments in Transferable Securities
UKAIT	UK Asylum and Immigration Tribunal
UKBA	UK Border Agency of the Home Office
UKCC	United Kingdom Central Council for Nursing, Midwifery and Health Visiting
UKFTT	United Kingdom First-tier Tribunal Tax Chamber
UKHL	United Kingdom House of Lords
U.K.H.R.R.	United Kingdom Human Rights Reports
UKSC	United Kingdom Supreme Court
UKUT	United Kingdom Upper Tribunal
Unemployment, Sickness and Invalidity Benefit Regs	Social Security (Unemployment, Sickness and Invalidity Benefit) Regulations 1983
USI Regs	Social Security (Unemployment, Sickness and Invalidity Benefit) Regulations 1983
UT	Upper Tribunal
VAMS	Veterans Agency Medical Service
VAT	Value Added Tax
VCM	vinyl chloride monomer
VERA 1992	Vehicle Excise and Registration Act 1992
VWF	Vibration White Finger
W	Welsh Decision
WAO	Wet op arbeidsongeschiktheidsverzekering (Dutch Act on Incapacity for Work)
WAZ	Wet arbeidsongeschiktheidsverzekering (Dutch Act on Self-employed Persons' Incapacity for Work)
WCA/WCAt	Work Capability Assessment
Welsh Regulations	Children (Leaving Care) (Wales) Regulations 2001 (SI 2001/2189)
WFHRAt	Work-Focused Health-Related Assessment
WFI	work-focused Interview
WFTC	Working Families Tax Credit

Table of Abbreviations used in this Series

WIA	Wet Werk en inkomen naar arbeidsvermogen (Dutch Act on Work and Income according to Labour Capacity)
Widow's Benefit and Retirement Pensions Regs	Social Security (Widow's Benefit and Retirement Pensions) Regulations 1979
Wikeley, Annotations	N. Wikeley, "Annotations to Jobseekers Act 1995 (c.18)" in *Current Law Statutes Annotated* (1995)
Wikeley, Ogus and Barendt	Wikeley, Ogus and Barendt, *The Law of Social Security* (5th ed., Butterworths, 2002)
W.L.R.	Weekly Law Reports
WLUK	Westlaw UK
Workmen's Compensation Acts	Workmen's Compensation Acts 1925 to 1945
WPS	War Pensions Scheme
W-RA Regs	Employment and Support Allowance (Work-Related Activity) Regulations 2011 (SI 2011/1349)
WRA 2007	Welfare Reform Act 2007
WRA 2009	Welfare Reform Act 2009
WRA 2012	Welfare Reform Act 2012
WRAAt	Work-Related Activity Assessment
WRPA 1999	Welfare Reform and Pensions Act 1999
WRP(NI)O 1999	Welfare Reform and Pensions (Northern Ireland) Order
WTC	Working Tax Credit
WTC (Entitlement and Maximum Rate) Regulations 2002	Working Tax Credit (Entitlement and Maximum Rate) Regulations 2002
WTC Regulations	Working Tax Credit (Entitlement and Maximum Rate) Regulations 2002
W.T.L.R.	Wills & Trusts Law Reports

TABLE OF CASES

Table of Cases

TABLE OF SOCIAL SECURITY COMMISSIONERS' DECISIONS

TABLE OF EUROPEAN LEGISLATION

TABLE OF STATUTES

TABLE OF STATUTORY INSTRUMENTS

PART I

NEW LEGISLATION

NEW REGULATIONS

The Welfare Reform Act 2012 (Commencement No. 17, 19, 22, 23 and 24 and Transitional and Transitory Provisions (Modification)) Order 2018

SI 2018/532 (C.43)

Made 26th April 2018

The Secretary of State for Work and Pensions makes the following Order in exercise of the powers conferred by section 150(3) and (4)(a), (b)(i) and (c) of the Welfare Reform Act 2012:

ARRANGEMENT OF ARTICLES

Citation

1. This Order may be cited as the Welfare Reform Act 2012 (Com- 1.002
mencement No. 17, 19, 22, 23 and 24 and Transitional and Transitory
Provisions (Modification)) Order 2018.

Interpretation

2.—(1) In this Order— 1.003
"claimant"—
  (a) in relation to an employment and support allowance, has the
      same meaning as in Part 1 of the Welfare Reform Act 2007;
  (b) in relation to a jobseeker's allowance, has the same meaning as
      in the Jobseekers Act 1995 (as it applies apart from the amend-
      ments made by Part 1 of Schedule 14 to the Welfare Reform Act
      2012 that remove references to an income-based jobseeker's
      allowance);

(c) in relation to universal credit, has the same meaning as in Part 1 of the Welfare Reform Act 2012;

"the Claims and Payments Regulations 1987" means the Social Security (Claims and Payments) Regulations 1987;

"employment and support allowance" means an employment and support allowance under Part 1 of the Welfare Reform Act 2007;

"jobseeker's allowance" means a jobseeker's allowance under the Jobseekers Act 1995;

"the No. 17 Order" means the Welfare Reform Act 2012 (Commencement No. 17 and Transitional and Transitory Provisions) Order 2014;

"the No. 19 Order" means the Welfare Reform Act 2012 (Commencement No. 19 and Transitional and Transitory Provisions and Commencement No. 9 and Transitional and Transitory Provisions (Amendment)) Order 2014;

"the No. 22 Order" means the Welfare Reform Act 2012 (Commencement No. 22 and Transitional and Transitory Provisions) Order 2015;

"the No. 23 Order" means the Welfare Reform Act 2012 (Commencement No. 23 and Transitional and Transitory Provisions) Order 2015;

"the No. 24 Order" means the Welfare Reform Act 2012 (Commencement No. 24 and Transitional and Transitory Provisions and Commencement No. 9 and Transitional and Transitory Provisions (Amendment)) Order 2015.

(2) For the purposes of this Order, the Universal Credit, Personal Independence Payment, Jobseeker's Allowance and Employment and Support Allowance (Claims and Payments) Regulations 2013 apply for the purpose of deciding—

(a) whether a claim for universal credit is made; and

(b) the date on which the claim is made.

(3) For the purposes of this Order, the Claims and Payments Regulations 1987 apply, subject to paragraphs (4) and (5), for the purposes of deciding—

(a) whether a claim for an employment and support allowance or a jobseeker's allowance is made; and

(b) the date on which the claim is made or treated as made.

(4) Subject to paragraph (5), for the purposes of this Order—

(a) a person makes a claim for an employment and support allowance or a jobseeker's allowance if that person takes any action which results in a decision on a claim being required under the Claims and Payments Regulations 1987; and

(b) it is irrelevant that the effect of any provision of those Regulations is that, for the purposes of those Regulations, the claim is made or treated as made at a date that is earlier than the date on which that action is taken.

(5) Where, by virtue of—

(a) regulation 6(1F)(b) or (c) of the Claims and Payments Regulations 1987, in the case of a claim for an employment and support allowance; or

(b) regulation 6(4ZA) to (4ZD) and (4A)(a)(i) and (b) of those Regulations,

in the case of a claim for a jobseeker's allowance, a claim for an employment and support allowance or a jobseeker's allowance is treated as made at a date that is earlier than the date on which the action referred to in paragraph (4)(a) is taken, the claim is treated as made on that earlier date.

Modification of the No. 17 Order, the No. 19 Order, the No. 22 Order and the No. 24 Order: removal of the gateway conditions

3. The provisions specified in the first column of the table in the Schedule have effect as though the reference in those provisions to meeting the gateway conditions were omitted, in respect of a claim for universal credit that is made, or a claim for an employment and support allowance or a jobseeker's allowance that is made or treated as made, by reference to the claimant's residence in any postcode district or part-district specified in the corresponding entry in the second column, on or after the date specified in the corresponding entry in the third column. **1.004**

Modifications of the No. 17 Order, the No. 19 Order, the No. 22 Order and the No. 24 Order in consequence of removal of the gateway conditions

4.—(1) This article applies in respect of claims in relation to which provisions of the No. 17 Order, the No. 19 Order, the No. 22 Order and the No. 24 Order are modified by article 3. **1.005**

(2) Where this article applies, the following modifications also have effect—

(a) those made to the No. 17 Order by article 10(2) of the Welfare Reform Act 2012 (Commencement No. 29 and Commencement No. 17, 19, 22, 23 and 24 and Transitional and Transitory Provisions (Modification)) Order 2017; and

(b) those made to the No. 19 Order, the No. 22 Order and the No. 24 Order by articles 13(2), 14(2) and 15(2) respectively of the Welfare Reform Act 2012 (Commencement No. 19, 22, 23 and 24 and Transitional and Transitory Provisions (Modification)) Order 2016.

Modification of the No. 23 Order: claims for housing benefit, income support or a tax credit

5.—(1) This article applies to claims in relation to which the provisions referred to in paragraph (2)(a) to (d) are modified by article 3. **1.006**

(2) Where this article applies, article 7 of the No. 23 Order (prevention of claims for housing benefit, income support or a tax credit) applies as though the reference in paragraph (1) of that article to article 3(1) and (2)(a) to (c) of that Order included a reference to—

(a) paragraph (1) and sub-paragraphs (g), (i) and (k) of paragraph (2) of article 3 of the No. 17 Order;

(b) paragraph (1) and sub-paragraphs (a), (b), (d), (f), (h), (j), (k), (m) and (n) of paragraph (2) of article 3 of the No. 19 Order;

(c) paragraph (1) and sub-paragraphs (a), (c), (e) to (j), (l) to (n), (p) to (r) and (t) of paragraph (2) of article 3 of the No. 22 Order; and

(d) paragraph (1) and sub-paragraphs (a) to (d), (f) to (u), (w) to (y), (bb) and (cc) of paragraph (2) of article 3 of the No. 24 Order.

Article 3

SCHEDULE

POSTCODE DISTRICTS AND PART-DISTRICTS WHERE GATEWAY CONDITIONS REMOVED

1.007

Provisions modified	Postcodes			Date
Articles 3(2)(t) and 4(2)(mm) and (nn) of the No. 22 Order	LL22 7.	LL22 9.		2nd May 2018
Articles 3(2)(c) and 4(2)(e) and (f) of the No. 24 Order	CV23 1.			2nd May 2018
Articles 3(2)(f) and 4(2)(k) and (l) of the No. 24 Order	B45 9.			2nd May 2018
Articles 3(2)(j) and 4(2)(s) and (t) of the No. 24 Order	NE6 4. NE26 1 to NE26 3. NE30.	NE12. NE28.	NE25 8. NE29.	2nd May 2018
Articles 3(2)(k) and 4(2)(u) and (v) of the No. 24 Order	LN7.			2nd May 2018
Articles 3(2)(t) and 4(2)(mm) and (nn) of the No. 24 Order	NE13 6.	NE25 9.	NE27.	2nd May 2018
Articles 3(2)(cc) and 4(2)(eee) and (fff) of the No. 24 Order	IV2 8.	MK43 1 and MK43 2.		2nd May 2018
Articles 3(2)(f) and 4(2)(k) and (l) of the No. 22 Order	SY8 2.	SY8 3.		9th May 2018
Articles 3(2)(h) and 4(2)(o) and (p) of the No. 22 Order	SY1. SY4 1 to SY4 3. SY6. SY11. SY14 7. TF12.	SY2. SY4 5. SY10 1. SY12. TF9 1. WV16.	SY3. SY5 6 to SY5 8. SY10 8. SY13. TF9 3.	9th May 2018
Articles 3(2)(n) and 4(2)(aa) and (bb) of the No. 22 Order	SY4 4. TF11 9.	TF9 2. TF13 6.	TF9 4.	9th May 2018
Articles 3(2)(t) and 4(2)(mm) and (nn) of the No. 22 Order	LL14 5.			9th May 2018

Provisions modified	Postcodes			Date
Articles 3(2)(a) and 4(2)(a) and (b) of the No. 24 Order	WV15 5			9th May 2018
Articles 3(2)(b) and 4(2)(c) and (d) of the No. 24 Order	IP14.			9th May 2018
Articles 3(2)(c) and 4(2)(e) and (f) of the No. 24 Order	HG14 7. NG24. NN10.	NG22 0. NG25.	NG23 6. NN9 6.	9th May 2018
Articles 3(2)(f) and 4(2)(k) and (l) of the No. 24 Order	SY5 0. SY10 7.	SY5 9. SY10 9.	SY9.	9th May 2018
Articles 3(2)(h) and 4(2)(o) and (p) of the No. 24 Order	IP20, IP23.	IP21. NR15 2.	IP22.	9th May 2018
Articles 3(2)(i) and 4(2)(q) and (r) of the No. 24 Order	IP6 8.			9th May 2018
Articles 3(2)(k) and 4(2)(u) and (v) of the No. 24 Order	NG23 7.			9th May 2018
Articles 3(2)(l) and 4(2)(w) and (x) of the No. 24 Order	TF11 8.	WV15 6.		9th May 2018
Articles 3(2)(r) and 4(2)(ii) and (jj) of the No. 24 Order	WV5 7.			9th May 2018
Articles 3(2)(s) and 4(2)(kk) and (ll) of the No. 24 Order	NG23 5.			9th May 2018
Articles 3(2)(i) and 4(2)(i) of the No. 17 Order	L10 0. L10 8. L33 0 to L33 2. L35 1 to L35 3. L36 0 to L36 4.	L10 2 and L10 3. L28 3 to L28 7. L33 5 to L33 9. L35 5. L36 6 to L36 9.	L10 6. L32. L34. L35 7.	16th May 2018
Articles 3(2)(a) and 4(2)(a) of the No. 19 Order	L33 3 and L33 4. OL10. OL12 9. OL16.	M24 0 to M24 2. OL11. OL15 0.	M24 5 and M24 6. OL12 6. OL15 8.	16th May 2018
Articles 3(2)(b) and 4(2)(b) of the No. 19 Order	L10 1. L14. L36 5.	L10 4 and L10 5. L28 0 and L28 1. M24 4.	L10 7. L28 8.	16th May 2018
Articles 3(2)(d) and 4(2)(d) of the No. 19 Order	OL12 0.	OL12 7.		16th May 2018
Articles 3(2)(c) and 4(2)(e) and (f) of the No. 22 Order	EN5 1 and EN5 2. HA8 4. N2 8. N20. NW9 0 and NW9 1.	EN5 5. HA8 9. N3. NW4. NW9 5 to NW9 8.	HA8 0. N2 2. N12. NW7. NW11.	16th May 2018

7

Provisions modified	Postcodes			Date
Articles 3(2)(i) and 4(2)(q) and (r) of the No. 22 Order	DG1. DG4. DG7. DG9. DG12.	DG2. DG5. DG8 0 and DG8 1. DG10. DG13.	DG3. DG6. DG8 7 to DG8 9. DG11. DG14.	16th May 2018
Articles 3(2)(l) and 4(2)(w) and (x) of the No. 22 Order	E10 7.	E10 9.	E17.	16th May 2018
Articles 3(2)(t) and 4(2)(mm) and (nn) of the No. 22 Order	EN4 8 and EN4 9. N18 9.	N9 0 and N9 1.	N18 2.	16th May 2018
Articles 3(2)(a) and 4(2)(a) and (b) of the No. 24 Order	DG16 5. L10 9.	EN4 0. N18 3.	EN5 3 and EN5 4. OL15 9.	16th May 2018
Articles 3(2)(c) and 4(2)(e) and (f) of the No. 24 Order	HA8 5 to HA8 8.	ML12 6.	NW9 9.	16th May 2018
Articles 3(2)(d) and 4(2)(g) and (h) of the No. 24 Order	DG8 6.			16th May 2018
Articles 3(2)(i) and 4(2)(q) and (r) of the No. 24 Order	EH27. EH47. EH52. EH55.	EH28. EH48. EH53. FK1 2.	EH29. EH49 6. EH54. ML7 5.	16th May 2018
Articles 3(2)(w) and 4(2)(ss) and (tt) of the No. 24 Order	N2 0.	N2 9.		16th May 2018
Articles 3(2)(cc) and 4(2)(eee) and (fff) of the No. 24 Order	NW9 4.			16th May 2018
Articles 3(2)(l) and 4(2)(w) and (x) of the No. 22 Order	PL22. PL25.	PL23. PL26.	PL24.	23rd May 2018
Articles 3(2)(p) and 4(2)(ee) and (ff) of the No. 22 Order	PL27. PL30. PL33. TR3 6. TR6.	PL28. PL31. TR1. TR4.	PL29. PL32. TR2. TR5.	23rd May 2018
Articles 3(2)(t) and 4(2)(mm) and (nn) of the No. 22 Order	TR7.	TR8.	TR9.	23rd May 2018
Articles 3(2)(b) and 4(2)(c) and (d) of the No. 24 Order	GU47 0. RG10 8. RG41. SL1 7.	GU47 9. RG12. RG42. SL5 8.	RG10 0. RG40. RG45. SL6 1 to SL6 9.	23rd May 2018
Articles 3(2)(i) and 4(2)(q) and (r) of the No. 24 Order	SL8.2			3rd May 2018
Articles 3(2)(u) and 4(2)(oo) and (pp) of the No. 24 Order	SL5 0.	SL5 7.	SL5 9.	23rd May 2018

Provisions modified	Postcodes			Date
Articles 3(2)(y) and 4(2)(ww) and (xx) of the No. 24 Order	RG21. RG24. RG27.	RG22. RG25. RG28 9.	RG23. RG26. RG29.	23rd May 2018
Articles 3(2)(l) and 4(2)(w) and (x) of the No. 22 Order	DA11 0.	DA11 7.	DA12.	30th May 2018
Articles 3(2)(d) and 4(2)(g) and (h) of the No. 24 Order	DA13 0. ME3. ME7.	ME1. ME4. ME8.	ME2. ME5.	30th May 2018
Articles 3(2)(h) and 4(2)(o) and (p) of the No. 24 Order	LS25 6. YO11. YO14.	YO8 3 to YO8 5. YO12. YO21.	YO8 8 and YO8 9. YO13. YO22.	30th May 2018
Articles 3(2)(o) and 4(2)(cc) and (dd) of the No. 24 Order	DN14 0.			30th May 2018
Articles 3(2)(p) and 4(2)(ee) and (ff) of the No. 24 Order	CT18. CT21. DA13 9. TN29.	CT19. DA10. TN25 5 to TN25 7. TN26 2.	CT20. DA11 8 and DA11 9. TN28.	30th May 2018
Articles 3(2)(t) and 4(2)(mm) and (nn) of the No. 24 Order	NE31. NE34. SR6 7.	NE32. NE35.	NE33. NE36.	30th May 2018
Articles 3(2)(a) and 4(2)(a) and (b) of the No. 22 Order	BS20.	BS49.		6th June 2018
Articles 3(2)(j) and 4(2)(s) and (t) of the No. 22 Order	LL24 LL27. LL30. LL34.	LL25. LL28. LL31.	LL26. LL29. LL32.	6th June 2018
Articles 3(2)(l) and 4(2)(w) and (x) of the No. 22 Order	TR14.	TR15.	TR16.	6th June 2018
Articles 3(2)(p) and 4(2)(ee) and (ff) of the No. 22 Order	TR17. TR20.	TR18. TR26.	TR19. TR27.	6th June 2018
Articles 3(2)(r) and 4(2)(ii) and (jj) of the No. 22 Order	CF31. CF34.	CF32 7 to CF32 9. CF36.	CF33.	6th June 2018
Articles 3(2)(t) and 4(2)(mm) and (nn) of the No. 22 Order	LL2 8. TR11.	TR3 7. TR12.	TR10. TR13.	6th June 2018
Articles 3(2)(a) and 4(2)(a) and (b) of the No. 24 Order	BN5. RH10 4 to RH10 9. RH12 5. RH15. RH18. RH20 9 TB6.	BN6. RH11. RH13. RH16. RH19 1 RH19 4. TN7.	RH10 1. RH12 1 and RH12 2. RH14 9. RH17. RH20 2 to RH20 4.	6th June 2018
Articles 3(2)(d) and 4(2)(g) and (h) of the No. 24 Order	RH20 1.	TN3 9.		6th June 2018

9

Provisions modified	Postcodes			Date
Articles 3(2)(f) and 4(2)(k) and (l) of the No. 24 Order	L33.			6th June 2018
Articles 3(2)(g) and 4(2)(m) and (n) of the No. 24 Order	BS1. BS4. BS9 1. BS40 6 to BS40 9.	BS2. BS6 5. BS13. BS41.	BS3. BS8. BS14.	6th June 2018
Articles 3(2)(l) and 4(2)(w) and (x) of the No. 24 Order	PO30. PO38. PO41. O40 9.	PO31. PO39. SO40 4. SO45.	PO32. PO40. SO40 7.	6th June 2018
Articles 3(2)(m) and 4(2)(y) and (z) of the No. 24 Order	BN45.			6th June 2018
Articles 3(2)(s) and 4(2)(kk) and (ll) of the No. 24 Order	RH6 6. RH12 3 and RH142 4.	RH7 9. RH14 0.	RH10 3. RH19 2 and RH19 3.	6th June 2018
Articles 3(2)(t) and 4(2)(mm) and (nn) of the No. 24 Order	CF32 0.			6th June 2018
Articles 3(2)(x) and 4(2)(uu) and (vv) of the No. 24 Order	CF35.			6th June 2018
Articles 3(2)(cc) and 4(2)(eee) and (fff) of the No. 24 Order	RH12 0.			6th June 2018
Articles 3(2)(f) and 4(2)(k) and (l) of the No. 22 Order	HR1. HR6. SY8 1.	HR2. HR9 5 and HR9 6.	HR4. SY7 0.	13th June 2018
Articles 3(2)(g) and 4(2)(m) and (n) of the No. 22 Order	IP25. PE37.	NR19.	NR20 4.	13th June 2018
Articles 3(2)(i) and 4(2)(q) and (r) of the No. 22 Order	EH38. EH45. TD3. TD6. TD9 1. TD11.	EH43. TD1. TD4. TD7. TD9 7 to TD9 9. TD13.	EH44. TD2. TD5. TD8. TD10. TD14.	13th June 2018
Articles 3(2)(j) and 4(2)(s) and (t) of the No. 22 Order	HR9 7.			13th June 2018
Articles 3(2)(a) and 4(2)(a) and (b) of the No. 24 Order	TD9 0.			13th June 2018
Articles 3(2)(f) and 4(2)(k) and (l) of the No. 24 Order	DE5 DE56 4. HR3. HR8 1.	DE55 1. DE56 9. HR5. SY7 8.	DE56 0 and DE56 1. DE75. HR7. SY8 4.	13th June 2018
Articles 3(2)(g) and 4(2)(m) and (n) of the No. 24 Order	LN12 2. LN13 9. PE23.	LN12 9. NG16 2 to NG16 5. PE24.	LN13 3. PE22 8. PE25.	13th June 2018

10

Provisions modified	Postcodes			Date
Articles 3(2)(h) and 4(2)(o) and (p) of the No. 24 Order	NR20 3.			13th June 2018
Articles 3(2)(j) and 4(2)(s) and (t) of the No. 24 Order	DE55 2 to DE55 7. S42 5 and S42 6.	DE56 2. S45.	NG16 6.	13th June 2018
Articles 3(2)(l) and 4(2)(w) and (x) of the No. 24 Order	NR20 5.			13th June 2018
Articles 3(2)(p) and 4(2)(ee) and (ff) of the No. 24 Order	LE1. LE4. LE7. LE9 6. LE18.	LE2. LE5. LE8 4 to LE8 6. LE9 9. LE19.	LE3. LE6. LE9 1 to LE9 3. LE17 4 and LE17 5. LE87.	13th June 2018
Articles 3(2)(q) and 4(2)(gg) and (hh) of the No. 24 Order	ST1. ST4 1 to ST4 3. ST9. ST12.	ST2. ST6 1 to ST6 4. ST10. ST13.	ST3. ST6 6 to ST6 9. ST11.	13th June 2018
Articles 3(2)(w) and 4(2)(ss) and (tt) of the No. 24 Order	PE32 2.			13th June 2018
Articles 3(2)(bb) and 4(2)(ccc) and (ddd) of the No. 24 Order	KY13 0. PH2. PH5. PH8. PH11. PH14. PH17.	KY14. PH3. PH6. PH9. PH12. PH15. PH18.	PH1. PH4. PH7. PH10. PH13. PH16.	13th June 2018
Articles 3(2)(g) and 4(2)(m) and (n) of the No. 22 Order	TN23. TN26 1. TN30.	TN24. TN26 3.	TN25 4. TN27 0.	20th June 2018
Articles 3(2)(a) and 4(2)(a) and (b) of the No. 24 Order	DH1. DH6 1. DL5 4 and DL5 5. DL17.	DH2. DH6 4 and DH6 5. DL5 7.	DH3 2 to DH3 4. DH7 DL16.	20th June 2018
Articles 3(2)(d) and 4(2)(g) and (h) of the No. 24 Order	TN27 8.			20th June 2018
Articles 3(2)(g) and 4(2)(m) and (n) of the No. 24 Order	KT1. KT3 5. KT9 2. TW2. TW11.	KT2. KT5. SW13 SW14. TW9. TW12 1.	KT3 3. KT6 7. TW1. TW10. TW12 3.	20th June 2018
Articles 3(2)(h) and 4(2)(o) and (p) of the No. 24 Order	EC1A. EC1R 3. EC1V 7 and EC1V 8. N1 8. N19 3 and N19 4. SW1E. SW1V. SW1Y. W1C. W1G.	EC1M 4 to EC1M 7. EC1V 0. EC1Y. N5 1. NW8 8 and NW8 9. SW1H. SW1W. W1A. W1D. W1H.	EC1R 0 and EC1R 1. EC1V 2 and EC1V 4. N1 1 and N1 2. N7 6 to N7 8. SW1 A. SW1P. SW1X. W1B. W1F. W1J.	20th June 2018

11

Provisions modified	Postcodes			Date
	W1K. W1U. W9 2. WC2N.	W1S. W1W. WC2E. WC2R.	W1T 3. W2. WC2H 7.	
Articles 3(2)(j) and 4(2)(s) and (t) of the No. 24 Order	DL1. DL4 2.	DL2 2 and DL2 3. DL5 6.	DL3. DL12 8.	20th June 2018
Articles 3(2)(k) and 4(2)(u) and (v) of the No. 24 Order	BD1. BD3 9. BD5. BD8. BD12. BD15. BD18. BD20 9.	BD2. BD4 6 and BD4 7. BD6. BD9. BD13. BD16. BD20 0. BD21.	BD3 0. BD4 9. BD7. BD10 8 and BD10 9. BD14. BD17. BD20 5 and BD20 6. BD22.	20th June 2018
Articles 3(2)(l) and 4(2)(w) and (x) of the No. 24 Order	DL2 1.	TS21 2.		20th June 2018
Articles 3(2)(o) and 4(2)(cc) and (dd) of the No. 24 Order	KT3 4. SW19 1 to SW19 5.	KT3 6. SW19 7 to SW19 9.	KT4 8.	20th June 2018
Articles 3(2)(q) and 4(2)(gg) and (hh) of the No. 24 Order	BD3 8.	BD4 0.	BD10 0.	20th June 2018
Articles 3(2)(s) and 4(2)(kk) and (ll) of the No. 24 Order	IG1. IG4. IG7 4. KT4 7. RM3. RM7. RM13.	IG2. IG5. IG8 0 and IG8 1. RM1. RM5. RM11. RM14 1 and RM14 2.	IG3. IG6. IG8 7 and IG8 8. RM2. RM6 4. RM12. RM14 9.	20th June 2018
Articles 3(2)(u) and 4(2)(oo) and (pp) of the No. 24 Order	KT6 4 to KT6 6.	KT9 1.	TW12 2.	20th June 2018
Articles 3(2)(w) and 4(2)(ss) and (tt) of the No. 24 Order	EC1M 3. N1C. N6. N19 5. NW8 6 and NW8 7. W9 1. WC1E. WC1R. WC2A. Wc2H 8 and WC2H 9.	EC1 N. N1 0. N7 0. NW1 1 to NW1 6. W1T1 and W1T 2. WC1A. WC1H. WC1V. WC2B.	EC1R 4 and EC1R 5. N1 9. N7 9. NW8 0. W1T4 to W1T 7. WC1B. WC1N. WC1X. WC2H 0.	20th June 2018
Articles 3(2)(y) and 4(2)(ww) and (xx) of the No. 24 Order	EC1V 1. N4.	EC1V 9. N5 2.	N1 3.	20th June 2018
Articles 3(2)(m) and 4(2)(y) and (z) of the No. 22 Order	AB41 8. AB44. AB53 4 to AB53 6.	AB42. AB45 1.	AB43. AB45 3.	27th June 2018
Articles 3(2)(a) and 4(2)(a) and (b) of the No. 24 Order	CF46. CF48 3 and CF48 4. NP7 8 and NP7 9. NP16.	CF47. NP7 0 and NP7 1. NP12 4. NP25.	CF48 1. NP7 5 and NP7 6. NP15. NP26.	27th June 2018

Provisions modified	Postcodes			Date
Articles 3(2)(f) and 4(2)(k) and (l) of the No. 24 Order	NP7 7.	NP8.		27th June 2018
Articles 3(2)(i) and 4(2)(q) and (r) of the No. 24 Order	AB37. AB54. IV30. IV36.	AB38. AB55. IV31.	AB45 2. AB56. IV32.	27th June 2018
Articles 3(2)(x) and 4(2)(uu) and (vv) of the No. 24 Order	CF48 2.			27th June 2018
Articles 3(2)(e) and 4(2)(i) and (j) of the No. 22 Order	CO1. CO4 0. CO5 7 and CO5 8.	CO2. CO4 3.	CO3. CO4 5.	4th July 2018
Articles 3(2)(g) and 4(2)(m) and (n) of the No. 22 Order	CO4 9.	CO11 2.	CO12.	4th July 2018
Articles 3(2)(a) and 4(2)(a) and (b) of the No. 24 Order	CO7 7. SO21 1 and SO21 2. SP9.	CO7 9. SO22. SP10.	SO20. SO23. SP11 7 to SP11 9.	4th July 2018
Articles 3(2)(b) and 4(2)(c) and (d) of the No. 24 Order	CO5 0. CO11 1.	CO6 3 and CO6 4.	CO7 6.	4th July 2018
Articles 3(2)(c) and 4(2)(e) and (f) of the No. 24 Order	CO5 9. HA2 HA7.	CO6 1. HA3.	HA1. HA5 5.	4th July 2018
Articles 3(2)(d) and 4(2)(g) and (h) of the No. 24 Order	BN11 BN14. BN17. BN44. PO10 8. PO20.	BN12. BN15. BN18. GU28. PO18. PO21.	BN13. BN16. BN43. GU29. PO19. PO22.	4th July 2018
Articles 3(2)(g) and 4(2)(m) and (n) of the No. 24 Order	HA5 1 to HA5 3.	HA6 1.		4th July 2018
Articles 3(2)(h) and 4(2)(o) and (p) of the No. 24 Order	EX10. EX13. EX16. EX24. EX33. EX36. EX39.	EX11. EX14. EX19. EX31. EX34. EX37.	EX12. EX15. EX22 7. EX32. EX35. EX38.	4th July 2018
Articles 3(2)(j) and 4(2)(s) and (t) of the No. 24 Order	HA5 4.	HA6 2 and HA6 3.		4th July 2018
Articles 3(2)(m) and 4(2)(y) and (z) of the No. 24 Order	BN42.			4th July 2018
Articles 3(2)(p) and 4(2)(ee) and (ff) of the No. 24 Order	CT1. CT3 4. CT6.	CT2. CT4.	CT3 1 and CT3 2. CT5.	4th July 2018

Provisions modified	Postcodes			Date
Articles 3(2)(r) and 4(2)(ii) and (jj) of the No. 24 Order	SE4. SE8 3 and SE8 4. SE23.	SE6 4. SE13. SE26.	SE6 9. SE19 2 and SE19 3. SO24 0.	4th July 2018
Articles 3(2)(y) and 4(2)(ww) and (xx) of the No. 24 Order	RG28 7. SP11 0.	SO21 3. SP11 6.	SO24 9.	4th July 2018
Articles 3(2)(cc) and 4(2)(eee) and (fff) of the No. 24 Order	CO4 6.			4th July 2018
Articles 3(2)(n) and 4(2)(aa) and (bb) of the No. 22 Order	LE11.	LE12 7 and LE12 8.		11th July 2018
Articles 3(2)(b) and 4(2)(c) and (d) of the No. 24 Order	LE12 9.			11th July 2018
Articles 3(2)(g) and 4(2)(m) and (n) of the No. 24 Order	PE11.	PE12 2.	PE12 6 to PE12 9.	11th July 2018
Articles 3(2)(j) and 4(2)(s) and (t) of the No. 24 Order	S21 1 to S21 3.	S43 3.	S44.	11th July 2018
Articles 3(2)(l) and 4(2)(w) and (x) of the No. 24 Order	CV1. CV4. CV7 7. S26. S61 3 and S61 4. S66. TS17 0. TS18. TS21 1. TS23.	CV2. CV5. CV8 3. S60. S62. TS15. TS17 5 and TS17 6. TS19. TS21 3.	CV3. CV6. S25. S61 1. S65. TS16. TS17 8 TS20. TS22.	11th July 2018
Articles 3(2)(m) and 4(2)(y) and (z) of the No. 24 Order	PE6 0.			11th July 2018
Articles 3(2)(o) and 4(2)(cc) and (dd) of the No. 24 Order	DN14 4 to DN14 9. HU13 3. HU18. YO8 6. YO25.	HU10. HU14 HU15. S21 4 and S21 5. YO15. YO43.	HU13 0. HU17. S61 2. YO16.	11th July 2018
Articles 3(2)(p) and 4(2)(ee) and (ff) of the No. 24 Order	DE1. DE6 9. DE23. SE72 2.	DE3. DE21. DE24. DE73 6 and DE73 7.	DE6 1 to DE6 4. DE22. DE65.	11th July 2018
Articles 3(2)(r) and 4(2)(ii) and (jj) of the No. 24 Order	TS17 7.	TS17 9.		11th July 2018
Articles 3(2)(s) and 4(2)(kk) and (ll) of the No. 24 Order	DE74.	LE12 5.		11th July 2018
Articles 3(2)(u) and 4(2)(oo) and (pp) of the No. 24 Order	HU4 7.	HU13 9.		11th July 2018

Provisions modified	Postcodes			Date
Articles 3(2)(w) and 4(2)(ss) and (tt) of the No. 24 Order	PE12 0.			11th July 2018
Articles 3(2)(g) and 4(2)(g) of the No. 17 Order	PR0. PR4 4 and PR4 5. PR25 1 to PR25 3.	PR1. PR5 4 and PR5 5. PR25 9.	PR2. PR11. PR26 6.	18th July 2018
Articles 3(2)(i) and 4(2)(i) of the No. 17 Order	L35 0. WA9. WA11 8 and WA11 9.	L35 4. WA10. WA12.	L35 8 and L35 9. WA11 0.	18th July 2018
Articles 3(2)(k) and 4(2)(k) of the No. 17 Order	CW12 1 and CW12 2. SK9.	CW12 4. WA16.	CW12 9.	18th July 2018
Articles 3(2)(a) and 4(2)(a) of the No. 19 Order	WA11 7.			18th July 2018
Articles 3(2)(f) and 4(2)(f) of the No. 19 Order	SK10.	SK11 6 to SK11 9.		18th July 2018
Articles 3(2)(h) and 4(2)(h) of the No. 19 Order	PR4 0.			18th July 2018
Articles 3(2)(j) and 4(2)(j) of the No. 19 Order	L35 6.			18th July 2018
Articles 3(2)(k) and 4(2)(k) of the No. 19 Order	PR5 0. PR6. PR26 7 to PR26 9.	PR5 6. PR7.	PR5 8. PR25 4 and PR25 5.	18th July 2018
Articles 3(2)(m) and 4(2)(m) of the No. 19 Order	PR3.			18th July 2018
Articles 3(2)(n) and 4(2)(aa) and (bb) of the No. 22 Order	SK11 0.			18th July 2018
Articles 3(2)(q) and 4(2)(gg) and (hh) of the No. 22 Order	B74 2 and B74 3. WS2. WS5 3.	WS1 1 to WS1 3. WS3 1 to WS3 3. WS9 0 and WS9 1.	WS1 9. WS4. WS9 8.	18th July 2018
Articles 3(2)(a) and 4(2)(a) and (b) of the No. 24 Order	CW12 3.			18th July 2018
Articles 3(2)(f) and 4(2)(k) and (l) of the No. 24 Order	NP13. NP23.	NP22 3 and NP22 4.	NP22 9.	18th July 2018
Articles 3(2)(g) and 4(2)(m) and (n) of the No. 24 Order	BS5 7 and BS5 8. BS7 8.	BS6 6 and BS6 7.	BS6 9.	18th July 2018
Articles 3(2)(i) and 4(2)(q) and (r) of the No. 24 Order	B43 7.			18th July 2018

Provisions modified	Postcodes			Date
Articles 3(2)(j) and 4(2)(s) and (t) of the No. 24 Order	WS1 4.			18th July 2018
Articles 3(2)(l) and 4(2)(w) and (x) of the No. 24 Order	BS5 0. BS16 3.	BS5 6. WS3 5.	BS5 9.	18th July 2018
Articles 3(2)(n) and 4(2)(aa) and (bb) of the No. 24 Order	BS7 9.	BS16 1 and BS16 2.		18th July 2018
Articles 3(2)(r) and 4(2)(ii) and (jj) of the No. 24 Order	WS10 8.			18th July 2018
Articles 3(2)(g) and 4(2)(g) of the No. 17 Order	BL0 9. BL9 0. M25 1. M26 1 and M26 2.	BL8 1 to BL8 3. BL9 5. M25 3. M26 4.	BL8 9. BL9 8 and BL9 9. M25 9. M45.	25th July 2018
Articles 3(2)(a) and 4(2)(a) of the No. 19 Order	BL9 7.			25th July 2018
Articles 3(2)(b) and 4(2)(b) of the No. 19 Order	M7 4. M22 0 to M22 2. M23.	M8. M22 5. M25 0.	M9. M22 8 and M22 9. M25 2.	25th July 2018
Articles 3(2)(d) and 4(2)(d) of the No. 19 Order	BL9 6.			25th July 2018
Articles 3(2)(j) and 4(2)(j) of the No. 19 Order	M22 4.			25th July 2018
Articles 3(2)(k) and 4(2)(k) of the No. 19 Order	BL8 4.			25th July 2018
Articles 3(2)(n) and 4(2)(n) of the No. 19 Order	CA1. CA4. CA7 0. CA8 0 and CA8 1. CA11.	CA2. CA5. CA7 5. CA8 9. CA16.	CA3. CA6. CA& 7 to CA7 9. CA10 1 to CA10 3. CA17.	25th July 2018
Articles 3(2)(g) and 4(2)(m) and (n) of the No. 22 Order	CO7 0. CO13. CO16.	CO7 5. CO14.	CO7 8. CO15.	25th July 2018
Articles 3(2)(l) and 4(2)(w) and (x) of the No. 22 Order	E4 6. E11 4. SS8.	E4 8 and E4 9. E11 9.	E10 5 and E10 6. SS7.	25th July 2018
Articles 3(2)(g) and 4(2)(m) and (n) of the No. 24 Order	DH4. NE37 9. SR2. SR5 2 to SR5 5.	DH5. NE38. SR3. SR5 9.	NE37 1 and NE37 2. SR1. SR4.	25th July 2018
Articles 3(2)(o) and 4(2)(cc) and (dd) of the No. 24 Order	BR1 1 to BR1 3. BR3 3 to BR3 6. BR5. SE20.	BR1 9. BR3 9. BR6. TN16 3.	BR2. BR4. BR7.	25th July 2018

Provisions modified	Postcodes			Date
Articles 3(2)(p) and 4(2)(ee) and (ff) of the No. 24 Order	BR8. DA2. DA9.	DA1 1 and DA1 2. DA3. TN14 7.	DA1 9. DA4. TN15 6 and TN15 7	25th July 2018
Articles 3(2)(q) and 4(2)(gg) and (hh) of the No. 24 Order	E4 7. SS6.	SS4.	SS5. 2018	25th July
Articles 3(2)(r) and 4(2)(ii) and (jj) of the No. 24 Order	BR1 4 and BR1 5. DA1 5.	BR3 1. SE6 1 to SE6 3.	DA1 3.	25th July 2018
Articles 3(2)(s) and 4(2)(kk) and (ll) of the No. 24 Order	E6 1. E6 9. E12. E16. IG8 9.	E6 3. E7. E13. E18.	E6 5 to E6 7. E11 1 to E11 3. E15. E20 1 and E20 2.	25th July 2018
Articles 3(2)(t) and 4(2)(mm) and (nn) of the No. 24 Order	CA8 2. SR5 1.	CA9 3. SR6 0.	NE37 3. SR6 8 and SR6 9.	
Articles 3(2)(y) and 4(2)(ww) and (xx) of the No. 24 Order	E20 3.			25th July 2018

The Welfare Reform Act 2012 (Commencement No. 17, 19, 22, 23 and 24 and Transitional and Transitory Provisions (Modification) (No. 2)) Order 2018

SI 2018/881 (C.68)

Made 19th July 2018

The Secretary of State for Work and Pensions makes the following Order in exercise of the powers conferred by section 150(3) and (4)(a), (b)(i) and (c) of the Welfare Reform Act 2012:

ARRANGEMENT OF ARTICLES

Citation

1.009   **1.** This Order may be cited as the Welfare Reform Act 2012 (Commencement No. 17, 19, 22, 23 and 24 and Transitional and Transitory Provisions (Modification) (No. 2)) Order 2018.

Interpretation

1.010   **2.**—(1) In this Order—
"claimant"—

(a) in relation to an employment and support allowance, has the same meaning as in Part 1 of the Welfare Reform Act 2007;

(b) in relation to a jobseeker's allowance, has the same meaning as in the Jobseekers Act 1995 (as it applies apart from the amendments made by Part 1 of Schedule 14 to the Welfare Reform Act 2012 that remove references to an income-based jobseeker's allowance);

(c) in relation to universal credit, has the same meaning as in Part 1 of the Welfare Reform Act 2012;

"the Claims and Payments Regulations 1987" means the Social Security (Claims and Payments) Regulations 1987;
"employment and support allowance" means an employment and support allowance under Part 1 of the Welfare Reform Act 2007;
"jobseeker's allowance" means a jobseeker's allowance under the Jobseekers Act 1995;

"the No. 17 Order" means the Welfare Reform Act 2012 (Commencement No. 17 and Transitional and Transitory Provisions) Order 2014;

"the No. 19 Order" means the Welfare Reform Act 2012 (Commencement No. 19 and Transitional and Transitory Provisions and Commencement No. 9 and Transitional and Transitory Provisions (Amendment)) Order 2014;

"the No. 22 Order" means the Welfare Reform Act 2012 (Commencement No. 22 and Transitional and Transitory Provisions) Order 2015;

"the No. 23 Order" means the Welfare Reform Act 2012 (Commencement No. 23 and Transitional and Transitory Provisions) Order 2015;

"the No. 24 Order" means the Welfare Reform Act 2012 (Commencement No. 24 and Transitional and Transitory Provisions and Commencement No. 9 and Transitional and Transitory Provisions (Amendment)) Order 2015.

(2) For the purposes of this Order, the Universal Credit, Personal Independence Payment, Jobseeker's Allowance and Employment and Support Allowance (Claims and Payments) Regulations 2013 apply for the purpose of deciding—

(a) whether a claim for universal credit is made; and

(b) the date on which the claim is made.

(3) For the purposes of this Order, the Claims and Payments Regulations 1987 apply, subject to paragraphs (4) and (5), for the purposes of deciding—

(a) whether a claim for an employment and support allowance or a jobseeker's allowance is made; and

(b) the date on which the claim is made or treated as made.

(4) Subject to paragraph (5), for the purposes of this Order—

(a) a person makes a claim for an employment and support allowance or a jobseeker's allowance if that person takes any action which results in a decision on a claim being required under the Claims and Payments Regulations 1987; and

(b) it is irrelevant that the effect of any provision of those Regulations is that, for the purposes of those Regulations, the claim is made or treated as made at a date that is earlier than the date on which that action is taken.

(5) Where, by virtue of—

(a) regulation 6(1F)(b) or (c) of the Claims and Payments Regulations 1987(**11**), in the case of a claim for an employment and support allowance; or

(b) regulation 6(4ZA) to (4ZD) and (4A)(a)(i) and (b) of those Regulations(**12**), in the case of a claim for a jobseeker's allowance,

a claim for an employment and support allowance or a jobseeker's allowance is treated as made at a date that is earlier than the date on which the action referred to in paragraph (4)(a) is taken, the claim is treated as made on that earlier date.

Modification of the No. 17 Order, the No. 19 Order, the No. 22 Order and the No. 24 Order: removal of the gateway conditions

1.011   **3.** The provisions specified in the first column of the table in the Schedule have effect as though the reference in those provisions to meeting the gateway conditions were omitted, in respect of a claim for universal credit that is made, or a claim for an employment and support allowance or a jobseeker's allowance that is made or treated as made, by reference to the claimant's residence in any postcode district or part-district specified in the corresponding entry in the second column, on or after the date specified in the corresponding entry in the third column.

Modifications of the No. 17 Order, the No. 19 Order, the No. 22 Order and the No. 24 Order in consequence of removal of the gateway conditions

1.012   **4.**—(1) This article applies in respect of claims in relation to which provisions of the No. 17 Order, the No. 19 Order, the No. 22 Order and the No. 24 Order are modified by article 3.

(2) Where this article applies, the following modifications also have effect—

(a) those made to the No. 17 Order by article 10(2) of the Welfare Reform Act 2012 (Commencement No. 29 and Commencement No. 17, 19, 22, 23 and 24 and Transitional and Transitory Provisions (Modification)) Order 2017; and

(b) those made to the No. 19 Order, the No. 22 Order and the No. 24 Order by articles 13(2), 14(2) and 15(2) respectively of the Welfare Reform Act 2012 (Commencement No. 19, 22, 23 and 24 and Transitional and Transitory Provisions (Modification)) Order 2016.

Modification of the No. 23 Order: claims for housing benefit, income support or a tax credit

1.013   **5.**—(1) This article applies to claims in relation to which the provisions referred to in paragraph (2)(a) to (d) are modified by article 3.

(2) Where this article applies, article 7 of the No. 23 Order (prevention of claims for housing benefit, income support or a tax credit) applies as though the reference in paragraph (1) of that article to article 3(1) and (2)(a) to (c) of that Order included a reference to—

(a) paragraph (1) and sub-paragraphs (c) and (i) of paragraph (2) of article 3 of the No. 17 Order;

(b) paragraph (1) and sub-paragraphs (b) to (h) and (j) to (n) of paragraph (2) of article 3 of the No.19 Order;

(c) paragraph (1) and sub-paragraphs (a), (c) to (e), (g) to (k), (m) to (q), and (t) of paragraph (2) of article 3 of the No. 22 Order; and

(d) paragraph (1) and sub-paragraphs (a) to (d), (f) to (y), (aa) and (cc) of paragraph (2) of article 3 of the No. 24 Order.

Article 3

SCHEDULE

POSTCODE DISTRICTS AND PART-DISTRICTS WHERE GATEWAY CONDITIONS REMOVED

1.014

Provisions modified	*Postcodes*			*Date*
Articles 3(2)(i) and 4(2)(q) and (r) of the No. 22 Order	SW11 2 SW15 9	SW15 2 SW17 6 and SW17 7	SW15 4 SW18 1 to SW18 3	5th September 2018
Articles 3(2)(j) and 4(2)(s) and (t) of the No. 22 Order	CF81 NP11 3 and NP11 4 NP24	CF83 2 to CF83 4 NP11 6 and NP11 7	CF83 8 and CF83 9 NP12 0 to NP12 3	5th September 2018
Articles 3(2)(a) and 4(2)(a) and (b) of the No. 24 Order	CF82			5th September 2018
Articles 3(2)(f) and 4(2)(k) and (l) of the No. 24 Order	NP11 5	NP22 5		5th September 2018
Articles 3(2)(g) and 4(2)(m) and (n) of the No. 24 Order	SW15 1	SW15 3	SW15 5 and SW15 6	5th September 2018
Articles 3(2)(h) and 4(2)(o) and (p) of the No. 24 Order	EX7 SA63 SA66 SA69 SA72 TQ7 TQ10 TQ12 5 and TQ12 6	SA61 SA64 SA67 SA70 SA73 TQ8 TQ11 TQ13	SA62 SA65 SA68 SA71 TQ6 TQ9 TQ12 1 to TQ12 3 TQ14	5th September 2018
Articles 3(2)(i) and 4(2)(q) and (r) of the No. 24 Order	HP9 HP12 HP15 SL2 3 and SL2 4 SL9 7 to SL9 98	HP10 HP13 HP16 SL7	HP11 HP14 SL0 SL9 1	5th September 2018
Articles 3(2)(j) and 4(2)(s) and (t) of the No. 24 Order	SL9 0			5th September 2018
Articles 3(2)(l) and 4(2)(w) and (x) of the No. 24 Order	BS9 2 to BS9 4	BS10 5 BS11		5th September 2018
Articles 3(2)(n) and 4(2)(aa) and (bb) of the No. 24 Order	BS7 0 BS34	BS10 6 and BS10 7 BS35	BS32	5th September 2018
Articles 3(2)(o) and 4(2)(cc) and (dd) of the No. 24 Order	SW17 0	SW18 4 and SW18 5	SW19 6	5th September 2018
Articles 3(2)(p) and 4(2)(ee) and (ff) of the No. 24 Order	TQ1 TQ4	TQ2 TQ5	TQ3 TQ12 4	5th September 2018

Provisions modified	*Postcodes*			*Date*
Articles 3(2)(x) and 4(2)(uu) and (vv) of the No. 24 Order	CF83 1			5th September 2018
Articles 3(2)(g) and 4(2)(m) and (n) of the No. 22 Order	IP24 PE21	IP27 0 PE22 9	PE20 1 and PE20 2	12th September 2018
Articles 3(2)(n) and 4(2)(aa) and (bb) of the No. 22 Order	SK13 SK23	SK17 6 and SK17 7	SK22	12th September 2018
Articles 3(2)(a) and 4(2)(a) and (b) of the No. 24 Order	NR16 2			12th September 2018
Articles 3(2)(c) and 4(2)(e) and (f) of the No. 24 Order	NG15 9 NG19 6 NG21	NG18 NG19 9 NG22 8 and NG22 9	NG19 0 NG20 0 NG70	12th September 2018
Articles 3(2)(f) and 4(2)(k) and (l) of the No. 24 Order	B60 B78 1 HR8 2 WR13	B61 CV9 HR8 9 WR14	B76 0 CV13 6 WR8 0	12th September 2018
Articles 3(2)(g) and 4(2)(m) and (n) of the No. 24 Order	LN11 PE22 0	LN12 1 PE22 7	LN13 0	12th September 2018
Articles 3(2)(j) and 4(2)(s) and (t) of the No. 24 Order	DE4 SK17 0	DE45 SK17 8 and SK17 9	NG19 7	12th September 2018
Articles 3(2)(k) and 4(2)(u) and (v) of the No. 24 Order	DN10 4 PE20 3	DN21	LN8 6	12th September 2018
Articles 3(2)(u) and 4(2)(oo) and (pp) of the No. 24 Order	CB6 3	CB7		12th September 2018
Articles 3(2)(w) and 4(2)(ss) and (tt) of the No. 24 Order	CB6 1 and CB6 2 PE14	IP26 PE15	PE13 PE16	12th September 2018
Articles 3(2)(o) and 4(2)(cc) and (dd) of the No. 22 Order	G51 1 to G51 3	G51 9	G52 1	19th September 2018
Articles 3(2)(q) and 4(2)(gg) and (hh) of the No. 22 Order	G51 4 PA1 PA2 9 PA5 PA8 PA12	G52 2 to G52 4 PA2 PA3 PA6 PA9	G52 9 PA2 6 and PA2 7 PA4 PA7 PA10	19th September 2018
Articles 3(2)(s) and 4(2)(kk) and (ll) of the No. 24 Order	PA2 8			19th September 2018

Provisions modified	*Postcodes*			*Date*
Articles 3(2)(v) and 4(2)(qq) and (rr) of the No. 24 Order	G83 7 PA21 PA24 PA27 PA30 PA33 PA36 PA41 PA44 PA47 PA60 PA63 PA66 PA69 PA72 PA75 PA78	G84 PA22 PA25 PA28 PA31 PA34 PA37 PA42 PA45 PA48 PA61 PA64 PA67 PA70 PA73 PA76	PA20 PA23 PA26 PA29 PA32 PA35 PA38 PA43 PA46 PA49 PA62 PA65 PA68 PA71 PA74 PA77	19th September 2018
Articles 3(2)(i) and 4(2)(i) of the No. 17 Order	M27 0 M28	M27 5 M30	M27 8 and M27 9 M38	26th September 2018
Articles 3(2)(g) and 4(2)(g) of the No. 19 Order	L16 L18 3 and L18 4 L24 0 to L24 3 L26	L17 0 L18 6 to L18 9 L24 6 to L249 L27	L17 5 and L17 6 L19 L25	26th September 2018
Articles 3(2)(j) and 4(2)(j) of the No. 19 Order	L24 4 and L24 5			26th September 2018
Articles 3(2)(l) and 4(2)(l) of the No. 19 Order	M1 M5 M27 4	M2 M6 M27 6	M3 M7 1 to M7 3 M50	26th September 2018
Articles 3(2)(m) and 4(2)(m) of the No. 19 Order	LA5 0 LA8 LA11 9 M44	LA6 1 and LA6 2 LA9 LA22	LA7 LA11 6 LA23	26th September 2018
Articles 3(2)(k) and 4(2)(u) and (v) of the No. 22 Order	HS1 HS4 HS7 KW15 LA10 5 ZE3	HS2 HS5 HS8 KW16 ZE1	HS3 HS6 HS9 KW17 ZE2	26th September 2018
Articles 3(2)(n) and 4(2)(aa) and (bb) of the No. 22 Order	BN7 BN10	BN8 5 and BN8 6 BN25	BN9 TN22	26th September 2018
Articles 3(2)(o) and 4(2)(cc) and (dd) of the No. 22 Order	G5 G43 G53 6	G41 G44 5 G53 9	G42 G44 9	26th September 2018
Articles 3(2)(p) and 4(2)(ee) and (ff) of the No. 22 Order	TR21 TR24	TR22 TR25	TR23	26th September 2018
Articles 3(2)(a) and 4(2)(a) and (b) of the No. 24 Order	BN8 4			26th September 2018

Provisions modified	Postcodes			Date
Articles 3(2)(c) and 4(2)(e) and (f) of the No. 24 Order	G44 4			26th September 2018
Articles 3(2)(h) and 4(2)(o) and (p) of the No. 24 Order	EX1 EX4 EX8 EX18	EX2 EX5 EX9 EX20	EX3 EX6 EX17 EX21	26th September 2018
Articles 3(2)(i) and 4(2)(q) and (r) of the No. 24 Order	HP5 HP8 HP19 HP22 MK18	HP6 HP17 HP20 HP27	HP7 HP18 HP21 MK17 0	26th September 2018
Articles 3(2)(l) and 4(2)(w) and (x) of the No. 24 Order	BH21 6 BH25 SO42	BH23 8 BH31 SP6	BH24 SO41	26th September 2018
Articles 3(2)(s) and 4(2)(kk) and (ll) of the No. 24 Order	G44 3 G76 0 G78	G46 G76 6 to G76 8	G53 7 G77 2018	26th September
Articles 3(2)(y) and 4(2)(ww) and (xx) of the No. 24 Order	PO1 PO4 PO7	PO2 PO5 PO8	PO3 PO6	26th September 2018
Articles 3(2)(o) and 4(2)(cc) and (dd) of the No. 24 Order	SE7 SE9 9 SE12 2	SE9 1 SE10 0 and SE10 1 SE18	SE9 5 and SE9 6 SE10 9	3rd October 2018
Articles 3(2)(q) and 4(2)(gg) and (hh) of the No. 24 Order	CM21 0 and CM21 1 EN11 SG3 SG5 9 SG9 SG12	CM22 7 SG1 SG4 SG6 SG10 SG13	CM23 SG2 SG5 1 and SG5 2 SG8 1 SG11 SG14	3rd October 2018
Articles 3(2)(r) and 4(2)(ii) and (jj) of the No. 24 Order	SE3 SE12 0 TS1 TS4 TS8	SE9 2 to SE9 4 SE12 8 and SE12 9 TS2 TS5	SE10 8 SE28 TS3 TS7 8	3rd October 2018
Articles 3(2)(u) and 4(2)(oo) and (pp) of the No. 24 Order	SG7	SG8 5	SG8 8 and SG8 9	3rd October 2018
Articles 3(2)(y) and 4(2)(ww) and (xx) of the No. 24 Order	E2 E9	E5 N1 4 to N1 7	E8 N16	3rd October 2018
Articles 3(2)(f) and 4(2)(k) and (l) of the No. 24 Order	LD1 LD4 LD7 LL36 SY15 SY18 SY21	LD2 LD5 LD8 SA9 SY16 SY19 SY22	LD LD6 LL35 SY10 0 SY17 SY20 9	10th October 2018

Provisions modified	Postcodes			Date
Articles 3(2)(h) and 4(2)(o) and (p) of the No. 24 Order	SY20 8			10th October 2018
Articles 3(2)(k) and 4(2)(u) and (v) of the No. 24 Order	LS29 0	LS29 7 to LS29 9		10th October 2018
Articles 3(2)(q) and 4(2)(gg) and (hh) of the No. 24 Order	BD3 7 LS1 LS4 LS7 LS10 LS13 LS16 LS18 LS21 LS24 8 and LS24 9 LS26 0 LS29 6	BD4 8 LS2 LS5 LS8 LS11 LS14 LS17 1 LS19 LS22 LS25 3 LS27 WF3 2	BD11 1 LS3 LS6 LS9 LS12 LS15 LS17 5 to LS17 9 LS20 LS23 LS25 5 LS28	10th October 2018
Articles 3(2)(t) and 4(2)(mm) and (nn) of the No. 24 Order	CF61 CF64	CF62 CF71	CF63	10th October 2018
Articles 3(2)(aa) and 4(2)(aaa) and (bbb) of the No. 24 Order	LS26 8	WF3 1		10th October 2018
Articles 3(2)(g) and 4(2)(m) and (n) of the No. 22 Order	IP11 IP13 6 IP16	IP12 IP13 9 IP17	IP13 0 IP15	17th October 2018
Articles 3(2)(n) and 4(2)(aa) and (bb) of the No. 22 Order	NN14 2 NN16 0	NN14 6 NN16 8 and NN16 9	NN15	17th October 2018
Articles 3(2)(q) and 4(2)(gg) and (hh) of the No. 22 Order	WS3 4 WS9 9	WS7 4	WS8 6	17th October 2018
Articles 3(2)(b) and 4(2)(c) and (d) of the No. 24 Order	IP13 7 and IP13 8 NR26	NR11 8 NR27	NR25	17th October 2018
Articles 3(2)(c) and 4(2)(e) and (f) of the No. 24 Order	B94 CV23 8 CV33 CV47 NN16 6	CV8 1 and CV8 2 CV31 CV34 NN14 1 WR1	CV23 0 CV32 CV35 8 NN14 3 and NN14 4 WR4 9	17th October 2018
Articles 3(2)(d) and 4(2)(g) and (h) of the No. 24 Order	WR3 WR7	WR4 0 WR9 0	WR5 1 WR9 8 and WR9 9	17th October 2018
Articles 3(2)(f) and 4(2)(k) and (l) of the No. 24 Order	WR2 WR9 7	WR5 2 and WR5 3	WR6	17th October 2018

Provisions modified	Postcodes			Date
Articles 3(2)(g) and 4(2)(m) and (n) of the No. 24 Order	NG16 1			17th October 2018
Articles 3(2)(l) and 4(2)(w) and (x) of the No. 24 Order	CV35 7 NR3 NR6 NR9 NR12 7 and NR12 8 NR15 1 NR18	NR1 NR4 NR7 NR10 NR13 4 to NR13 6 NR16 1 WS8 7	NR2 NR5 NR8 NR11 7 NR14 NR17	17th October 2018
Articles 3(2)(r) and 4(2)(ii) and (jj) of the No. 24 Order	WV12	WV13		17th October 2018
Articles 3(2)(s) and 4(2)(kk) and (ll) of the No. 24 Order	LE12 6 NG3 NG6 NG11 NG14 5	NG1 NG4 NG7 NG12 NG15 5 to NG15 8	NG2 NG5 1 and NG5 2 NG8 NG13 8 and NG13	17th October 2018
Articles 3(2)(u) and 4(2)(oo) and (pp) of the No. 24 Order	CB1 CB4 CB22 CB25 9 PE27 PE28 4 and PE28 5 SG8 0	CB2 CB5 CB23 PE19 PE28 0 PE28 9 SG8 6 and SG8 7	CB3 CB21 5 and CB21 6 CB24 PE26 1 PE28 2 PE29	17th October 2018
Articles 3(2)(w) and 4(2)(ss) and (tt) of the No. 24 Order	PE26 2	PE28 3		17th October 2018
Articles 3(2)(g) and 4(2)(m) and (n) of the No. 24 Order	HA4 UB7 UB10	UB3 UB8 UB11	UB4 UB9 4 and UB9 5	24th October 2018
Articles 3(2)(j) and 4(2)(s) and (t) of the No. 24 Order	UB9 6			24th October 2018
Articles 3(2)(l) and 4(2)(w) and (x) of the No. 24 Order	PO33 PO36	PO34 PO37	PO35	24th October 2018
Articles 3(2)(n) and 4(2)(aa) and (bb) of the No. 24 Order	BS15 BS30 GL9	BS16 4 to BS16 7 BS36 GL12 8	BS16 9 BS37 GL13	24th October 2018
Articles 3(2)(r) and 4(2)(ii) and (jj) of the No. 24 Order	DA1 4 DA7 DA15 DA18 GU14 GU34 9 GU52	DA5 DA8 DA16 GU11 GU30 GU35 SE2	DA6 DA14 DA17 GU12 4 GU34 1 to GU34 3 GU51	24th October 2018

Provisions modified	Postcodes			Date
Articles 3(2)(s) and 4(2)(kk) and (ll) of the No. 24 Order	CR3 6 and CR3 7 GU3 1 and GU3 2 GU6 GU9 GU26 KT18 KT21 KT23 RH2 RH5 RH7 6 SM7 1 and SM7 2	GU1 GU4 8 GU7 GU10 GU27 KT19 KT22 2 KT24 RH3 RH6 0 RH8 SM7 9	GU2 GU5 GU8 GU12 6 KT17 KT20 KT22 7 to KT22 9 RH1 RH4 RH6 7 to RH6 9 RH9	24th October 2018
Articles 3(2)(t) and 4(2)(mm) and (nn) of the No. 24 Order	LU1	LU2	LU5 5 and LU5 6	24th October 2018
Articles 3(2)(u) and 4(2)(oo) and (pp) of the No. 24 Order	GU3 3 GU21 GU24	GU4 7 GU22 KT14 6	GU12 5 GU23	24th October 2018
Articles 3(2)(w) and 4(2)(ss) and (tt) of the No. 24 Order	N8 N17	N10 N22	N15 3 to N15 5	24th October 2018
Articles 3(2)(y) and 4(2)(ww) and (xx) of the No. 24 Order	GU34 4 and GU 34 5	N15 6		24th October 2018
Articles 3(2)(o) and 4(2)(cc) and (dd) of the No. 22 Order	G12 G4 G13 G21 G33 6	G2 G11 G14 G22	G3 G11 G20 G23	31st October 2018
Articles 3(2)(i) and 4(2)(q) and (r) of the No. 24 Order	AB10 AB13 AB16 AB23 AB31 AB34 AB39 AB51	AB11 AB14 AB21 AB24 AB32 AB35 AB41 6 and AB41 7 AB52	AB12 AB15 AB22 AB25 AB33 AB36 AB41 9 AB53 8	31st October 2018
Articles 3(2)(m) and 4(2)(y) and (z) of the No. 24 Order	G61	G62	G64 1 to G64 3	31st October 2018
Articles 3(2)(c) and 4(2)(c) of the No. 17 Order	BL1 BL4 BL6 4	BL2 BL5 1 BL6 9	BL3 BL5 3 M263	7th November 2018
Articles 3(2)(b) and 4(2)(b) of the No. 19 Order	L15	L18 0 to L18 2	L18 5	7th November 2018
Articles 3(2)(c) and 4(2)(c) of the No. 19 Order	L1 L6 0 and L6 1 L7 L17 7 to L17 9	L2 L6 3 and L6 4 L8	L3 L6 6 to L6 9 L17 1 to L17 4	7th November 2018

Provisions modified	Postcodes			Date
Articles 3(2)(e) and 4(2)(e) of the No. 19 Order	BL5 2			7th November 2018
Articles 3(2)(k) and 4(2)(k) of the No. 19 Order	BL6 5 to BL6 7	BL7		7th November 2018
Articles 3(2)(o) and 4(2)(cc) and (dd) of the No. 24 Order	S1 S4 S6 3 S9 S12 S32 S35 8 and S35 9	S2 S5 0 S7 S10 S14 S33	S3 S5 5 to S5 7 S8 S11 S17 S35 0 to S35 4	7th November 2018
Articles 3(2)(t) and 4(2)(mm) and (nn) of the No. 24 Order	NE20 NE61 NE65 7 and NE65 8 NE67 NE70 TD15	NE23 NE63 NE66 5 NE68 NE71	NE25 0 NE64 NE66 9 NE69 TD12	7th November 2018
Articles 3(2)(x) and 4(2)(uu) and (vv) of the No. 24 Order	CF37 CF40 CF43 CF72	CF38 CF41 CF44	CF39 CF42 CF45	7th November 2018
Articles 3(2)(n) and 4(2)(aa) and (bb) of the No. 22 Order	TF1 TF4 TF7	TF2 TF5 TF8	TF3 TF6 TF10 7	14th November 2018
Articles 3(2)(q) and 4(2)(gg) and (hh) of the No. 22 Order	NG5 0	NG5 7		14th November 2018
Articles 3(2)(a) and 4(2)(a) and (b) of the No. 24 Order	SY7 9			14th November 2018
Articles 3(2)(d) and 4(2)(g) and (h) of the No. 24 Order	DY10 1 and DY10 2 DY12 1 DY14 0 WR12	DY10 4 DY12 3 WR10	DY11 6 and DY11 7 DY13 8 and DY13 9 WR11	14th November 2018
Articles 3(2)(f) and 4(2)(k) and (l) of the No. 24 Order	DY12 2 WR8 9	DY13 0 WR15	DY14 8 and DY14 9	14th November 2018
Articles 3(2)(g) and 4(2)(m) and (n) of the No. 24 Order	NG9 1	NG9 3 to NG9 9		14th November 2018
Articles 3(2)(i) and 4(2)(q) and (r) of the No. 24 Order	B21 8 B66 B69 DY4	B43 5 and B43 6 B67 B70 WS5 4	B65 9 B68 B71 WS10 0	14th November 2018
Articles 3(2)(j) and 4(2)(s) and (t) of the No. 24 Order	MK16 8 NN2 NN5 NN12 OX17	MK19 NN3 NN7 1 to NN7 3 NN13 6 and NN13 7 WS10 7	NN1 NN4 NN7 9 NN13 9 WS10 9	14th November 2018

Provisions modified	Postcodes			Date
Articles 3(2)(k) and 4(2)(u) and (v) of the No. 24 Order	LN4 3 and LN4 4	LN10 6	NG32 3	14th November 2018
Articles 3(2)(l) and 4(2)(w) and (x) of the No. 24 Order	DY10 3	DY11 5	TF10 8 and TF10 9	14th November 2018
Articles 3(2)(s) and 4(2)(kk) and (ll) of the No. 24 Order	NG5 3 to NG5 6 NG4 6	NG5 8 and NG5 9	NG9 2	14th November 2018
Articles 3(2)(w) and 4(2)(ss) and (tt) of the No. 24 Order	PE30 PE33 PE36	PE31 6 and PE31 7 PE34 PE38	PE32 1 PE35	14th November 2018
Articles 3(2)(d) and 4(2)(d) of the No. 19 Order	BB4 BB9 4 and BB9 5 BB18 9 OL13	BB8 NN9 7 to BB9 9 BL0 O	BB9 0 BB18 5 OL12 8	21st November 2018
Articles 3(2)(j) and 4(2)(j) of the No. 19 Order	SK1 SK4 SK7	SK2 SK5 SK8	SK3 SK6 SK12	21st November 2018
Articles 3(2)(k) and 4(2)(k) of the No. 19 Order	BB9 6			21st November 2018
Articles 3(2)(n) and 4(2)(n) of the No. 19 Order	BB7			21st November 2018
Articles 3(2)(a) and 4(2)(a) and (b) of the No. 22 Order	BB18 6			21st November 2018
Articles 3(2)(c) and 4(2)(e) and (f) of the No. 22 Order	NW2 1 NW6 9	NW2 4 to NW2 7 NW10 2 and NW10 3	NW6 6 and NW6 NW10 8 and NW10 9	21st November 2018
Articles 3(2)(e) and 4(2)(i) and (j) of the No. 22 Order	ME14 ME17 1	ME15 ME17 3 and ME17 4	ME16 8 ME18 6	21st November 2018
Articles 3(2)(g) and 4(2)(m) and (n) of the No. 22 Order	ME17 2			21st November 2018
Articles 3(2)(h) and 4(2)(o) and (p) of the No. 22 Order	DE13 0 ST14 7	DE13 8 ST14 9	DE14	21st November 2018
Articles 3(2)(q) and 4(2)(gg) and (hh) of the No. 22 Order	NG15 0	NG17 0 to NG17 3	NG17 5 to NG17 9	21st November 2018
Articles 3(2)(t) and 4(2)(mm) and (nn) of the No. 22 Order	NW10 4	NW10 7		21st November 2018

Provisions modified	Postcodes			Date
Articles 3(2)(a) and 4(2)(a) and (b) of the No. 24 Order	TN12 9			21st November 2018
Articles 3(2)(b) and 4(2)(c) and (d) of the No. 24 Order	NN8 2 to NN8 6	NN8 9		21st November 2018
Articles 3(2)(c) and 4(2)(e) and (f) of the No. 24 Order	NG17 4 NN29	NN8 1	NN9 5	21st November 2018
Articles 3(2)(d) and 4(2)(g) and (h) of the No. 24 Order	ME6 ME18 5 TN1 TN3 8 TN10 TN13 TN15 8 and TN15 9 TN27 9	ME16 0 ME19 TN2 TN4 TN11 TN14 5 and TN14 6 TN17	ME16 9 ME20 TN 3 0 TN9 TN12 5 to TN12 8 TN15 0 TN18	21st November 2018
Articles 3(2)(f) and 4(2)(k) and (l) of the No. 24 Order	DE11 DE13 9 ST15 ST17 9 ST21	DE12 6 DE15 ST16 ST18 0	DE12 8 ST14 8 ST17 4 ST20	21st November 2018
Articles 3(2)(h) and 4(2)(o) and (p) of the No. 24 Order	NW10 5	W10 4		21st November 2018
Articles 3(2)(j) and 4(2)(s) and (t) of the No. 24 Order	DE6 5 NN6 0	NG19 8 ST14 5	NG20 8 and NG20 9	21st November 2018
Articles 3(2)(l) and 4(2)(w) and (x) of the No. 24 Order	ST17 0 WS6 WS15 1 and Ws15 2	ST18 9 WS11 WS15 4	ST19 WS12 WS15 9	21st November 2018
Articles 3(2)(o) and 4(2)(cc) and (dd) of the No. 24 Order	TN16 1			21st November 2018
Articles 3(2)(p) and 4(2)(ee) and (ff) of the No. 24 Order	DE73 5	DE73 8		21st November 2018
Articles 3(2)(r) and 4(2)(ii) and (jj) of the No. 24 Order	WV11 9			21st November 2018
Articles 3(2)(s) and 4(2)(kk) and (ll) of the No. 24 Order	TN8	TN16 2		21st November 2018
Articles 3(2)(t) and 4(2)(mm) and (nn) of the No. 24 Order	LU3 LU6 SG15 SG18	LU4 LU7 SG16 SG19 1	LU5 4 SG5 3 and SG5 4 SG17	21st November 2018
Articles 3(2)(u) and 4(2)(oo) and (pp) of the No. 24 Order	SG19 2 and SG19 3			21st November 2018

Provisions modified	Postcodes			Date
Articles 3(2)(w) and 4(2)(ss) and (tt) of the No. 24 Order	NW2 2 and NW2 3 W9 3	NW61 and NW6 2	NW6 5	21st November 2018
Articles 3(2)(d) and 4(2)(gg) and (hh) of the No. 22 Order	EH1 EH4 EH7 EH10 4 to EH10 6 EH12 EH15 G60 G82 1 to G82 4 G83 3	EH2 EH5 EH8 EH10 9 EH13 EH16 5 and EH16 6 G81 1 to G81 4 G82 9	EH3 EH6 EH9 EH11 EH14 EH17 7 G81 6 G83 0	28th November 2018
Articles 3(2)(i) and 4(2)(q) and (r) of the No. 22 Order	EH10 7	EH16 4	EH17 8	28th November 2018
Articles 3(2)(m) and 4(2)(y) and (z) of the No. 22 Order	G83 9			28th November 2018
Articles 3(2)(i) and 4(2)(q) and (r) of the No. 24 Order	EH30			28th November 2018
Articles 3(2)(m) and 4(2)(y) and (z) of the No. 24 Order	G81 5			28th November 2018
Articles 3(2)(r) and 4(2)(ii) and (jj) of the No. 24 Order	GU31	GU32	GU33	28th November 2018
Articles 3(2)(u) and 4(2)(oo) and (pp) of the No. 24 Order	GU15 GU18 GU25 KT7 KT11 KT14 7 KT16 TW17 TW20	GU16 GU19 GU46 KT8 KT12 KT14 9 KT22 0 TW18	GU17 GU20 GU47 7 and GU47 8 KT10 KT13 KT15 TW15 TW19	28th November 2018 TW16
Articles 3(2)(v) and 4(2)(qq) and (rr) of the No. 24 Order	G63 0	G82 5	G83 8	28th November 2018
Articles 3(2)(w) and 4(2)(ss) and (tt) of the No. 24 Order	TS6 TS9 6 TS12	TS7 0 TS10 TS13	TS7 9 TS11 TS14	28th November 2018
Articles 3(2)(y) and 4(2)(ww) and (xx) of the No. 24 Order	PO9 PO12 PO15 SO31 0 and SO31 1 SO32 3	PO10 7 PO13 PO16 SO31 6 and SO31 7	PO11 PO14 PO17 SO31 9	28th November 2018

Provisions modified	Postcodes			Date
Articles 3(2)(aa) and 4(2)(aaa) and (bbb) of the No. 24 Order	LS25 1 and LS25 2 LS26 9 WF3 3 and WF3 4 WF6 WF9	LS25 4 WF1 WF4 WF7 WF10	LS25 7 WF2 WF5 WF8 WF11	28th November 2018
Articles 3(2)(c) and 4(2)(c) of the No. 19 Order	L4 0 to L4 4 L62	L4 7 L6 5	L5	5th December 2018
Articles 3(2)(f) and 4(2)(f) of the No. 19 Order	L4 6	L4 8 and L4 9	L11	5th December 2018
Articles 3(2)(g) and 4(2)(g) of the No. 19 Order	L12	L13		5th December 2018
Articles 3(2)(h) and 4(2)(h) of the No. 19 Order	FY5	FY6	FY7	5th December 2018
Articles 3(2)(m) and 4(2)(m) of the No. 19 Order	FY1 FY4 LA12 LA15 LA18 LA21	FY2 FY8 LA13 LA16 LA19 PR4 1 to PR4 3	FY3 LA11 7 LA14 LA17 LA20	5th December 2018
Articles 3(2)(c) and 4(2)(e) and (f) of the No. 22 Order	HA0 2 to HA0 4	HA9	NW10 0 and NW10 1	5th December 2018
Articles 3(2)(o) and 4(2)(cc) and (dd) of the No. 22 Order	G1 1 G15 G33 1 to G33 5 G40 G69 6 to G69 8	G1 3 to G1 5 G31 G33 9 G45	G1 9 G32 G34 G69 1	5th December 2018
Articles 3(2)(t) and 4(2)(mm) and (nn) of the No. 22 Order	HA0 1			5th December 2018
Articles 3(2)(a) and 4(2)(a) and (b) of the No. 24 Order	HP1 LL58 LL62 LL65 LL68 LL71 LL74 LL77 7 and L77 8 WD7	HP2 LL60 LL63 LL66 LL69 LL72 LL75 LL78	HP3 9 LL61 LL64 LL67 LL70 LL73 LL76 WD6	5th December 2018
Articles 3(2)(b) and 4(2)(c) and (d) of the No. 24 Order	CM0 CM1 9 CM9 4 and CM9 5	CM1 to CM1 3 CM2 CM9 8	CM1 6 and CM1 7 CM3 5 to CM3 8 CM11 1	5th December 2018
Articles 3(2)(c) and 4(2)(e) and (f) of the No. 24 Order	CM1 4 CM9 6	CM3 1	CM3 3 and CM3 4	5th December 2018
Articles 3(2)(f) and 4(2)(k) and (l) of the No. 24 Order	LL59	LL77 9		5th December 2018

Provisions modified	*Postcodes*			*Date*
Articles 3(2)(h) and 4(2)(o) and (p) of the No. 24 Order	SA35 SA38 SA43 SA45 SA48 SY25	SA36 SA41 SA44 6 SA46 SY23	SA37 SA42 SA44 9 SA47 SY24	5th December 2018
Articles 3(2)(i) and 4(2)(q) and (r) of the No. 24 Order	HP4 2 and HP4 3 MK2 MK5 MK8 MK11 MK14 MK16 6	HP23 MK3 MK6 MK9 MK12 MK15 MK16 9	MK1 MK4 MK7 MK10 MK13 MK16 0 MK46	5th December 2018
Articles 3(2)(j) and 4(2)(s) and (t) of the No. 24 Order	HP3 0	HP3 8		5th December 2018
Articles 3(2)(q) and 4(2)(gg) and (hh) of the No. 24 Order	CM5 EN9 3	CM16 IG10	EN9 1	5th December 2018
Articles 3(2)(s) and 4(2)(kk) and (ll) of the No. 24 Order	IG7 5 and IG7 6	IG9	RM4	5th December 2018
Articles 3(2)(t) and 4(2)(mm) and (nn) of the No. 24 Order	HP4 1	MK17 8 and MK17 9		5th December 2018
Articles 3(2)(w) and 4(2)(ss) and (tt) of the No. 24 Order	NW1 0 NW5	NW1 7 to NW1 9 NW6 3 and NW6 4	NW3	5th December 2018
Articles 3(2)(g) and 4(2)(m) and (n) of the No. 22 Order	CB8 1	IP28 6 and IP28 7		12th December 2018
Articles 3(2)(h) and 4(2)(o) and (p) of the No. 22 Order	CW2 5 ST5 5 to ST5 9	CW3 9 ST7 1	ST5 2 and ST5 3 ST7 8	12th December 2018
Articles 3(2)(n) and 4(2)(aa) and (bb) of the No. 22 Order	ST7 3	ST8 6	ST8 9	12th December 2018
Articles 3(2)(b) and 4(2)(c) and (d) of the No. 24 Order	NR12 0 NR21 7 and NR21 8	NR12 9 NR24	NR21 0 NR28	12th December 2018
Articles 3(2)(f) and 4(2)(k) and (l) of the No. 24 Order	LL23 LL39 LL42 LL45 LL48 LL52 LL55 SA14 SA17 SA20 SA33	LL37 LL40 LL43 LL46 LL49 LL53 LL56 SA15 SA18 SA31 ST5 4	LL38 LL41 LL44 LL47 LL51 LL54 LL57 SA16 SA19 SA32	12th December 2018

Provisions modified	Postcodes			Date
Articles 3(2)(h) and 4(2)(o) and (p) of the No. 24 Order	SA34 SA44 4 and SA44 5	SA39	SA40	12th December 2018
Articles 3(2)(l) and 4(2)(w) and (x) of the No. 24 Order	NR11 6			12th December 2018
Articles 3(2)(o) and 4(2)(cc) and (dd) of the No. 24 Order	S5 8 and S5 9 S6 9 S36 1 to S36 4	S6 1 and S6 2 S13	S6 4 to S6 6 S20	12th December 2018
Articles 3(2)(q) and 4(2)(gg) and (hh) of the No. 24 Order	ST4 4 to ST4 9 ST7 4	ST5 0 and ST5 1 ST8 7	ST6 5	12th December 2018
Articles 3(2)(t) and 4(2)(mm) and (nn) of the No. 24 Order	CA8 7 NE24 NE43 NE46 NE49 NE65 9	NE19 NE26 4 NE44 NE47 NE62 NE66 1 to NE66 4	NE22 NE42 5 and NE42 6 NE45 NE48 NE65 0	12th December 2018
Articles 3(2)(u) and 4(2)(oo) and (pp) of the No. 24 Order	CB8 0 HU1 HU4 6 HU6 HU9 HU16 IP28 8	CB8 7 to CB8 9 HU2 HU4 9 HU7 HU11 HU19	CB25 0 HU3 HU5 HU8 HU12 HU20	12th December 2018
Articles 3(2)(w) and 4(2)(ss) and (tt) of the No. 24 Order	IP27 9 NR23	NR21 9 PE31 8	NR22	12th December 2018
Articles 3(2)(cc) and 4(2)(eee) and (fff) of the No. 24 Order	All further postcode districts and part-districts in England and Wales, and Scotland			12th December 2018

PART II

UPDATING MATERIAL
VOLUME I

NON MEANS TESTED BENEFITS AND EMPLOYMENT AND SUPPORT ALLOWANCE

Commentary by

Ian Hooker

John Mesher

Edward Mitchell

Richard Poynter

Christopher Ward

Nick Wikeley

p.27, *correction to the Social Security Contributions and Benefits Act 1992 s.1 (Outline of contributory system)*

ERRATUM: With effect from October 12, 2015, Sch.15(1), para.2 of   2.001
the Pensions Act 2014 added to s.1(2):

"(da) Class 3A, payable by eligible people voluntarily under section 14A with a view to obtaining units of additional pension; and"

A consequential amendment was made to include a reference to Class 3A contributions in the list in s.1(4)(a).

p.49, *correction to the Social Security Contributions and Benefits Act 1992 s.38(1) (Widow's pension (deaths before 9 April 2001))*

ERRATUM: Delete the words "[² pensionable age]" at the end of   2.002
s.38(1)(a) and replace with "the age of 65". The deleted amendment should have been made by the Pensions Act 2007 Sch.1 para.40 but was overlooked; see further the Explanatory Memorandum to the Social Security (Miscellaneous Amendments No. 4) Regulations 2017 (SI 2017/1015).

p.75, *annotation to the Social Security Contributions and Benefits Act 1992 s.48A (Category B retirement pension for married person or civil partner)*

A challenge to s.48A's general exclusion of those who attained pen-   2.003
sionable age on or after 6 April 2016 was made in *FY v SSWP* (RP) [2018] UKUT 146 (AAC). The Appellant attained pensionable age on 21 April 2016 and his wife, for whom the Appellant wished to secure a category B pension, would attain pensionable age on 11 January 2021. The condition in s.48A(1)(a) was not met because the wife had not attained pensionable age by 6 April 2016. While the wife's entitlement to a Category B pension was in issue, the proceedings were brought by the husband and followed the Secretary of State's decision on his own claim for retirement pension. Upper Tribunal Judge Wikeley held that no decision had been made about the wife's entitlement to a Category B pension. In the absence of such a decision, there was nothing to be challenged before the First-tier Tribunal and, in turn, the Upper Tribunal. The Upper Tribunal could not, therefore, consider the Appellant's substantive arguments.

In *FY*, the Appellant husband did, in fact, apply without success to the First-tier Tribunal for his wife to be made a party to the proceedings. Judge Wikeley rejected the husband's challenge to the First-tier Tribunal's refusal to make his wife a party to the proceedings. In the absence of a decision as to her entitlement to a Category B pension, the First-tier Tribunal rightly refused to make the wife to a party to the proceedings. Judge Wikeley went on to observe that, in advance of a decision as to the wife's entitlement to a Category B pension, which could not possibly be given before 2021 when she attained pensionable age, the only potential means of challenging what the Appellant described as the 'abolition' of

Category B pensions was a claim for judicial review in the High Court.

p.225, *annotation to the Social Security Contributions and Benefits Act 1992 s.113 (General provisions as to disqualification and suspension)*

2.004   For a further decision on the EU-Morocco Agreement, see *HMRC v HEH and SSWP (TC and CHB)* [2018] UKUT 237 (AAC).

p.235, *amendments to the Social Security Contributions and Benefits Act 1992 s.122 (Interpretation of Parts I to VI and supplementary provisions)*

2.005   With effect from November 15, 2018, reg.2 of the Social Security (Updating of EU References) (Amendment) Regulations 2018 (SI 2018/1084) amended s.122(1) by inserting the words "as amended from time to time"–
  (a) in the definition of "Regulation (EC) No 1408/71", after "14 June 1971"; and
  (b) in the definition of "Regulation (EC) No 883/2004", after "29 April 2004".

p.239, *amendments to the Social Security Contributions and Benefits Act 1992 s.149 (Provisions supplementary to section 148)*

2.006   With effect from December 6, 2018, para.43 of Sch.1(VIII) to the Pensions Act 2007 amended s.149(4) by replacing "the age of 65" with "pensionable age".

p.343, *correction to the Welfare Reform Act 2007 s.1 (Employment and support allowance)*

2.007   ERRATUM: In s.1(3)(aa) delete "as accepted" and replace with "has accepted".

pp.396-397, *annotation to the Welfare Reform Act 2007 Sch.1 para.6(1)(g) (Income related allowance)*

2.008   See further *MW v SSWP (ESA)* [2018] UKUT 304 (AAC), discussed in the note to the ESA Regulations 2008, reg.33, below.

p.424, *annotation to the Welfare Reform Act 2012 s.78 (Personal independence payment)*

2.009   In *KM v SSWP (PIP)* [2018] UKUT 296 (AAC) Judge Rowland adopted a novel approach to the problem that arises where the claimant has claimed PIP successfully in respect of one element and appealed against refusal of the other. If the judge in the UT upholds that appeal but directs that there should be a rehearing of the matter before a fresh tribunal the claimant may lose their income from the part to which they are entitled pending the outcome of the whole appeal. He observes that the ability of DWP to make payment on account of benefit is more limited in relation to PIP than was the case in DLA. In this case he agreed, unusually, to set aside only the part of the decision that was wrong in law and return that decision to an FTT to, in effect, complete the decision. And note that Judge Wright refers, in passing, to his having followed that course of action in other cases in his decision in *AW v SSWP (PIP)* [2018] UKUT 76 (AAC).

p.430, *amendment to the Welfare Reform Act 2012 s.84 (No entitlement to daily living component where UK is not competent state)*

With effect from November 15, 2018, reg.3(a) and (b) of the Social Security (Updating of EU References) (Amendment) Regulations (SI 2018/1084) amended this section as follows: (i) in subs.(2)(a), after "14 June 1971", by inserting ", as amended from time to time," and (ii) in subs.(2)(b), after "29 April 2004", by inserting ", as amended from time to time,". 2.010

p.462, *annotation to the Pensions Act 2014 s.30 (General Note cohabiting partners)*

The case of *McLaughlin, Re Judicial Review (Northern Ireland)* [2018] UKSC 48 in the Supreme Court has restored, effectively, the decision of Treacy J. in the High Court. The Supreme Court held, by a majority, that s.39A of the Contributions and Benefits Act is incompatible with article 14 read with article 8 of the ECHR insofar as it precluded entitlement to Widowed Parent's Allowance by the surviving partner of the deceased. The decision does not necessarily establish the claimant's entitlement to the benefit, because the effect of a declaration of incompatibility is just that–it remains for the DWP to determine what they will do in relation to the claim. At the time of writing this note the response of DWP is not known. However, it seems reasonably clear that some claimants, at least, should become entitled to Widowed Parent's Allowance, although Lady Hale, in the leading judgment, does observe that the case is strongest in respect of children of whom both spouses are a parent, as was the case here. The decision makes clear that the other old-style bereavement benefits (except conceivably Widowed Mother's Allowance) are not affected by this decision. In a separate judgment Lord Mance (with whom the rest of the majority agree) finds that *Shackell* was wrongly decided in making no distinction between benefits intended for support of children of the couple and other benefits. It was notable that in all other European countries (except Malta) the benefit was paid as a benefit of the child directly, and not via the surviving spouse. In Malta the benefit is paid to the survivor, but without regard to the legitimacy of the child. The court specifically makes no reference to the new Bereavement Support Payment. It is arguable that the difference in the rate at which that benefit is paid when the surviving spouse has responsibility for children might equally be incompatible with the ECHR, but (depending on the response that the DWP makes) that may require further litigation. 2.011

p.464, *annotation to the Pensions Act 2014 (Proof of a valid marriage)*

2.012   The case of *Akhter v Khan and the Attorney General* [2018] EWFC 54 has raised the question of whether religious ceremonies in this country other than those in the Church of England should be regarded as creating a marriage recognised for any purpose by the law. In this case it was an Islamic marriage ceremony (a Nikah) in which both parties regarded it as being the first step in formalising their relationship and intended to be followed by a civil ceremony in accordance with English law. Although the parties lived together for 18 years and had 4 children together, the civil ceremony never took place. The "wife" contended that she had constantly pressed her partner to complete the process, but that he had refused to do so. These proceedings were brought seeking divorce and consequent orders for matrimonial relief. Williams J. concluded that, on these facts, there had been a marriage that was void under the Matrimonial Causes Act 1973 and in respect of which the wife was entitled to a decree of nullity. That decree could give access to further orders for matrimonial relief. This decision does not however give any right to claim a Bereavement Support Payment. On the contrary, the marriage was found to be void. It was not a valid marriage at all; its status as a void marriage has effect only to support the action under the Matrimonial Causes Act.

p.572, *annotation to the Social Security Benefit (Computation of Earnings) Regulations 1996 (SI 1996/2745) reg.13 (Calculation of net profit of self-employed earners)*

2.013   The decision referred to as "CIB/4174/2003, decision of January 26, 2007" is reported as R(IB)3/07.

p.761, *annotation to the Social Security (Personal Independence Payment) Regulations 2013 (SI 2013/377) reg.2 (Interpretation—aid or appliance)*

2.014   The reasoning adopted by Judge Jacobs in *CW v SSWP (PIP)* [2016] UKUT 197 (AAC) has been applied too in *DR v SSWP (PIP)* [2018] UKUT 209 (AAC). There, the claimant had been awarded 2 points by the FTT for needing a "perching stool" to use while preparing a meal (Descriptor 1b). On appeal Judge Lane found that this was an error. On the facts before her she found that the claimant had no greater need to sit while preparing food and cooking a meal than might any person without a disability. Consequently, she said, applying the reasoning of the *CW* case, his need to sit from time to time was no evidence of a need to use an aid or appliance; it was, in effect, no evidence of any disability.

p.764, *annotation to the Social Security (Personal Independence Payment) Regulations 2013 (SI 2013/377) (Prior award of DLA)*

2.015   The circumstances in which an FTT is obliged to consider evidence that may have been relevant to an earlier claim for benefit, usually on entitlement to DLA, when they are considering an appeal for PIP have been reviewed by Judge Markus QC in two cases heard together, *CH and KN v SSWP (PIP)* [2018] UKUT 330 (AAC). These were both cases arising on the transfer of former DLA claimants to PIP, but similar issues can arise where the claimant seeks to involve as evidence on the claim for PIP evidence from earlier or contemporaneous claims for ESA, and even from claims for industrial injuries benefit.

Judge Markus found that she was required to answer two questions. First, in what circumstances should an FTT obtain evidence of an earlier award of DLA, and secondly, when will the FTT be required to give reasons that explain a difference that arises when the claimant's award of PIP is less beneficial than their previous award of DLA.

In answering the first question the Judge offers detailed advice on when the evidence from the earlier claim will be relevant followed by advice on the circumstances in which an FTT should call for evidence from an earlier claim. This advice can be found in paragraphs 45 to 66 of her judgment. (Judge Markus had been given details of the improved procedures that should now be followed by DWP so that the evidence should already be before the FTT on transfer cases, such as these, if the claimant has requested it.)

In answering the second question Judge Markus supports the remarks that had been made by Judge Ward in *YM v SSWP (PIP)* [2018] UKUT 16 (AAC). She says that she supports Judge Ward's approach in saying that there is no rule of law that requires a difference of outcome to be explained and that it is for the tribunal to determine in the circumstances of a particular case whether there is such an apparent inconsistency that reasons for it, are called for.

On the facts of these two cases she found that, in the first case, the Secretary of State had failed to include medical evidence in the file, even though it had been requested (at the FTT the claimant had not complained of its absence), but Judge Markus thought the evidence before the FTT was so complete, and given that the DLA evidence would have been 12 years old, that there was no error of law in failing to adjourn for that evidence. Nor in those circumstances was there any need for the FTT to explain the reasons for the difference between the claimant's awards. The reason that he did not succeed on the PIP claim was clear, though she does suggest that a brief single sentence to explain why the FTT had preferred the evidence on the current claim might have been desirable.

In the second case the judge found that there was sufficient overlap between what was probably the basis of the DLA claim and hence on which that was based and the current evidence of panic attacks suffered by the claimant and affecting her ability to go out alone, that the FTT had made an error of law in failing to call for the DLA evidence. The case was remitted for reconsideration by a new tribunal.

In *AW v SSWP (PIP)* [2018] UKUT 76 (AAC) Judge Wright has considered another case where the evidence on which an award of DLA had been made was not available to the FTT. In that case, however, he felt able on the basis of what could be inferred from the claimant's condition (which counsel for the Secretary of State agreed was unlikely to have changed) to decide the case himself and award the mobility component at the standard rate.

Two further cases deal with these issues. Both are decisions of Judge May QC. In the first, *AR v SSWP (PIP)* [2018] UKUT 313 (AAC) the judge decided that even applying what was said by Judge Ward in the *YM* case that the appeal failed because, as Judge Ward had expressed it in the *YM* case, the evidence from the one claim would need to be "reasonably capable of being material" to the other. In this case the claimant suffered from epilepsy, but the FTT found no evidence that he was at risk of a seizure when he was out. Judge May thought that the DLA claim must have been based on him being "unable or virtually unable to walk" for it to have awarded at the higher rate and could have no relevance to his PIP claim. Again in *SM v SSWP (PIP)* [2018] UKUT 314 (AAC) Judge May observes that the requirement to explain the award of PIP when it differs from an earlier award of DLA as set out by Judge Ward in *YM v SSWP (PIP)* [2018] UKUT 16 (AAC) was obiter, but, in any case, he finds that the principle should not apply in this appeal because the reasons for which the earlier benefit were awarded (unable or virtually unable to walk) were not relevant to the criteria that the FTT had applied in the present case. The claimant, who suffered from arthritis, was found to satisfy Descriptor 2(d) of the Mobility Activities. It does not appear that she disputed this conclusion; her appeal was based on the fact that she had an abdominal stoma which made it impossible, she said, to use public transport. There was no evidence to suggest that she could walk only 20 metres so as to satisfy Descriptor 2(e) and qualify for the higher rate of mobility.

p.767, *annotation to the Social Security (Personal Independence Payment) Regulations 2013 (SI 2013/377) reg. 4 (Meaning of 'safely')*

2.016   In *SH v SSWP (PIP)* [2018] UKUT 251 (AAC) Judge Hemingway has made some observations about the functioning of the test for a claimant being able to accomplish an activity safely. The claimant was a profoundly deaf young woman. She had been fitted with cochlear implants that gave a good degree of hearing when she was wearing the external part of the appliance, but those had to be removed when she was bathing or taking a shower. It was argued that she could not bathe or shower safely without some supervision because, in the event of a fire or other catastrophe, she would not be able to hear any alarm or other warning sound. Her circumstances were the same as those of one of the claimants in the *RJ* case. In that case the three-judge tribunal had observed:

"On our analysis of regulation 4 and "supervision", these facts would indicate that she needed supervision to bathe".

It seemed that, initially, counsel for the present claimant had argued before the UT that this meant that her client was entitled to succeed in respect of Activity 4b (need for supervision when washing and bathing) but subsequently accepted that a determination on the facts of the case was still required. Judge Hemingway agreed with that position and noted that even in the *RJ* case itself the matter had been remitted to a new tribunal for determination. In the present case he thought that the FTT had applied the correct test in relation to the risk apparent and that their conclusion rejecting the claim was one that they were entitled to reach, except in one respect; in deciding that the claimant could bathe safely without the need for supervision they had suggested that she could reduce the risk of harm occurring by limiting the time spent in the bath or in a shower. This, he decided they were not entitled to do. He refers to *EG v SSWP (PIP)* [2017] UKUT 101 (AAC) in which it was held that the claimant should be assessed in accordance with what they would choose to do and not circumscribe their activities. Doubtless there are limits to a claimant's choice of behaviour but this accords with the approach taken in *Secretary of State v Fairey* [1997] 1 W.L.R. 799 for DLA.

p.776, *annotation to Social Security (Personal Independence Payment) Regulations 2013 (SI 2013/377) reg.8 (Information or evidence required for determining limited or severely limited ability to carry out activities— effect of a prior award of DLA)*

The circumstances in which it will be appropriate for a FTT to call for evidence from a prior award of another benefit, usually a prior award of DLA in the case of a claimant who is transferring from that benefit to PIP, has been examined and explained by Judge Markus QC in *CH and KN v SSWP (PIP)* [2018] UKUT 330 (AAC). That case, and others, is discussed in the General Note following reg.4 above. Members of FTT will find the guidance offered by Judge Markus and the information provided by the Secretary of State regarding the current process used in transfer cases very helpful.   2.017

p.777, *annotation to the Social Security (Personal Independence Payment) Regulations 2013 (SI 2013/377) reg.9 (Good cause for non-attendance)*

Judge Wikeley has dealt with this issue (twice) in respect of the same claimant, the second appeal being *TC v SSWP (No.2) (PIP)* [2018] UKUT 286 (AAC). On both occasions he emphasises the importance of FTT examining thoroughly the evidence on which the decision to reach a negative determination has been made.   2.018

p.797, *annotation to the Social Security (Personal Independence Payment) Regulations 2013 (SI 2013/377) Sch.1 (Interpretation)*

The Secretary of State agreed to withdraw the appeal against the decision in *SSWP v LB (PIP)* [2016] UKUT 530 (AAC). Appeals to a FTT from decisions made on the original version of these regulations should be determined in accordance with that decision. The Secretary of State at the same time also withdrew her appeals against two decisions of the FTT that were to have been heard before a three-judge panel of the UT. In *KM v SSWP (PIP)* [2018] UKUT 296 (AAC) Judge Rowland has given helpful guidance to tribunals applying the original version of   2.019

the Schedule in accordance with the decision of Judge Mesher in *SSWP v LB (PIP)* [2016] UKUT 530 (AAC).

p.802, *annotation to the Social Security (Personal Independence Payment) Regulations 2013 (SI 2013/377) Sch.1 (General Note)*

2.020   In *KM v SSWP (PIP)* [2018] UKUT 296 (AAC) Judge Rowland has given helpful guidance to tribunals applying the original version of the Schedule in accordance with the decision of Judge Mesher in *SSWP v LB (PIP)* [2016] UKUT 530 (AAC).

p.804, *annotation to the Social Security (Personal Independence Payment) Regulations 2013 (SI 2013/377) Sch.1 (General Note—aid or appliance)*

2.021   Note that the use of a perching stool as an aid when preparing food in Activity 1 has been questioned in the decision of Judge Lane in *DR v SSWP (PIP)* [2018] UKUT 209 (AAC). The decision does not deny that a stool might be an aid in some appropriate cases, but it does affect how often that will be so. Judge Lane adopts the reasoning used by Judge Jacobs in *CW v SSWP (PIP)* [2016] UKUT 197 (AAC). She found that on the facts of this case the claimant had not shown that he needed to sit more often than might be the case for any other person and hence he did not need the stool as an aid in relation to that activity.

p.807, *annotation to the Social Security (Personal Independence Payment) Regulations 2013 (SI 2013/377) Sch.1 (Activity 1—Preparing food)*

2.022   The commentary has been confirmed by a decision of a Commissioner in Northern Ireland in *EH v Department for Communities (PIP)* [2018] NI Comm 55. The claimant suffered from depression. He admitted that he had never learned to cook and that now he lived apart from his family he ate only sandwiches and takeaway meals. He said he did not know how to turn a cooker on and did not use the kettle. On appeal it had been contended that this meant that he required prompting to prepare a meal. The Commissioner found that the FTT had been correct in concluding that the claimant was capable of cooking a meal; his failure to do so was the result of cultural or behavioural choice when he had lived as part of a family when his meals were prepared by his mother and then by his wife. Because he had never learned to cook, there was no evidence before the FTT of a connection between his mental health and his ability to cook.

p.810, *annotation to the Social Security (Personal Independence Payment) Regulations 2013 (SI 2013/377) Sch.1 (Activity 1—Preparing food)*

2.023   Note that the use of a perching stool as an aid when preparing food in Activity 1 has been questioned in the decision of Judge Lane in *DR v SSWP (PIP)* [2018] UKUT 209 (AAC). The decision does not deny that a stool might be an aid in some appropriate cases, but it does affect how often that will be so. Judge Lane adopts the reasoning used by Judge

Jacobs in *CW v SSWP (PIP)* [2016] UKUT 197 (AAC). She found that on the facts of this case the claimant had not shown that he needed to sit more often than might be the case of any person without a disability and hence he did not need the stool as an aid in that activity. Given that she observes that most food preparation and cooking can be accomplished with relatively little time spent standing, and that most people sit at frequent stages while cooking, it seems that the need to use a stool as an appliance might seldom be shown.

p.812, *annotation to the Social Security (Personal Independence Payment) Regulations 2013 (SI 2013/377) Sch.1 (Activity 2—Taking nutrition)*

The problem of whether neglecting to eat or even a reluctance to eat   2.024
so as to require prompting by another person can satisfy Descriptor 2d has been referred to by Judge Hemingway in *JW v SSWP (PIP)* [2018] UKUT 169 (AAC). The claimant was autistic. He was currently studying at university for a degree in Game Design. The evidence given to the FTT suggested that he became so engrossed in his work that he would neglect to eat or drink for long periods unless he was prompted by another person to do so. The FTT did not award points in this respect, but they did so on the basis that he had said that he ate when he was hungry and they observed that he appeared well nourished. They concluded that he did not need prompting to take nutrition. Judge Hemingway, however, thought that the FTT had also accepted that sometimes the claimant might neglect to eat for so long as to become weak with hunger, and that sometimes he was distracted from eating even when the pains of hunger might tell him to do so. He felt that no clear finding had been made on that matter and returned the case on that, and other grounds, for reconsideration by a fresh tribunal.

In doing so he does remark that if the meaning of this Activity is to be confined by the strict definition as suggested in the *MM* and *BJ* cases, it may be difficult to see how neglect or disinclination to eat can lead to a need for prompting to take nutrition since that involves only the process of getting food to the mouth, chewing and swallowing it. But he did accept that those earlier cases were concerned with the quality of the food taken and did not involve the issue when the claimant might fail to eat at all.

p.813, *annotation to the Social Security (Personal Independence Payment) Regulations 2013 (SI 2013/377) Sch.1 (Managing therapy or monitoring a health condition)*

The Secretary of State has withdrawn the appeal against the decision   2.025
in *SSWP v LB (PIP)* [2016] UKUT 530 (AAC). Any appeal to an FTT that is to be heard now where the decision is based on the original version of the regulations should be determined in accordance with that decision. See further *AH v SSWP (PIP)* [2018] UKUT 262 (AAC) where this was held to apply also to a decision of an FTT that had been made in the interval between the new version of the regulation coming into force and the decision of Mostyn J quashing the regulation. The UT

held that the Judge's decision had retrospective effect so as to mean that the FTT decision (correct when made) was now an error of law.

p.814, *annotation to the Social Security (Personal Independence Payment) Regulations 2013 (SI 2013/377) Sch.1 (Managing therapy or monitoring a health condition)*

2.026   The meaning to be given to the word "therapy" and the distinction between that and other forms of care and support that might be given to a claimant has arisen in several cases. To begin with the judges are agreed that the word "therapy", in the absence of any more helpful statutory definition must be given its ordinary dictionary meaning which is "the medical treatment of disease; curative medical or psychiatric treatment" (Oxford English Dictionary). In the first of these cases, *DC v SSWP (PIP)* [2016] UKUT 11 (AAC), Judge Jacobs decides that therapy must involve something more than keeping an eye on the claimant and giving support to general living activities. Nor, he suggests would providing employment for the claimant amount to therapy; it might be described as being therapeutic for him, but would not be therapy in this sense. In *KM v SSWP (PIP)* [2018] UKUT 296 (AAC) Judge Rowland agrees with that conclusion though on the case before him he returned the matter to a fresh tribunal to take evidence as to the forms of support that the family provided. In *AH v SSWP (PIP)* [2016] UKUT 276 (AAC) the emphasis was on the need for therapy to have occurred on the advice of a health care professional and "at home". In that case, the encouragement of friends to give up smoking and the attendance at keep-fit classes in a gym, failed for one or both of those reasons. The judge found also that, even if the action had been taken on the advice of her GP, it would not be therapy unless there was a direct correlation to a disease or condition for which it was curative treatment. In *KM*, Judge Rowland adds a gloss to this by saying that he thought the requirement that the activity be "at home" was intended to exclude things done at a hospital or other specialist venues as had been the case in *AH*, rather than to confine activity to being in the house. In other words, support that was given by family members on the advice of a medical professional that took place out of doors, such as walking for exercise in the park might also qualify if it could be shown to be a part of a curative treatment programme.

     In *KM v SSWP (PIP)* [2018] UKUT 296 (AAC) Judge Rowland also gives useful advice in relation to the way that attention given to the claimant in relation to more than one PIP Activity and hence, therefore, suggest the possibility of double counting, must be approached. He summarises the effect of these and other cases as follows:

     "20. The overall effect of the case law as it applies for the purposes of this case is therefore that a need for "prompting . . . to be able to manage therapy" must be a need for something more than, or different from, ordinary interactions within a household and also more than, or different from, a need for supervision, prompting or assistance such as would score points either under descriptor 3(b)(ii) as construed in LB or under any of the other daily living or mobility activities.

21. Subject to that qualification, it seems to me that, insofar as engaging with other people may be therapeutic for a claimant and is in a form recommended by a relevant health professional, engagement by those other people with the claimant may amount to prompting the claimant to undertake therapy for the purposes of descriptors 3(c) to 3(f)"

A wide meaning to the terms "manage therapy" and within that "health" has been suggested by Judge Hemingway in *MM v SSWP (PIP)* [2018] UKUT 193 (AAC). The claimant was a young person who was pro-foundly deaf. She had been fitted with cochlear implants that improved her ability to hear, but on the advice of her audiologist she undertook exercises, with which her mother assisted, to train her brain so as to take full advantage of the implants. It was contended that this assistance should score under Activity 3 c or d depending on the time taken each week. The judge did not make a conclusive decision on the point because he had not had full argument on it; he did reject a suggestion put on behalf of the Secretary of State that the mother's help amounted to no more than encouragement to give up a bad habit or to take up a good pastime, but the question of whether training the brain could be therapy to avoid a deterioration in health was not argued. Judge Hemingway thought that it possibly could be. He refers to *RH v SSWP (PIP)* [2015] UKUT 281 (AAC) where the UT judge had accepted that a TENS machine that relieved the claimant's pain could be regarded as therapy because it improved his health in the sense of making him more comfort-able and hence its absence might be regarded as a deterioration in health. In the present case the judge thought it was arguable that the exercises might amount to therapy (they were advised by a health professional) if they facilitated her ability to hear and that, without them, her hearing would be reduced by more than a minimal degree.

The meaning of "therapy" has been touched on by Judge Perez in *PM v SSWP (PIP)* [2018] UKUT 138 (AAC). There the claimant, who suffered extensively from arthritis had been advised by her consultant to apply a compression bandage to her lower leg daily. She said that doing so caused her pain and that she was slow in doing it. It was not suggested that the bandage was medicated. The UT judge found that there were sufficient findings of fact in the case file to be able to award 2 points under Descriptor c—needs assistance to manage therapy that takes no more than 3.5 hours a week.

By contrast the meaning of "manage medication" might appear to be narrow. This point has emerged in *EH v Department for Communities (PIP)* [2018] NI Com 55, a decision of the Commissioner in Northern Ireland. The Commissioner observed that the definition in Part 1 of the schedule applied only to a "failure" to take medication "so as to result in a deterioration in the claimant's health". He thought that this might mean that where a claimant requires supervision so as to prevent them overdosing, the definition would not apply. Even if the phrase "deteriora-tion in C's health" could be read, broadly, to include an attempted suicide, the words "failure to [take]" would be difficult to apply to an overdose. Only if "take medication" could be read as meaning, implicitly, taking it correctly, could taking an excess be regarded as a failure to take.

p.817, *annotation to the Social Security (Personal Independence Payment) Regulations 2013 (SI 2013/377) Sch.1 (Activity 4—Washing and bathing)*

2.027   A decision of Judge Mitchell in *MB v SSWP (PIP)* [2018] UKUT 139 (AAC) has considered the meaning of Descriptor f in this Activity. The claimant had said that she could not wash the upper part of her back satisfactorily and therefore needed assistance to do so. The FTT had found that most people are unable to reach the upper spinal region of their body and that therefore the claimant's inability to do so could not score points under this descriptor. The Judge finds that this was an error of law. He says that doubtless the tribunal was correct in their assumption about the ability of most people, but that such people are able to wash their back to a satisfactory extent by the use of a sponge or other appliance. The question that they should have considered was whether the claimant was unable to do that in a similar way so as to achieve a similar result without requiring the assistance of another. The claimant had raised a separate point about her ability to dry her back. Although neither the definitions of wash or bathe nor the words of Activity 4 refer to drying oneself, the judge was able to conclude that in this case (and probably in almost all others) the two activities are so closely related in functional terms that an ability to do the one will inevitably include an ability to do the other.

Note that in *SH v SSWP (PIP)* [2018] UKUT 251 (AAC) Judge Hemingway has made the point that just because the claimant may have to remove cochlear implants when washing and bathing does not mean that they must always qualify to have a need for supervision. That was the same situation in *RJ and others v SSWP (PIP)* [2017] UKUT 105 (AAC); [2017] AACR 32 where the judges had suggested that supervision might be necessary to ensure the safety of the claimant when her implants were removed. In the present case Judge Hemingway suggests that so long as the question of safety is considered correctly in accordance with the meaning of safety in reg.4, and on the evidence before them, an FTT might still conclude that the claimant does not require supervision while bathing.

p.822, *annotation to the Social Security (Personal Independence Payment) Regulations 2013 (SI 2013/377) Sch.1 (Activity 7—Communicating verbally)*

2.028   The matter of whether lip-reading should be taken account of in assessing a claimant's ability to communicate has been considered again in *MM v SSWP (PIP)* [2018] UKUT 193 (AAC) and also in *SB v SSWP (PIP)* [2018] UKUT 122 (AAC). In both cases the UT has held that for an FTT to take lip-reading into account amounts to an error of law so long as the Secretary of State continues to direct DM that it is not an acceptable means of communication.

p.830, *annotation to the Social Security (Personal Independence Payment) Regulations 2013 (SI 2013/377) Sch.1 (Mobility—Activity 1 Planning and following journeys)*

Several issues arising from the application of psychological distress and anxiety under the Descriptors to Activity 1 have been considered in *AA v SSWP (PIP)* [2018] UKUT 339 (AAC). The claimant suffered from paranoid schizophrenia. He had periods of low mood, lacked motivation and suffered high levels of anxiety. His evidence, which was accepted by the FTT, was that he would usually need encouragement to venture out of doors at all; that he could sometimes accomplish familiar journeys on his own, but that he would never go somewhere unfamiliar without someone to accompany him. Evidence was given that when he did go out alone he wore earphones and looked at the ground. Even when accompanied he might wear the earphones—his companion was there to provide what he described as "moral support" rather than to tell him where to go. The FTT allowed him 4 points under Descriptor 1b. Judge Hemingway, in the UT, observed that this meant that they accepted that he did need at least encouraging to avoid overwhelming psychological distress in order to leave his home. But they did not think that he qualified under Descriptor 1d or 1f. (It seems that they did not consider 1e because it was clear that he could undertake journeys so long as he had a companion). Judge Hemingway thought that they had probably refused his claim under 1d or 1f because they thought that his companion should need to provide some more positive intervention, that was more than just passive presence, to satisfy those Descriptors. 2.029

Judge Hemingway thought that two questions arose—does the companion have to play an active role when he accompanies the claimant; and can a claim succeed under Descriptor 1f if the claimant can undertake some familiar journeys but not others.

As to the first Judge Hemingway decided that active intervention was not necessary; with this the representative of the Secretary of State agreed and as the judge demonstrated this was in accordance with the reasoning of the UT in the *MH* case.

As to the second, the representative of the Secretary of State had observed that the wording of both 1d and 1f is "a" journey rather than "any" journey; therefore she said it should suffice that the claimant was sometimes unable to accomplish that journey without support. The judge held that thereafter the matter would be governed by reg.7—does the situation apply on more than 50% of the days on which it might arise.

This was a helpful conclusion for the claimant in this case but the judge anticipated a further argument that could arise from this distinction between "a" journey and "any" journey. He thought that in applying the same reasoning to Descriptors 1b and 1e that the claimant might fail if they were able to make a journey occasionally because the wording suggests that they would need to be incapable of "any" journey. He suggests that he would reject that argument; the use of the word "any" in that context means, he suggests, simply there is no distinction between familiar and unfamiliar journeys.

He then goes on to consider the case of a claimant who can make some familiar journeys on most, but not on all days, and other familiar journeys on some but not most days! This is not a case for the application of reg.7 because it is not a matter of the days so much as the various journeys. Judge Hemingway says that the answer is to approach the question as a broad assessment of the claimant's ability to tackle familiar routes in general.

p.832, *annotation to the Social Security (Personal Independence Payment) Regulations 2013 (SI 2013/377) Sch.1 (Planning and following journeys)*

2.030   Note that where the claim is based upon an argument that the claimant needs to be accompanied when undertaking a journey, it is necessary to demonstrate with evidence in support that without that company the claimant would be at risk of harm in some way. See the decision of Judge May QC in *AR v SSWP (PIP)* [2018] UKUT 313 (AAC). The claimant suffered from epilepsy, but there was no evidence that he was prone to having a seizure when he was out.

p.864, *amendment to the Social Security (Maternity Allowance) (Working Abroad) Regulations 1987 (SI 1987/417) reg.2 (Special provision for persons who have been working abroad)*

2.031   With effect from November 15, 2018, reg.4(1)(a) of the Social Security (Updating of EU References) (Amendment) Regulations 2018 (SI 2018/1084) amended reg.2 as follows: (i) in para.(2)(b)(ii) after "EEC" by inserting ", as amended from time to time," and (ii) at the end of para.(2)(b)(ii) by adding "or Regulation (EC) No. 883/2004 of the European Parliament and of the Council of 29 April 2004, as amended from time to time, on the coordination of social security systems".

p.865, *amendment to Social Security (Maternity Allowance) (Working Abroad) Regulations 1987 (SI 1987/417) reg.2 (Special provision for persons who have been working abroad)*

2.032   With effect from November 15, 2018, reg.4(1)(b) of the Social Security (Updating of EU References) (Amendment) Regulations 2018 (SI 2018/1084) amended reg.2 as follows: (i) in sub-para.(a) after "EEC" by inserting ", as amended from time to time, or Regulation (EC) No. 883/2004 of the European Parliament and of the Council of 29 April 2004, as amended from time to time"; (ii) in sub-para.(c) after "Council Resolution" by inserting "or Regulation of the European Parliament and of the Council"; (iii) and in the words after sub-para.(c) after the words "Council Regulation" by inserting "or Regulation of the European Parliament and of the Council".

p.921, *annotation to the Social Security (Widow's Benefit and Retirement Pensions) Regulations 1979 (SI 1979/642) reg.7 (Category B retirement pension for certain widows by virtue of husband's contributions)*

ERRATUM: insert heading 'AMENDMENT' after the text of reg.7   2.032.1
and before the footnote.

p.1036, *annotation to the Employment Support Allowance Regulations 2008 (SI 2008/794) reg.18 (Circumstances in which the condition that the claimant is not receiving education does not apply)*

See further *MW v SSWP (ESA)* [2018] UKUT 304 (AAC), discussed   2.033
in the note to reg.33 below.

p.1072, *annotation to the Employment Support Allowance Regulations 2008 (SI 2008/794) reg.29(2)(b)*

Judge Hemingway in *HT v SSWP (ESA)* [2018] UKUT 174 (AAC)   2.034
has agreed with Judge Ward in *PD v SSWP (ESA)* [2014] UKUT 148
(AAC) that the risk within reg.29 with respect to travelling to work is
likely to be rare in the context of physical problems:

> "19. But I stress that, in general terms, I think it would be rare (though
> not impossible) for a claimant to succeed simply on the basis of risk on
> the journey to and from a workplace in consequence only of physical
> health difficulties in circumstances where those same difficulties do
> not lead to the risk arising in the workplace itself. So a failure to refer
> to the possibility of any such risk on the part of a tribunal is unlikely,
> absent unusual circumstances, to justify a finding that there has been
> an error of law of a material nature. Further, for the agoraphobic the
> facility of public transport will almost certainly not be a solution. But
> that cannot necessarily be said of a person who only has substantial
> physical health difficulties. There will thus be cases where, depending
> on the circumstances, all that will need to be assessed will be risk to
> and from a hypothetical bus stop at either end of the journey. Put
> another way there may depending on the facts only be a need to assess
> risk on the basis that a claimant will have to journey under his/her own
> steam on relatively short journeys. Following the reasoning in *PD*,
> cited above, the prospect of third party assistance on the journey will
> be a potentially relevant consideration though the availability of such
> cannot simply, without evidence, be assumed. Where the arguments
> as to risk relate to falling the use of such as walking sticks and walking
> frames will need to be considered."

p.1079, *annotation to the Employment Support Allowance Regulations 2008 (SI 2008/794) reg.29(2)(b) (The (in)applicability of the Equality Act 2010)*

SB v SSWP (ESA) [2015] UKUT 88 (AAC) has been considered and   2.035
followed in *SP v SSWP (ESA)* [2018] UKUT 205 (AAC), where the
claimant had a latex allergy and appealed a refusal to award ESA on the

basis of reg.29(2)(b). The tribunal dismissed her appeal, noting the duty of an employer to make adjustments under the Equality Act 2010, the claimant's responsibility to also consider making adjustments at work to minimise risk, and the claimant's failure to check for latex the chair she sat on at the tribunal hearing. Judge Poole QC held that the tribunal had made adequate findings of fact to supported its conclusion under reg.29(2)(b). These included identifying the gravity of risk to health from the potential effects of allergic reactions to latex, the likelihood of the risk occurring, and risk mitigation measures (such as the claimant's use of medication and her experience in monitoring the environment around her to check for latex). Judge Poole QC observed (at para.21):

"While I accept that it would have been an impermissible approach for the tribunal to make a decision that, because the Equality Act 2010 requires an employer to make reasonable adjustments to accommodate a disabled person, there is therefore no risk, or proceed itself to make an assessment of whether duties are owed by employers under the 2010 Act, this is not what the tribunal did in this case. Instead, the tribunal considered a number of adjustments that could be made by both the appellant and employers . . . In doing so it completed the 'claimant specific risk assessment' referred to in *SB v SSWP (ESA)* [2015] UKUT 88 (AAC) . . . ".

p.1079, *annotation to the Employment Support Allowance Regulations 2008 (SI 2008/794) reg.29(3)(a) (Reasonable adjustments in the claimant's workplace)*

2.036   See now *SP v SSWP (ESA)* [2018] UKUT 205 (AAC), where the claimant had a latex allergy and had appealed a refusal to award ESA on the basis of reg.29(2)(b) (discussed above). Judge Poole QC held as follows (at para.11):

"The wording of regulation 29(3)(a) refers to reasonable adjustments in the claimant's workplace, without confining its application to adjustments made only by an employer. It is normal in the workplace to expect both employer and employee to play their parts in keeping the working environment as risk free as practicable. In my view both employer and employee can be expected to take reasonable measures. Accordingly, measures that a claimant may reasonably take to reduce risk are relevant either under the reasonable adjustment wording in regulation 29(3)(a), or even if that was wrong to the general consideration of whether a risk is substantial under regulation 29(2)(b)."

p.1085, *annotation to the Employment Support Allowance Regulations 2008 (SI 2008/794) reg.33 (Additional circumstances where claimants are to be treated as having limited capability for work)*

2.037   See *MW v SSWP (ESA)* [2018] UKUT 304 (AAC), confirming that although there is a general entitlement condition that a claimant "is not receiving education" (see Welfare Reform Act 2007, Sch.1, para. 6(1)(g)) this is disapplied to a claimant entitled to DLA (since reg.18 of the 2008 Regulations disapplies Sch.1, para.6(1)(g)). Moreover, reg.33(2) provides that, for the purposes of income-related ESA, a claimant is to be treated as having limited capability for work where they are (a) not a qualifying young person, (b) receiving education and (c) not subject to Sch.1, para.6(1)(g) in accordance with reg.18.

pp.1090-1100, *annotation to the Employment Support Allowance Regulations 2008 (SI 2008/794) reg.35 (Certain claimants to be treated as having limited capability for work-related activity)*

See further *JL v SSWP (ESA)* [2018] UKUT 346 (AAC) for an extreme example of reg.35(2) being found to apply. The claimant had previously been placed in the support group. The evidence of two ESA medical assessments and the claimant's own GP showed that the claimant's blood pressure was indisputably high and uncontrolled. Moreover, the DWP's own guidance to decision-makers (Memo DMG 17/15, paragraph 25(3)) gives the example of a claimant with hypertension which is uncontrolled despite medication as an instance of "immediate substantial risk" in the context of reg.35(2). The FTT's decision (upholding the conclusion that reg.35(2) did not apply, despite the HCP terminating the assessment and advising the claimant to attend A&E forthwith) was set aside for inadequate reasoning and the decision re-made. **2.038**

p.1099, *annotation to the Employment Support Allowance Regulations 2008 (SI 2008/794) reg.35 (Certain claimants to be treated as having limited capability for work-related activity)*

ERRATUM: The correct citation for *PD v SSWP (ESA)* is [2014] UKUT 148 (AAC). **2.038.1**

p.1140, *annotation to the Employment Support Allowance Regulations 2008 (SI 2008/794) reg.75 (Payments treated as not being payments to which section 3 applies)*

ERRATUM: Delete the text under the heading 'MODIFICATION' and replace with the following: **2.038.2**

"Regulation 75 is modified by Sch.1, para.11 (and see also Sch.2, para.14) of the Employment and Support Allowance (Transitional Provisions, Housing Benefit and Council Tax Benefit) (Existing Awards) (No.2) Regulations 2010 (SI 2010/1907) (as amended) for the purposes specified in reg. 16(1). For details of these modifications, see the text of those Regulations below."

pp.1261-1262, *annotation to the Employment Support Allowance Regulations 2008 (SI 2008/794) Sch. 2 (Assessment of whether a claimant has limited capability for work)*

The decision in *AS v SSWP (ESA)* [213] UKUT 587 (AAC) was approved by the Northern Ireland Court of Appeal in *O'Neill v Department for Communities* [2018] NICA 29 (a ruling refusing permission to appeal). **2.039**

p.1266, *annotation to the Employment Support Allowance Regulations 2008 (SI 2008/794) Sch. 2 (Assessment of whether a claimant has limited capability for work)*

2.040　　See now, following *AG v SSWP (ESA)* [2017] UKUT 413 (AAC) on the possible linkage between ESA and PIP, Judge Poole QC's decision in *MH v SSWP (ESA)* [2018] UKUT 194 (AAC), where she held that the tribunal did not act in error of law by failing to adjourn (or to record its reasons for not adjourning) for evidence about the PIP award, nor in either determining the ESA appeal without having before it that evidence or in failing directly to address the claimant's PIP award in its statement of reasons.

ERRATUM: the correct citation for *KB v SSWP (ESA)* is [2014] UKUT 126 (AAC).

pp.1274-1277, *annotation to the Employment Support Allowance Regulations 2008 (SI 2008/794) Sch. 2 (Activity 5(b)—Manual dexterity)*

2.041　　An Upper Tribunal Judge has expressed the view (obiter) that the reference to a £1 coin in descriptor 5(b) includes "the £1 coin in the form in which it exists whenever the assessment is applied in an individual case" (para.26) and so can include the new-style £1 coin: *R v SSWP* [2018] UKUT 326 (AAC).

p.1278, *annotation to the Employment Support Allowance Regulations 2008 (SI 2008/794) Sch. 2 (Activity 9—Absence or loss of control)*

2.042　　See, for a successful reasons challenge, *VH v SSWP (ESA)* [2018] UKUT 290 (AAC) (at paras.15 and 16).

p.1286, *annotation to the Employment Support Allowance Regulations 2008 (SI 2008/794) Sch. 2 (Activity 13—Initiating and completing personal action)*

2.043　　See, for a successful reasons challenge, *VH v SSWP (ESA)* [2018] UKUT 290 (AAC) (at paras 17-20).

p.1298, *annotation to the Employment Support Allowance Regulations 2008 (SI 2008/794) Sch. 3 (Assessment of whether a claimant has limited capability for work-related activity)*

2.044　　On the importance of a consistent approach to the descriptors under Sch.2 and Sch.3 respectively, see *SSWP v JL (ESA)* [2018] UKUT 291 (AAC).

p.1340, *amendment to the Employment and Support Allowance Regulations 2008 (SI 2008/794) Sch.8 para.18(c) (Sums to be disregarded in the calculation of income other than earnings)*

2.045　　With effect from December 6, 2018, reg.8 of the Social Security (Miscellaneous Amendments No.5) Regulations 2017 (SI 2017/1187) amended para.18(c) by inserting the words "or, if it was higher at that time, pensionable age" after the words "the age of 65".

p.1343, *amendment to the Employment and Support Allowance Regulations 2008 (SI 2008/794) Sch.8 para.31 (Sums to be disregarded in the calculation of income other than earnings)*

With effect from April 5, 2018, reg.2(18)(b) of the Loans for Mort- 2.045.1
gage Interest and Social Fund Maternity Grant (Amendment) Regulations 2018 (SI 2018/307) substituted a new paragraph 31 as follows:

"**31.** Any payment received under an insurance policy taken out to insure against the risk of being unable to maintain repayments on a loan which qualifies under Part 1 of Schedule 1 to the Loans for Mortgage Interest Regulations 2017 (legacy benefit claimants and SPC claimants) and used to meet such repayments."

p.1343, *amendment to the Employment and Support Allowance Regulations 2008 (SI 2008/794) Sch.8 para.32 (Sums to be disregarded in the calculation of income other than earnings)*

With effect from April 5, 2018, reg.2(18)(b) of the Loans for Mort- 2.045.2
gage Interest and Social Fund Maternity Grant (Amendment) Regulations 2018 (SI 2018/307) amended paragraph 32 so that it now reads as
follows:

"**32.**—(1) Except where paragraph 31 (or 33) applies, and subject to sub-paragraph (2), any payment made to the claimant which is intended to be used and is used as a contribution towards—
(a) any payment due on a loan if secured on the dwelling occupied as the home which does not qualify under Part 1 of Schedule 1 to the Loans for Mortgage Interest Regulations;
(b) any charge which qualifies in accordance with paragraph 18 of Schedule 6 (housing costs) to these Regulations or any interest payment on a loan which qualifies under Part 1 of Schedule 1 to the Loans for Mortgage Interest Regulations, to the extent that the charge or payment is not met under these Regulations or by loan payments (as the case may be);
(c) any payment due on a loan which qualifies under Part 1 of Schedule 1 to the Loans for Mortgage Interest Regulations attributable to the payment of capital;
(d) any amount due by way of premiums on—
(i) an insurance policy taken out to insure against the risk of being unable to make the payments referred to in (a) to (c) above; or
(ii) a policy of insurance taken out to insure against loss or damage to any building or part of a building which is occupied by the claimant as the claimant's home;
(e) the claimant's rent in respect of the dwelling occupied by the claimant as the home but only to the extent that it is not met by

housing benefit; or the claimant's accommodation charge but only to the extent that the actual charge exceeds the amount payable by a local authority in accordance with Part 3 of the National Assistance Act 1948 or Part 1 of the Care Act 2014 (care and support) or Part 4 of the Social Services and Well-being (Wales) Act 2014 (meeting needs) other than any direct payment made in accordance with regulations made under section 50 or 52 of that Act.

(2) This paragraph does not apply to any payment which is treated as possessed by the claimant by virtue of regulation 107(3)(c).

(3) In this paragraph—

(a) "Loans for Mortgage Interest Regulations" means the Loans for Mortgage Interest Regulations 2017;

(b) "loan payments" has the meaning given in the Loans for Mortgage Interest Regulations."

p.1346, *amendment to the Employment and Support Allowance Regulations 2008 (SI 2008/794) Sch.8 para.45(2) (Sums to be disregarded in the calculation of income other than earnings)*

2.046   With effect from April 11, 2018, para.21(o) of Sch. to the Secretaries of State for Health and Social Care and for Housing, Communities and Local Government and Transfer of Functions (Commonhold Land) Order 2018 (SI 2018/378) amended para.45(2) by inserting the words "and Social Care" after the words "for Health".

p.1348, *amendment to the Employment and Support Allowance Regulations 2008 (SI 2008/794) Sch.8 (Sums to be disregarded in the calculation of income other than earnings)*

2.047   With effect from September 3, 2018, art.7 of the Social Security (Scotland) Act 2018 (Consequential Modifications) Order 2018 (SI 2018/872) added the following after para.69 of Sch.8:

"**70.** Any payment of carer's allowance supplement made under section 81 of the Social Security (Scotland) Act 2018."

With effect from December 10, 2018, art.10(2) of the Social Security (Scotland) Act 2018 (Best Start Grants) (Consequential Modifications and Saving) Order 2018 (SI 2018/1138) added the following after para.69 (presumably meaning the para.70 inserted by the previous amendment) of Sch.8:

"**70.** Any early years assistance given in accordance with section 32 of the Social Security (Scotland) Act 2018."

Since the Scottish early years assistance, including best start grants, will take the form of lump sum payments it would probably not constitute income in any event.

p.1353, *amendment to the Employment and Support Allowance Regulations 2008 (SI 2008/794) Sch.9 para.11(2) (Capital to be disregarded)*

With effect from September 11, 2018, reg.7 of the Social Security   **2.048**
(Treatment of Arrears of Benefit) Regulations 2018 (SI 2018/932) amended para.11(2) by substituting the following for head (a):

"(a) paid in order to rectify, or to compensate for—
    (i) an official error as defined in regulation 1(2) of the Social Security and Child Support (Decisions and Appeals) Regulations 1999, or
    (ii) an error on a point of law; and"

See the entry for p.666 of Vol.II for discussion of the effect of the amendment.

p.1357, *amendment to the Employment and Support Allowance Regulations 2008 (SI 2008/794) Sch.9 para.37(2) (Capital to be disregarded)*

With effect from April 11, 2018, art.15 and para.21(o) of the Schedule   **2.049**
to the Secretaries of State for Health and Social Care and for Housing, Communities and Local Government and Transfer of Functions (Commonhold Land) Order 2018 (SI 2018/378) amended para.37(2) by inserting the words "and Social Care" after the words "for Health".

p.1360, *amendment to the Employment and Support Allowance Regulations 2008 (SI 2008/794) Sch.9 (Capital to be disregarded)*

With effect from December 10, 2018, art.10(3) of the Social Security   **2.050**
(Scotland) Act 2018 (Best Start Grants) (Consequential Modifications and Saving) Order 2018 (SI 2018/1138) amended Sch.9 by renumbering the second para.61 as 62 and adding the following after para.62, as renumbered, of Sch.9:

"**63.** Any early years assistance given in accordance with section 32 of the Social Security (Scotland) Act 2018."

p.1380, *annotation to the Employment and Support Allowance (Transitional Provisions, Housing Benefit and Council Tax Benefit) (Existing Awards) (No. 2) Regulations 2010 (SI 2010/1907) (Existing awards that qualify for conversion)*

In *DS v SSWP* [2018] UKUT 270 (AAC), the Secretary of State   **2.051**
accepted formally that the unitary nature of ESA was not established by the decision in *LH v SSWP (ESA)* [2014] UKUT 480 (AAC); [2015] AACR 14 and that *SK v SSWP* (ESA) [2018] UKUT 267 (AAC) was therefore in error of law. A three-judge panel of the Upper Tribunal has issued a consent order including a declaration to that effect.

PART III

UPDATING MATERIAL
VOLUME II

INCOME SUPPORT, JOBSEEKER'S ALLOWANCE, STATE PENSION CREDIT AND THE SOCIAL FUND

Commentary by

John Mesher

Richard Poynter

Nick Wikeley

p.60, *annotation to the old style Jobseekers Act 1995 s.6(1) (Availability for employment)*

In paras.22-25 of *RL v SSWP (JSA)* [2018] UKUT 177 (AAC) Judge   3.001
Lane shows cogently that the propositions in para.14 of *R(U) 5/80* that
being available means being available in an active, positive sense and that
"availability implies some active step by the person concerned to draw
attention to his availability" cannot survive the introduction of a discrete
condition of entitlement of actively seeking employment. She also suggests that many decisions still being based on availability should properly
be considered by reference to the actively seeking employment test.

p.75, *annotation to the old style Jobseekers Act 1995 s.9 (Actively seeking employment)*

RL v SSWP (JSA) [2018] UKUT 177 (AAC), para.38(i), and *CH v*   3.002
SSWP (JSA) (No.2) [2018] UKUT 320 (AAC), para.8, both reiterate
that a jobseeker's agreement is not an enforceable civil contract, so that
the terms of the old style JSA legislation are determinative rather than
the principles of the law of contract. The reiteration is no doubt only
necessary because of claimants' continuing (but understandable) failure
to grasp that a jobseeker's agreement is not an agreement (and that a
claimant commitment is not a commitment).

p.78, *annotation to the old style Jobseekers Act 1995 s.9 (Actively seeking employment)*

CH v SSWP (JSA) (No.2) [2018] UKUT 320 (AAC) concerns the   3.003
appeal from the decision of the Secretary of State on the reference of the
questions in s.9(6) directed to be referred by Judge Ward in *CH v SSWP
(JSA)* [2015] UKUT 373 (AAC). There were a number of modifications in the revised proposed initial agreement referred by the employment officer, as compared with the proposed agreement that had been
before Judge Ward. Although the types of job to be looked for were the
same, the requirement to access the jobseekers.direct.gov.uk was
reduced from three times to twice a week and the requirement to access
the internet daily was reduced to weekly, such access being for periods
acceptable to the claimant in view of his problems with spending too
long in front of a screen. A right of review by a disability employment
adviser at the request of either party was also written in. The First-tier
Tribunal had erred in law by failing to explain why it considered that it
was reasonable to expect the claimant to comply with the proposed
agreement. In substituting his own decision that the claimant was not
entitled to old style JSA for the weeks in question (by reason of not
having entered into a jobseeker's agreement) Judge Wikeley first concluded that compliance would mean that the claimant satisfied the
conditions of entitlement of availability for and actively seeking employment. The jobs listed were appropriate and realistic in the light of the
claimant's experience and the proposed hours and travelling time were
not onerous. The job search activities were suitably calibrated to the

claimant's circumstances. By contrast, the qualifications and restrictions suggested by the claimant would not have allowed him to satisfy those conditions. As to reasonableness, the proposed agreement was not unduly onerous or insufficiently focused on the claimant's individual suitability for types of work and did not rely on standard-form job search requirements. It was a reasonably bespoke agreement for the claimant's own circumstances. The claimant had failed to explain how it would be unreasonable to expect him to comply with it.

pp.121-122, *annotation to the old style Jobseekers Act 1995 s.19(2)(e) (Higher-level sanctions)*

3.004   *SN v SSWP (JSA)* [2018] UKUT 279 (AAC) discusses, from para.42 onwards, what can amount to a failure to participate in a scheme (at a time when the consequent sanction was under reg.8 of the MWAS Regulations, rather than s.19(2)(e)). It confirms that conduct of the claimant related to the ordinary requirements of the work activity in question leading to the termination of their placement can amount to a failure to participate. In particular, it is held in paras.59-62 that actions before the start of the scheme can be relevant. In *SN* the claimant was required to work for four weeks as a retail assistant in a charity shop. As found by Upper Tribunal Judge Wright in substituting a decision on the appeal, the claimant visited the shop about a week before the placement was due to start, to find out what would be entailed. During the visit he used offensive language to one member of staff and about the nature of the work involved, that was unreasonable in any work setting. He attended at the shop at the specified time for the start of the placement, but, as the representative of the programme provider was not to arrive for about 20 minutes, retired to a changing cubicle to sit down, took off his shoes and appeared to go to sleep. When the representative arrived, the deputy manager of the shop told him that the claimant would not be allowed to work there in view of his earlier offensive conduct. The judge concludes that the combination of the claimant's behaviour on the earlier visit and his attitude of antagonism and lack of interest on the first day of the placement meant that he had failed to meet the notified requirements for participation in the scheme. There was no good cause for the failure. Some doubt is expressed in para.45 about the result in *SA v SSWP (JSA)* [2015] UKUT 454 (AAC).

p.214, *annotation to the Jobseekers (Back to Work Schemes) Act 2013*

3.005   On October 31, 2018 the House of Commons and House of Lords Joint Committee on Human Rights issued a report (HC 1451, HL paper 209) welcoming the government's action in proposing the remedial Order mentioned at the end of para.1.433. It concluded that the procedural requirements of the Human Rights Act 1998 were met and that the reasons for proceeding by way of a non-urgent order rather than by way of a Bill were sufficiently compelling. However, it regretted the delay between the making of the declaration of incompatibility by Lang J and the laying of the order.

p.216, *annotation to the Jobseekers (Back to Work Schemes) Act 2013*

In *SN v SSWP (JSA)* [2018] UKUT 279 (AAC), para.91, it was 3.006
confirmed that, despite the failure to issue the claimant with a MWA05
letter, he had been sufficiently notified of the requirement to participate
in a mandatory work activity scheme within reg.4 of the MWAS Regulations by a combination of information given in an interview with an
adviser and a letter from the programme provider about the specific
placement as a retail assistant in a charity shop.

p.329, *amendment to the Income Support (General) Regulations 1987 (SI
1987/1967) reg.21AA(3) (Special cases: supplemental—persons from
abroad)*

With effect from November 15, 2018, reg.4 and Sch. para.6 of the 3.007
Social Security (Updating of EU References) (Amendment) Regulations
2018 (SI 2018/1084) amended reg.21AA(3)(d) by substituting the
words "Article 45 of the Treaty on the Functioning of the European
Union" for the words "Article 39 of the Treaty establishing the European Community".

p.331, *annotation to the Income Support (General) Regulations 1987 (SI
1987/1967) reg.21AA (Special cases: supplemental—persons from abroad—
Habitual residence test—Who is exempt?)*

The Immigration Act 2016, s.67(1) requires the Secretary of State "as 3.008
soon as possible after the passing of this Act, make arrangements to
relocate to the United Kingdom and support a specified number of
unaccompanied refugee children from other countries in Europe." Once
relocated to the UK, such children claim asylum in the normal way. If
that claim is successful, the person (who may no longer be a child) will
either be granted refugee status or humanitarian protection and will
therefore be exempt from the habitual residence test under para.(4)(g) or
(hh) of reg.21AA (and of the equivalent provisions in reg.85A of the JSA
Regulations 1996, reg.2 of the SPC Regulations, reg.7 of the Tax Credits
(Residence) Regulations 2003, reg.23 of the Child Benefit (General)
Regulations 2006, reg.70 of the ESA Regulations 2008, reg.9 of the
Universal Credit Regulations and reg.8 of the Childcare Payments (Eligibility) Regulations 2015).

Where, however, the person is not granted refugee status or humanitarian protection but satisfies certain other conditions, s/he will (where
his or her application was made on or after July 6, 2018), be granted a
five-year residence permit and the opportunity to apply for indefinite
leave to remain under rules 352ZG–352ZN of the Immigration Rules.
Permission to remain in the UK in these circumstances is known as
"section 67 leave".

With effect from July 20, 2018, the Child Benefit, Tax Credits and
Childcare Payments (Section 67 Immigration Act 2016 Leave) (Amend-
ment) Regulations 2018 amend reg.7 of the Tax Credits (Residence)
Regulations 2003, reg.23 of the Child Benefit (General) Regulations

2006, and reg.8 of the Childcare Payments (Eligibility) Regulations 2015 to add those with section 67 leave to the categories of people who are exempt from the habitual residence test for child benefit, tax credits and childcare payments. However, no equivalent amendment has been made to the rules for IS, housing benefit, IBJSA, ESA, SPC, or universal credit. People with section 67 leave who wish to claim one of those benefits will therefore have to establish that they are habitually resident as a matter of fact. Note, however, that all EEA nationals with section 67 leave will automatically satisfy the right to reside test by virtue of the residence permit issued under rule 352ZI of the Immigration Rules.

p.630, *amendment to the Income Support (General) Regulations 1987 (SI 1987/1967) Sch.9 para.17(c) (Sums to be disregarded in the calculation of income other than earnings)*

3.009   With effect from December 6, 2018, reg.2(3) of the Social Security (Miscellaneous Amendments No.5) Regulations 2017 (SI 2017/1187) amended para.17(c) by inserting the words "or, if it was higher at that time, pensionable age" after the words "the age of 65".

p.633, *amendment to the Income Support (General) Regulations 1987 (SI 1987/1967) Sch.9 para.29 (Sums to be disregarded in the calculation of income other than earnings)*

3.009.1   With effect from April 5, 2018, reg.2(18)(c) of the Loans for Mortgage Interest and Social Fund Maternity Grant (Amendment) Regulations 2018 (SI 2018/307) substituted a new paragraph 29 as follows:

"**29.** Any payment received under an insurance policy taken out to insure against the risk of being unable to maintain repayments on a loan which qualifies under Part 1 of Schedule 1 to the Loans for Mortgage Interest Regulations 2017 (legacy benefit claimants and SPC claimants) and used to meet such repayments."

p.633, *amendment to the Income Support (General) Regulations 1987 (SI 1987/1967) Sch.9 para.30 (Sums to be disregarded in the calculation of income other than earnings)*

3.009.2   With effect from April 5, 2018, reg.2(18)(c) of the Loans for Mortgage Interest and Social Fund Maternity Grant (Amendment) Regulations 2018 (SI 2018/307) amended paragraph 30 so that it now reads as follows:

30.—(1) Except where paragraph 29 or 30ZA applies, and subject to sub-paragraph (2), any payment made to the claimant which is intended to be used and is used as a contribution towards—
  (a) any payment due on a loan if secured on the dwelling occupied as the home which does not qualify under Part 1 of Schedule 1 to the Loans for Mortgage Interest Regulations;
  (b) any charge which qualifies in accordance with paragraph 17 of Schedule 3 (housing costs) to these Regulations or any interest payment on a loan which qualifies under Part 1 of Schedule 1 to

the Loans for Mortgage Interest Regulations, to the extent that the charge or payment is not met under these Regulations or by loan payments (as the case may be);

(c) any payment due on a loan which qualifies under Part 1 of Schedule 1 to the Loans for Mortgage Interest Regulations attributable to the payment or capital;

(d) any amount due by way of premiums on—

(i) an insurance policy taken out to insure against the risk of being unable to make the payments referred to in (a) to (c) above; or

(ii) a policy of insurance taken out to insure against loss or damage to any building or part of a building which is occupied by the claimant as his home.

(e) his rent in respect of the dwelling occupied by him as his home but only to the extent that it is not met by housing benefit; or his accommodation charge but only to the extent that the actual charge exceeds the amount payable by a local authority in accordance with Part III of the National Assistance Act 1948 or Part 1 of the Care Act 2014 (care and support) or Part 4 of the Social Services and Well-being (Wales) Act 2014 (meeting needs) other than any direct payment made in accordance with regulations made under section 50 or 52 of that Act.

(2) This paragraph shall not apply to any payment which is treated as possessed by the claimant by virtue of regulation 42(4)(a)(ii) (notional income).

(3) In this paragraph—

(a) "Loans for Mortgage Interest Regulations" means the Loans for Mortgage Interest Regulations 2017;

(b) "loan payments" has the meaning given in the Loans for Mortgage Interest Regulations."

p.637, *amendment to the Income Support (General) Regulations 1987 (SI 1987/1967) Sch.9 para.48(2) (Sums to be disregarded in the calculation of income other than earnings)*

With effect from April 11, 2018, para.21(a) of the Schedule to the 3.010
Secretaries of State for Health and Social Care and for Housing, Communities and Local Government and Transfer of Functions (Commonhold Land) Order 2018 (SI 2018/378) amended para.48(2) by inserting the words "and Social Care" after the words "for Health".

p.638, *amendment to the Income Support (General) Regulations 1987 (SI 1987/1967) Sch.9 (Sums to be disregarded in the calculation of income other than earnings)*

With effect from September 3, 2018, art.2 of the Social Security 3.011
(Scotland) Act 2018 (Consequential Modifications) Order 2018 (SI 2018/872) added the following after para.80 of Sch.9:

"**81.** Any payment of carer's allowance supplement made under section 81 of the Social Security (Scotland) Act 2018."

With effect from December 10, 2018, art.5(2) of the Social Security (Scotland) Act 2018 (Best Start Grants) (Consequential Modifications and Saving) Order 2018 (SI 2018/1138) added the following after para.81 of Sch.9:

"**82.** Any early years assistance given in accordance with section 32 of the Social Security (Scotland) Act 2018."

Since the Scottish early years assistance, including best start grants, will take the form of lump sum payments it would probably not constitute income in any event.

p.666, *amendment to the Income Support (General) Regulations 1987 (SI 1987/1967) Sch.10 para.7(2) (Capital to be disregarded)*

3.012 With effect from September 11, 2018, reg.2 of the Social Security (Treatment of Arrears of Benefit) Regulations 2018 (SI 2018/932) amended para.7(2) by substituting the following for head (a):

"(a) paid in order to rectify, or to compensate for—
  (i) an official error as defined in regulation 1(2) of the Social Security and Child Support (Decisions and Appeals) Regulations 1999, or
  (ii) an error on a point of law; and"

The amendment extends the effect of para.7(2) to arrears paid because there has been an error of law as well as those where there has been an official error. Errors of law revealed by a decision of the courts or the Upper Tribunal are excluded from the definition of official error in the Decisions and Appeals Regulations. The same has been done for the equivalent old style ESA and JSA provisions. Note that payments of arrears of a benefit that would have been income if paid on time will retain their character as income in relation to the period from the date on which they were due to be paid or in respect of which they were payable. Amounts left over after that period of attribution will be capital and therefore come within the potential scope of the para.7 disregard.

p.669, *amendment to the Income Support (General) Regulations 1987 (SI 1987/1967) Sch.10 para.38(2) (Capital to be disregarded)*

3.013 With effect from April 11, 2018, para.21(a) of the Schedule to the Secretaries of State for Health and Social Care and for Housing, Communities and Local Government and Transfer of Functions (Commonhold Land) Order 2018 (SI 2018/378) amended para.38(2) by inserting the words "and Social Care" after the words "for Health".

p.673, *amendment to the Income Support (General) Regulations 1987 (SI 1987/1967) Sch.10 (Capital to be disregarded)*

3.014 With effect from December 10, 2018, art.5(3) of the Social Security (Scotland) Act 2018 (Best Start Grants) (Consequential Modifications and Saving) Order 2018 (SI 2018/1138) added the following after para.74 of Sch.10:

"**75.** Any early years assistance given in accordance with section 32 of the Social Security (Scotland) Act 2018."

p.703, *amendment to the Social Security (Restrictions on Amounts for Children and Qualifying Young Persons) Amendment Regulations 2017 (SI 2017/376) reg.5(2) (Restrictions on amounts for children and young persons—consequential changes to the Income Support (General) Regulations 1987)*

With effect from November 28, 2018, reg.5(a) of the Universal Credit and Jobseeker's Allowance (Miscellaneous Amendments) Regulations 2018 (SI 2018/1129) amended reg.5(2) by substituting the words "the child element specified in regulation 24(1) of the Universal Credit Regulations 2013 would be payable" for the words "an exception in Schedule 12 of the Universal Credit Regulations 2013 would apply". **3.015**

p.704, *amendment to the Social Security (Restrictions on Amounts for Children and Qualifying Young Persons) Amendment Regulations 2017 (SI 2017/376) reg.6(2) (Restrictions on amounts for children and young persons—consequential changes to the Jobseeker's Allowance Regulations 1996)*

With effect from November 28, 2018, reg.5(b) of the Universal Credit and Jobseeker's Allowance (Miscellaneous Amendments) Regulations 2018 (SI 2018/1129) amended reg.6(2) by substituting the words "the child element specified in regulation 24(1) of the Universal Credit Regulations 2013 would be payable" for the words "an exception in Schedule 12 of the Universal Credit Regulations 2013 would apply". **3.016**

p.745, *annotation to the Social Security (Immigration and Asylum) Consequential Amendments Regulations 2000 (SI 2000/636) (General note—"Person subject to immigration control"—person who requires leave to enter or remain in the UK but does not have it)*

A person whose leave to remain was continued by the former s.3D of the Immigration Act 1971 (which was in force between August 31, 2006 and November 30, 2016) pending an appeal against a decision to revoke his leave to remain (or to vary it with the result that he has no leave to enter or remain in the United Kingdom) had leave to remain and was therefore not a person subject to immigration control: see *GO v HMRC (CHB)* [2018] UKUT 328 (AAC). Although not relevant in that case, the result would not seem to follow if the person also fell within one of the other heads of s.115(9). **3.017**

p.801, *amendment to the Immigration (European Economic Area) Regulations 2016 (SI 2016/1052) reg.2(1) (General interpretation— Definition of EEA National)*

With effect from July 24, 2018, reg.2 of, and para.1 of the Schedule to, the Immigration (European Economic Area) (Amendment) Regulations **3.018**

2018 (SI 2018/801) amended reg.2(1) by substituting the following for the definition of "EEA National":

""EEA national" means—
  (a) a national of an EEA State who is not also a British citizen; or
  (b) a national of an EEA State who is also a British citizen and who prior to acquiring British citizenship exercised a right to reside as such a national, in accordance with regulation 14 or 15,
save that a person does not fall within paragraph (b) if the EEA State of which they are a national became a member State after that person acquired British citizenship."

pp.805-806, *annotation to the Immigration (European Economic Area) Regulations 2016 (SI 2016/1052) (General note—The personal scope of the Citizenship Directive—scope of* Lounes v Secretary of State for the Home Department*)*

3.019   The scope of the right of residence under art.21 TFEU recognised by the Grand Chamber of the CJEU in *Toufik Lounes v Secretary of State for the Home Department* (Case C-165/16) was considered by the Immigration and Asylum Chamber of the Upper Tribunal in *Kovacevic (British citizen—Art 21 TFEU) Croatia* [2018] UKUT 273 (IAC). Ms Kovacevic is a national of Croatia who lawfully entered the UK in 1995 and naturalised as a British citizen in 2007 (i.e., before Croatia acceded to the EU on 1 July 2013). Since arriving in the UK, she had resided and worked lawfully under UK domestic law and she retained her Croatian nationality following naturalisation. In June 2014, (i.e., after Croatia acceded to the EU) she married an Algerian national. The Upper Tribunal distinguished *Lounes*. Although she was a dual British/Croatian national, Ms Kovacevic had neither lived nor worked in the UK in the exercise of her Treaty rights. Her rights were therefore analogous to those of the Mrs McCarthy in *McCarthy v Secretary of State for the Home Department* C-434/09 (noted at pp.804-805 of the main work) and no right arose under art.21. Mrs Kovacevic has applied to the Court of Appeal for permission to appeal against the Upper Tribunal's decision and, at the time of going to press, that application was proceeding under Case Reference C9/2018/2638.

pp.830-831, *amendment to the Immigration (European Economic Area) Regulations 2016 (SI 2016/1052) reg.6 (Qualified person)*

3.020   With effect from July 24, 2018, reg.2 of, and para.2 of the Schedule to, the Immigration (European Economic Area) (Amendment) Regulations 2018 (SI 2018/801) amended reg.6 by amending head (a) of the definition of "relevant period" in para.(1) to read as follows:

""relevant period" means—
  (a) in the case of a person retaining worker status under paragraph (2)(b) [or self-employed person status under paragraph (4)(b)], a continuous period of six months;";

by substituting the following for para.(4):

"(4) A person who is no longer in self-employment must continue to be treated as a self-employed person provided that the person—
    (a) is temporarily unable to engage in activities as a self-employed person as the result of an illness or accident;
    (b) is in duly recorded involuntary unemployment after having worked as a self-employed person in the United Kingdom for at least one year provided the person—
        (i) has registered as a jobseeker with the relevant employment office; and
        (ii) satisfies conditions D and E;
    (c) is in duly recorded involuntary unemployment after having worked as a self-employed person in the United Kingdom for less than one year, provided the person—
        (i) has registered as a jobseeker with the relevant employment office; and
        (ii) satisfies conditions D and E;
    (d) is involuntarily no longer in self-employment and has embarked on vocational training; or
    (e) has voluntarily ceased self-employment and has embarked on vocational training that is related to the person's previous occupation.

(4A) A person to whom paragraph (4)(c) applies may only retain self-employed person status for a maximum of six months.

(4B) Condition D is that the person—
    (a) entered the United Kingdom as a self-employed person or in order to seek employment as a self-employed person; or
    (b) is present in the United Kingdom seeking employment or self-employment, immediately after enjoying a right to reside under sub-paragraphs (c) to (e) of the definition of qualified person in paragraph (1) (disregarding any period during which self-employed status was retained pursuant to paragraph (4)(b) or (c)).

(4C) Condition E is that the person provides evidence of seeking employment or self-employment and having a genuine chance of being engaged.";

by substituting the words "sub-paragraphs (b), (d) or (e)" for the words "sub-paragraphs (b) to (e)" in para.(5)(b);

by omitting the word "or" at the end of para.(7)(a) and inserting the words "or (c) a self-employed person under paragraph (4)(b)" after para.(7)(b);

by amending para.(8) to read as follows:

"(8) Condition C applies where the person concerned has, previously, enjoyed a right to reside under this regulation as a result of satisfying conditions A and B [or, as the case may be, conditions D and E]—
    (a) in the case of a person to whom paragraph (2)(b) or (c) [or (4)(b) or (c)] applied, for at least six months; or
    (b) in the case of a jobseeker, for at least 91 days in total,

unless the person concerned has, since enjoying the above right to reside, been continuously absent from the United Kingdom for at least 12 months.";

and by inserting the words "or, as the case may be, condition E" after the words "condition B" in para.(10)(b).

pp.830-831, *amendment to the Immigration (European Economic Area) Regulations 2016 (SI 2016/1052) reg.9(2) (Family members of British citizens)*

3.021   With effect from July 24, 2018, reg.2 of, and para.3 of the Schedule to, the Immigration (European Economic Area) (Amendment) Regulations 2018 (SI 2018/801) amended reg.9(2) by omitting the word "and" at the end of para. (2)(b) and by inserting the following sub-paras after para.(2)(c):

"(d) F was a family member of BC during all or part of their joint residence in the EEA State; and

(e) genuine family life was created or strengthened during their joint residence in the EEA State".

p.839, *annotation to the Immigration (European Economic Area) Regulations 2016 (SI 2016/1052) reg.6 (Qualified person—Retaining worker status—Involuntary unemployment—Genuine chance of being engaged)*

3.022   The relationship between the inaccurately-named "genuine prospects of work" test and participation in the New Enterprise Allowance ("NEA") scheme was considered by the Upper Tribunal in *EG v SSWP* (JSA) [2018] UKUT 285 (AAC). Judge Poole QC accepted a concession by the Secretary of State that the First-tier Tribunal had erred in law by failing to consider "to consider the implications of the claimant's participation in the NEA scheme in relation to whether he had a genuine prospect of work and retained jobseeker's status" but rejected the claimant's submission that, while participating in the scheme he did not have to show that he had a genuine chance of being engaged.

As far as any right to reside the claimant may have had as a jobseeker is concerned, the decision cannot be faulted. However, it is strongly arguable that the First-tier Tribunal erred more fundamentally by failing to consider whether his participation in the NEA scheme had given rise to a separate right of residence as a self-employed person. The NEA scheme is established under Jobseeker's Act 1995, s.17A and the Jobseeker's Allowance (Schemes for Assisting Persons to Obtain Employment) Regulations 2013. As its name suggests, the NEA scheme is designed to help people into *self-employment*. Regulation 3(5) of those Regulations states that it is "designed to assist a claimant into self-employed earner's employment comprising guidance and support provided by a business mentor, access to a loan to help with start-up costs (subject to status) and a weekly allowance for a period of 26 weeks once the claimant starts trading." It is implicit in the definition that a claimant may have begun to trade as a self-employed person but still be participating in the NEA scheme: it cannot be assumed that, just because a claimant is claiming jobseeker's allowance and participating in a scheme under s.17A, he can only have a right of residence as a jobseeker. The point is a potentially important one for claimants. Claimants who are self-employed persons have a right of residence that counts for the purposes of *all* working-age means-tested benefits, not just JSA, and so can claim HB if they live in rented accommodation and can claim ESA if they become ill: see further p.832 of the main work in relation to the identical distinction between the rights of jobseekers and of those who retain worker status.

p.840, *annotation to the Immigration (European Economic Area) Regulations 2016 (SI 2016/1052) reg.6 (Qualified person—Retaining worker status—Involuntary unemployment—'Voluntary" and "Involuntary")*

An EEA national who retains worker status does not lose that status merely because his or her JSA is disallowed on the grounds of "not actively seeking work": see *SSWP v WN (rule 17)* (ESA) [2018] UKUT 268 (AAC).   3.023

p.857, *annotation to the Immigration (European Economic Area) Regulations 2016 (SI 2016/1052) reg.9 (Family members of British citizens—"Derived right of facilitation")*

In *Secretary of State for the Home Department v Christy* [2018] EWCA Civ 2378 the Court of Appeal rejected the Home Secretary's submission that, in order for the "derived right of facilitation" (i.e., the right of third country nationals in a durable relationship with an EU citizen, recognised by the CJEU in *Secretary of State for the Home Department v Banger* (Case C-89/17)) to arise for a third country national who is the durable partner of an EU citizen who returns to his home Member State following a period of residence in another Member State, the durable partner must have had her residence facilitated in that other Member State in accordance with Article 3(2) of the Directive.   3.024

p.857, *amendment to the Immigration (European Economic Area) Regulations 2016 (SI 2016/1052) reg.9A (Dual national: national of an EEA State who acquires British citizenship)*

With effect from July 24, 2018, reg.2 of, and para.4 of the Schedule to, the Immigration (European Economic Area) (Amendment) Regulations 2018 (SI 2018/801) inserted a new reg.9A as follows: 3.025

"Dual national: national of an EEA State who acquires British citizenship
9A.—(1) In this regulation "DN" means a person within paragraph (b) of the definition of "EEA national" in regulation 2(1).

(2) DN who comes within the definition of "qualified person" in regulation 6(1) is only a qualified person for the purpose of these Regulations if DN—

(a) came within the definition of "qualified person" at the time of acquisition of British citizenship; and

(b) has not at any time subsequent to the acquisition of British citizenship lost the status of qualified person.

(3) Regulation 15 only applies to DN, or to the family member of DN who is not an EEA national, if DN satisfies the condition in paragraph (4).

(4) The condition in this paragraph is that at the time of acquisition of British citizenship DN either—

(a) was a qualified person; or

(b) had acquired a right of permanent residence in accordance with these Regulations.".

p.861, *amendment to the Immigration (European Economic Area) Regulations 2016 (SI 2016/1052) reg.11 (Right of admission to the United Kingdom)*

3.026   With effect from July 24, 2018, reg.2 of, and para.5 of the Schedule to, the Immigration (European Economic Area) (Amendment) Regulations 2018 (SI 2018/801) amended reg.9 by inserting a new para.(9) as follows:

"(9) A person is not entitled to be admitted by virtue of this regulation where that person is subject to a decision under regulation 23(6)(b) (removal decision).".

p.863, *amendment to the Immigration (European Economic Area) Regulations 2016 (SI 2016/1052) reg.12 (Issue of EEA family permit)*

3.027   With effect from July 24, 2018, reg.2 of, and para.6 of the Schedule to, the Immigration (European Economic Area) (Amendment) Regulations 2018 (SI 2018/801) amended reg.12 by inserting a new para.(5A) as follows:

"(5A) An EEA family permit issued under this regulation may be issued in electronic form.".

p.863, *amendment to the Immigration (European Economic Area) Regulations 2016 (SI 2016/1052) reg.13(4) (Initial right of residence)*

3.028   With effect from July 24, 2018, reg.2 of, and para.7 of the Schedule to, the Immigration (European Economic Area) (Amendment) Regulations 2018 (SI 2018/801) amended reg.13(4) to read as follows:

"(4) A person who otherwise satisfies the criteria in this regulation is not entitled to a right to reside under this regulation where the Secretary of State or an immigration officer has made a decision under regulation 23(6)(b) (decision to remove on grounds of public policy, public security or public health), 24(1) (refusal to issue residence documentation etc), 25(1) (cancellation of a right of residence), 26(3) (misuse of right to reside) or 31(1) (revocation of admission), [or an order under regulation 23(5) (exclusion order) or 32(3) (deportation order), unless that decision or order, as the case may be, is set aside, revoked or otherwise no longer has effect]."

p.865, *amendment to the Immigration (European Economic Area) Regulations 2016 (SI 2016/1052) reg.14(4) (Extended right of residence)*

With effect from July 24, 2018, reg.2 of, and para.8 of the Schedule to, the Immigration (European Economic Area) (Amendment) Regulations 2018 (SI 2018/801) amended reg.14(4) to read as follows: **3.029**

"(4) A person who otherwise satisfies the criteria in this regulation is not entitled to a right to reside in the United Kingdom under this regulation where the Secretary of State or an immigration officer has made a decision under regulation 23(6)(b), 24(1), 25(1), 26(3) or 31(1), [or an order under regulation 23(5) (exclusion order) or 32(3) (deportation order), unless that decision or order, as the case may be, is set aside, revoked or otherwise no longer has effect]."

p.866, *amendment to the Immigration (European Economic Area) Regulations 2016 (SI 2016/1052) reg.15(4) (Permanent right of residence)*

With effect from July 24, 2018, reg.2 of, and para.9 of the Schedule to, the Immigration (European Economic Area) (Amendment) Regulations 2018 (SI 2018/801) amended reg.15(4) to read as follows: **3.030**

"(4) A person who satisfies the criteria in this regulation is not entitled to a right to permanent residence in the United Kingdom where the Secretary of State or an immigration officer has made a decision under regulation 23(6)(b), 24(1), 25(1), 26(3) or 31(1), [or an order under regulation 23(5) (exclusion order) or 32(3) (deportation order), unless that decision or order, as the case may be, is set aside, revoked or otherwise no longer has effect]."

p.877, *amendment to the Immigration (European Economic Area) Regulations 2016 (SI 2016/1052) reg.16(8) (Derivative right to reside)*

With effect from July 24, 2018, reg.2 of, and para.10 of the Schedule to, the Immigration (European Economic Area) (Amendment) Regulations 2018 (SI 2018/801) amended reg.16(8) by omitting the words "who is not an exempt person" from reg.16(8)(b)(ii).   **3.031**

p.877, *amendment to the Immigration (European Economic Area) Regulations 2016 (SI 2016/1052) reg.21 (Procedure for applications for documentation under this Part and regulation 12)*

With effect from July 24, 2018, reg.2 of, and para.11 of the Schedule to, the Immigration (European Economic Area) (Amendment) Regulations 2018 (SI 2018/801) amended reg.21 by omitting the words "or   **3.032** joined" in paragraphs (2)(a) and (5) and inserting the following paragraph after para.(4):

"(4A) An application for documentation under this Part, or for an EEA family permit under regulation 12, is invalid where the person making the application is subject to a removal decision made under regulation 23(6)(b), a deportation order made under regulation 32(3) or an exclusion order made under regulation 23(5)."

p.879, *annotation to the Immigration (European Economic Area) Regulations 2016 (SI 2016/1052) reg.16(5) (Derivative right to reside—Parents of British Children)*

3.032.1   In *DM v SSWP (PIP)* [2019] UKUT 26 (AAC), Upper Tribunal Judge Ward accepted a concession from the Secretary of State that "Regulation 16(5) of the Immigration (European Economic Area) Regulations 2016 (and regulation 15A(4A) of the 2006 Regulations) applies to carers of adult British citizens as well as children, and this reflects the relevant EU case law": see also the decision of the High Court (Lane J.) in *R (Hamid Saeed) v Secretary of State for the Home Department* [2018] EWHC 1707 (Admin).

In the light of that concession, the heading to the annotation should now read *Carers of British Citizens* rather than *Parents of British Children*.

pp.890-894, *annotation to the Immigration (European Economic Area) Regulations 2016 (SI 2016/1052) Sch.6 (Transitional Provisions)*

3.033   In *Oksuzoglu (EEA appeal—"new matter")* [2018] UKUT 385 (IAC), the Immigration and Asylum Chamber of the Upper Tribunal summarised the effect of the provisions in Sch.6 (taken together with the former transitory provisions in Sch.5) as being that:

(a) All decisions made on or after 1 February 2017 are to be treated as having been made under the 2016 Regs, whatever the date of the application;

(b) Regulation 9 of the 2016 Regs applies (through the medium of the transitory provisions) to all decisions made on or after 25 November 2016 whatever the date of the application;

(c) In all other respects the Immigration (EEA) Regulations 2006 apply if (i) the application was made before 25 November 2016 and (ii) the decision was made before 1 February 2017.

p.1264, *amendment to the Jobseeker's Allowance Regulations 1996 (SI 1996/207) Sch.1 para.12 (Applicable amounts—Higher pensioner premium)*

3.034   With effect from November 28, 2018, reg.2(a) of the Universal Credit and Jobseeker's Allowance (Miscellaneous Amendments) Regulations 2018 (SI 2018/1129) amended para.12(1)(a)(i) of Sch.1 to read as follows:

"Higher pensioner premium

12.—(1) Subject to sub-paragraph (5), the condition is that—

    (a) the claimant is a single claimant or lone parent who has attained the qualifying age for state pension credit and either—

        (i) satisfies one of the additional conditions specified in paragraph 14(1)(a), (c), [(ca), (cb),](e), (f)[, (fa)] or (h); or. . ."

p.1265, *amendment to the Jobseeker's Allowance Regulations 1996 (SI 1996/207) Sch.1, para.13(1) (Applicable amounts—Disability premium)*

With effect from November 28, 2018, reg.2(b) of the Universal Credit and Jobseeker's Allowance (Miscellaneous Amendments) Regulations 2018 (SI 2018/1129) amended para.13(1) of Sch.1 to read as follows: 3.035

"Disability premium

13.—(1) Subject to sub-paragraph (2), the condition is that the claimant—

    (a) is a single claimant or lone parent who has not attained the qualifying age for state pension credit and satisfies any one of the additional conditions specified in paragraph 14(1)(a), (c), [(ca), (cb),] (e), (f) [, (fa)] or (h); or

    (b) has not attained the qualifying age for state pension credit, has a partner and the claimant satisfies any one of the additional conditions specified in paragraph 14(1)(a), (c), [(ca), (cb),] (e), (f) [, (fa)] or (h); or

    (c) has a partner and the partner has not attained the qualifying age for state pension credit and also satisfies any one of the additional conditions specified in paragraph 14."

p.1318, *amendment to the Jobseeker's Allowance Regulations 1996 (SI 1996/207) Sch.7 para.18(c) (Sums to be disregarded in the calculation of income other than earnings)*

With effect from December 6, 2018, reg.3 of the Social Security (Miscellaneous Amendments No.5) Regulations 2017 (SI 2017/1187) amended para.18(c) by inserting the words "or, if it was higher at that time, pensionable age" after the words "the age of 65".   3.036

p.1321, *amendment to the Employment and Support Allowance Regulations 2008 (SI 2008/794) Sch.8 para.31 (Sums toamendment to the Jobseeker's Allowance Regulations 1996 (SI 1996/207) Sch.7 para.30 (Sums to be disregarded in the calculation of income other than earnings)*

With effect from April 5, 2018, reg.2(18)(d) of the Loans for Mortgage Interest and Social Fund Maternity Grant (Amendment) Regulations 2018 (SI 2018/307) substituted a new paragraph 30 as follows: 3.036.1

"**30.** Any payment received under an insurance policy taken out to insure against the risk of being unable to maintain repayments on a loan which qualifies under Part 1 of Schedule 1 to the Loans for Mortgage Interest Regulations 2017 (legacy benefit claimants and SPC claimants) and used to meet such repayments."

p.1321, *amendment to the Employment and Support Allowance Regulations 2008 (SI 2008/794) Sch.8 para.31 (Sums to amendment to the Jobseeker's Allowance Regulations 1996 (SI 1996/207) Sch.7 para.31 (Sums to be disregarded in the calculation of income other than earnings)*

3.036.2   With effect from April 5, 2018, reg.2(18)(d) of the Loans for Mortgage Interest and Social Fund Maternity Grant (Amendment) Regulations 2018 (SI 2018/307) amended paragraph 31 so that it now reads as follows:

31.—(1) Except where paragraph 30 or 31A applies, and subject to sub-paragraph (2), any payment made to the claimant which is intended to be used and is used as a contribution towards—

(a) any payment due on a loan if secured on the dwelling occupied as the home which does not qualify under Part 1 of Schedule 1 to the Loans for Mortgage Interest Regulations;

(b) any charge which qualifies in accordance with paragraph 16 of Schedule 2 (housing costs) to these Regulations or any interest payment on a loan which qualifies under Part 1 of Schedule 1 to the Loans for Mortgage Interest Regulations, to the extent that the charge or payment is not met under these Regulations or by loan payments (as the case may be);

(c) any payment due on a loan which qualifies under Part 1 of Schedule 1 to the Loans for Mortgage Interest Regulations attributable to the payment of capital;

(d) any amount due by way of premiums on—

(i) an insurance policy taken out to insure against the risk of being unable to make the payments referred to in (a) to (c) above, or

(ii) an insurance policy taken out to insure against loss or damage to any building or part of a building which is occupied by the claimant as his home;

(e) his rent in respect of the dwelling occupied by him as his home but only to the extent that it is not met by housing benefit; or his accommodation charge but only to the extent that the actual charge exceeds the amount payable by a local authority in accordance with Part III of the National Assistance Act 1948 or Part 1 of the Care Act 2014 (care and support) or Part 4 of the Social Services and Well-being (Wales) Act 2014 (meeting needs) other than any direct payment made in accordance with regulations made under section 50 or 52 of that Act.

(2) This paragraph shall not apply to any payment which is treated as possessed by the claimant by virtue of regulation 105(10)(a)(ii) (notional income).

(3) In this paragraph—

(a) "Loans for Mortgage Interest Regulations" means the Loans for Mortgage Interest Regulations 2017;

(b) "loan payments" has the meaning given in the Loans for Mortgage Interest Regulations."

p.1323, *amendment to the Jobseeker's Allowance Regulations 1996 (SI 1996/207) Sch.7 para.47(2) (Sums to be disregarded in the calculation of income other than earnings)*

With effect from April 11, 2018, para.21(d) of the Schedule to the Secretaries of State for Health and Social Care and for Housing, Communities and Local Government and Transfer of Functions (Commonhold Land) Order 2018 (SI 2018/378) amended para.47(2) by inserting the words "and Social Care" after the words "for Health".   3.037

p.1326, *amendment to the Jobseeker's Allowance Regulations 1996 (SI 1996/207) Sch.7 (Sums to be disregarded in the calculation of income other than earnings)*

With effect from September 3, 2018, art.3 of the Social Security (Scotland) Act 2018 (Consequential Modifications) Order 2018 (SI 2018/872) added the following after para.76 of Sch.7:   3.038

"**77.** Any payment of carer's allowance supplement made under section 81 of the Social Security (Scotland) Act 2018."

With effect from December 10, 2018, art.6(2) of the Social Security (Scotland) Act 2018 (Best Start Grants) (Consequential Modifications and Saving) Order 2018 (SI 2018/1138) added the following after para.77 of Sch.7:

"**78.** Any early years assistance given in accordance with section 32 of the Social Security (Scotland) Act 2018."

Since the Scottish early years assistance, including best start grants, will take the form of lump sum payments it would probably not constitute income in any event.

p.1335, *amendment to the Jobseeker's Allowance Regulations 1996 (SI 1996/207) Sch.8 para12(2) (Capital to be disregarded)*

With effect from September 11, 2018, reg.3 of the Social Security (Treatment of Arrears of Benefit) Regulations 2018 (SI 2018/932) amended para.12(2) by substituting the following for head (a):   3.039

"(a) paid in order to rectify, or to compensate for—
    (i) an official error as defined in regulation 1(2) of the Social Security and Child Support (Decisions and Appeals) Regulations 1999, or
    (ii) an error on a point of law; and"

See the entry for p.666 of Vol.II for discussion of the effect of the amendment.

p.1338, *amendment to the Jobseeker's Allowance Regulations 1996 (SI 1996/207) Sch.8 para.36(2) (Capital to be disregarded)*

3.040   With effect from April 11, 2018, para.21(d) of the Schedule to the Secretaries of State for Health and Social Care and for Housing, Communities and Local Government and Transfer of Functions (Commonhold Land) Order 2018 (SI 2018/378) amended para.36(2) by inserting the words "and Social Care" after the words "for Health".

p.1341, *amendment to the Jobseeker's Allowance Regulations 1996 (SI 1996/207) Sch.8 (Capital to be disregarded)*

3.041   With effect from December 10, 2018, art.5(3) of the Social Security (Scotland) Act 2018 (Best Start Grants) (Consequential Modifications and Saving) Order 2018 (SI 2018/1138) added the following after para.67 (presumably meaning the second para.66) of Sch.10:

"**68.** Any early years assistance given in accordance with section 32 of the Social Security (Scotland) Act 2018."

p.1347-9, *annotation to the Jobseeker's Allowance (Mandatory Work Activity Scheme) Regulations 2011 (SI 2011/688)*

3.041.1   *SSWP v DM (rule 17) (JSA)* [2018] UKUT 424 (AAC), a decision merely recording consent to the withdrawal of the Secretary of State's appeal to the Upper Tribunal, contains details of the Department's Operational Guidance (as in force in April 2012) about identifying when claimants were suitable for the MWAS, that had wrongly not been produced to the First-tier Tribunal. The Secretary of State accepted that, if that guidance had been properly applied, the claimant in *DM* should not, becuase of his complex barriers to employment, have been referred to the scheme.

p.1352, *annotation to the Jobseeker's Allowance (Schemes for Assisting Persons to Obtain Employment) Regulations 2013 (SI 2013/276)*

3.042   In *SN v SSWP (JSA)* [2018] UKUT 279 (AAC), para.91, it was confirmed that, despite the failure to issue the claimant with a MWA05 letter, he had been sufficiently notified of the requirement to participate in a mandatory work activity scheme within reg.4 of the MWAS Regulations by a combination of information given in an interview with an adviser and a letter from the programme provider about the specific placement.

p.1397, *amendments to the State Pension Credit Regulations 2002 (SI 2002/1792) reg.15(1) (Social security benefits which are not prescribed for the purpose of section 15(1)(e) of the State Pension Credit Act 2002)*

3.043   With effect from September 3, 2018, art.4 of the Social Security (Scotland) Act 2018 (Consequential Modifications) Order 2018 (SI

2018/872) inserted after sub-para.(r) the following new sub-paragraph:

"(ra) carer's allowance supplement payable under section 81 of the Social Security (Scotland) Act 2018;".

With effect from December 10, 2018, art.7(2) of the Social Security (Scotland) Act 2018 (Best Start Grants) (Consequential Modifications and Saving) Order 2018 (SI 2018/1138) inserted after sub-para.(ra)

"(rb) early years assistance given in accordance with section 32 of the Social Security (Scotland) Act 2018;".

p.1449, *amendment to the State Pension Credit Regulations 2002 (SI 2002/1792) Sch.V para.20 (Capital disregarded for the purpose of calculating income)*

With effect from December 10, 2018, art.7(3) of the Social Security (Scotland) Act 2018 (Best Start Grants) (Consequential Modifications and Saving) Order 2018 (SI 2018/1138) inserted after sub-para.(ra)   3.044

"(r) early years assistance given in accordance with section 32 of the Social Security (Scotland) Act 2018.".

p.1449, *amendment to the State Pension Credit Regulations 2002 (SI 2002/1792) Sch.V para.20A(1) (Income from capital)*

With effect from September 11, 2018, reg.4 of the Social Security (Treatment of Arrears of Benefit) Regulations 2018 (SI 2018/932) inserted "or an error on a point of law" after "error" in para.20A(1).   3.045

p.1478, *amendment to the Social Fund Winter Fuel Payment Regulations 2000 (SI 2000/729) reg.2(4) (Social fund winter fuel payments)*

With effect from November 15, 2018, reg.4 and Sch. para.9 of the Social Security (Updating of EU References) (Amendment) Regulations 2018 (SI 2018/1084) amended reg.2(4)(a) by inserting the words ", as amended from time to time," after "1408/71" and "883/2004".   3.046

pp.1491-1492, *amendment to the Social Fund Maternity and Funeral Expenses (General) Regulations 2005 (SI 2005/3061) reg.3A (Provision against double payment: Sure Start Maternity Grants)*

For the purposes of claims made on or after December 10, 2018, reg.3(2) of the Social Security (Scotland) Act 2018 (Best Start Grants) (Consequential Modifications and Saving) Order 2018 (SI 2018/1138) amended reg.3A by inserting the words "or a Best Start Grant" after the words "Sure Start Maternity Grant" in para.(1)(b) and by substituting the following for para.(1)(c):   3.047

"(c) "subsequent grant" is, in respect of C—
    (i) a second or subsequent Sure Start Maternity Grant; or

        (ii) if a Best Start Grant has been given, a first Sure Start Maternity Grant;

    (d) "Best Start Grant" is a grant given to a qualifying individual under Regulations made under section 32 of the Social Security (Scotland) Act 2018 in connection with having, or expecting to have, a new baby in the family.",

and by substituting "subsequent" for "second" in paras (2) and (3).

For Best Start Grants in Scotland on or after December 10, 2018, see the Early Years Assistance (Best Start Grants) (Scotland) Regulations 2018 (SSI 2018/370) in Part VII.

p.1493, *amendment to the Social Fund Maternity and Funeral Expenses (General) Regulations 2005 (SI 2005/3061) Pt.II (Heading—Payments for maternity expenses)*

3.048   For the purposes of claims made on or after December 10, 2018, reg.3(3) of the Social Security (Scotland) Act 2018 (Best Start Grants) (Consequential Modifications and Saving) Order 2018 (SI 2018/1138) amended the heading to Pt.II to read "Payments for maternity expenses [in England and Wales]'.

For payments for maternity expenses in Scotland on or after December 10, 2018, see the Early Years Assistance (Best Start Grants) (Scotland) Regulations 2018 (SSI 2018/370) in Part VII.

pp.1494-1495, *amendment to the Social Fund Maternity and Funeral Expenses (General) Regulations 2005 (SI 2005/3061) reg.5 (Entitlement)*

3.049   For the purposes of claims made on or after December 10, 2018, reg.3(4) of the Social Security (Scotland) Act 2018 (Best Start Grants) (Consequential Modifications and Saving) Order 2018 (SI 2018/1138) amended reg.5 by inserting a new para.(6) after para.(5) as follows:

"(6) The fifth condition is that the claimant lives in England or Wales."

For payments for maternity expenses in Scotland on or after December 10, 2018, see the Early Years Assistance (Best Start Grants) (Scotland) Regulations 2018 (SSI 2018/370) in Part VII.

p.1499, *annotation to the Social Fund Maternity and Funeral Expenses (General) Regulations 2005 (SI 2005/3061) reg.5(5) (Entitlement—Time limit for claims)*

3.050   With effect from October 18, 2018, reg.2 of the Social Security (Claims and Payments) (Social Fund Maternity Grant) (Amendment) Regulations 2018 (SI 2018/989), amended Sch. 4, para.8 (social fund payment in respect of maternity expenses) of the Social Security (Claims and Payments) Regulations 1987 (SI 1987/1968) (prescribed times for claiming benefit), by substituting the words "six months" for the words "three months". The effect is that all the three-month time limits referred to in the commentary have become six-month time limits from that date.

p.1506, *annotation to the Social Fund Maternity and Funeral Expenses (General) Regulations 2005 (SI 2005/3061) reg.7 (General Note—Time limit)*

Note that with effect from April 2, 2018, reg.2(4) of the Social **3.051** Security (Claims and Payments) (Social Fund Maternity Grant) (Amendment) Regulations 2018 (SI 2018/989), amended Sch. 4, para.9 (social fund payment in respect of funeral expenses) of the Social Security (Claims and Payments) Regulations 1987 (SI 1987/1968) (prescribed times for claiming benefit), by substituting "6 months" for "3 months". The effect is that the three-month time limits referred to in the commentary have become six-month time limits from that date.

p.1542, *annotation to the new style Jobseekers Act 1995 s.6A (Claimant commitment)*

See *JB v SSWP (UC)* [2018] UKUT 360 (AAC), discussed in detail **3.052** in the entry for p.60 of Vol.V, for discussion of the effect of the standard terms of claimant commitments and of the notification of requirements by other means.

p.1543, *annotation to the new style Jobseekers Act 1995 s.6B (Work-focused interview requirement)*

See *SN v SSWP (JSA)* [2018] UKUT 279 (AAC), detailed in the **3.053** entry for pp.121-2, for discussion of what might amount to a failure to participate (in that case in a mandatory work activity scheme) and the expression of some doubt about the result in *SA v SSWP (JSA)* [2015] UKUT 454 (AAC).

p.1551, *annotation to the new style Jobseekers Act 1995 s.6F (Imposition of work-related requirements)*

See *JB v SSWP (UC)* [2018] UKUT 360 (AAC), discussed in detail **3.054** in the entry for p.60 of Vol.V, for discussion of the effect of the standard terms of claimant commitments and of the notification of requirements by other means.

p.1552, *annotation to the new style Jobseekers Act 1995 s.6G (Contested requirements)*

See *SN v SSWP (JSA)* [2018] UKUT 279 (AAC), detailed in the **3.055** entry for pp.121-2, for discussion of what might amount to a failure to participate (in that case in a mandatory work activity scheme) and the expression of some doubt about the result in *SA v SSWP (JSA)* [2015] UKUT 454 (AAC).

p.1555, *annotation to the new style Jobseekers Act 1995 s.6H(4)*
(Imposition of work-related and connected requirements: supplementary)

3.056   See *JB v SSWP (UC)* [2018] UKUT 360 (AAC), discussed in detail
in the entry for p.60 of Vol.V, for discussion of the effect of the standard
terms of claimant commitments and of the notification of requirements
by other means.

PART IV

UPDATING MATERIAL
VOLUME III

ADMINISTRATION, ADJUDICATION AND
THE EUROPEAN DIMENSION

Commentary by

Mark Rowland

Christopher Ward

p.117, *Social Security Administration Act 1992 s.115C (Incorrect statements)*

ERRATUM: in s.115C(1)(a)(i) for "acclaim" substitute "a claim".   4.001

pp.183-184, *annotation to the Social Security (Recovery of Benefits) Act 1997 s.8 (Reduction of compensation payment)*

The fact that a compensator had no right to make a reduction under   4.002
s.8 does not preclude an injured person from appealing if one was in fact made in purported reliance on that provision, but the illegality of the reduction is not a relevant issue on any such appeal (*TC v SSWP (CR)* [2018] UKUT 272 (AAC)).

pp.189-191, *annotation to the Social Security (Recovery of Benefits) Act 1997 s.11 (Appeals against certificates of recoverable benefits)*

The fact that a compensator had no right to make a reduction under   4.003
s.8 because the claimant had not claimed compensation for lost earnings does not preclude an injured person from appealing if a reduction was in fact made in purported reliance on that provision. However, the illegality of the reduction is not a relevant issue on any such appeal. On the other hand, where there is a question whether employment and support allowance was paid in consequence of the relevant accident, consideration must be given not only to whether the claimant would have satisfied descriptors under Sch.2 or 3 to the Employment and Support Regulations 2008 but also whether the conditions of reg.29(2) or 35(2) would have been satisfied (*TC v SSWP (CR)* [2018] UKUT 272 (AAC)).

p.209, *annotation to the Social Security (Recovery of Benefits) Act 1998 Sch.2 (Calculation of compensation payment)*

See the supplementary annotation to s.11 of the 1997 Act (above).   4.004

p.225, *annotation to the Social Security Act 1998 s.9(5) (Revision of decisions)*

In *PH v SSWP (DLA)* [2018] UKUT 404 (AAC), it has been held   4.005
that, where it is a requirement that a person apply for revision before appealing, a refusal to revise on the ground of "official error" will have the effect of extending the time for appealing provided that the application on that ground was not spurious. This is because, as mentioned in the annotation to the main work, the time for appealing in a case where a notice has been issued under reg.3ZA(1) of the Social Security and Child Support (Decisions and Appeals) Regulations 1999 runs, under r.22(2)(d)(i) of the Tribunal Procedure (First-tier Tribunal) (Social Entitlement Chamber) 2008, from the date on which the "result of mandatory reconsideration" is issued. Because reg.3ZA(2) does not refer only to applications for revision within the scope of reg.3(1) or (3),

the constraints imposed by the terms of para.5(c) of Sch.1 to the Rules, a predecessor of which was the provision considered in *R(IS) 15/04,* also mentioned in the main work, do not apply.

pp.236-245, *annotation to the Social Security Act 1998 s.12(2) (Appeal to First-tier Tribunal)*

4.006   Regulation 31(2) of the Social Security and Child Support (Decisions and Appeals) Regulations 1999 was the provision, made under s.9(6), that was considered in *R(IS) 15/04* and a similar provision was considered in *Beltekian v Westminster City Council* [2004] EWCA Civ 1784 (reported as *R(H) 8/05*), both of which decisions are mentioned in the main work. However, as pointed out in *PH v SSWP (DLA)* [2018] UKUT 404 (AAC), those provisions have been replaced by r.22(2)(d) of, and para.5 of Sch.1 to, the Tribunal Procedure (First-tier Tribunal) (Social Entitlement Chamber) Rules 2008 and, while para.5(c) of Sch.1 replicates the former reg.31(2), it applies only where the original decision was not accompanied by a notice issued under reg.3ZA(1) of the 1999 Regs to the effect that the right of appeal is subject to an application for revision under s.9 being considered by the Secretary of State first. Where such a notice is issued, the time for appealing runs, under r.22(2)(d)(i), from the date on which the "result of mandatory reconsideration" is issued. Consequently, where the application for revision required by reg.3(ZA) is made on the ground of official error, the time for appealing is extended whether or not it is successful and, to that extent, what was said in *R(IS) 15/04* and *Beltekian* no longer applies. However, that does not affect the argument that, because there is a right of appeal against a supersession or refusal to supersede, but not against a revision or refusal to revise, the First-tier Tribunal cannot replace a supersession decision with a revision. On the other hand, a refusal to supersede a decision, or to uphold a supersession, on the ground that the original decision should be revised rather than superseded (see reg.6(3) of the 1999 Regulations, reg.15 of the Child Benefit and Guardian's Allowance (Decisions and Appeals) Regulations 2003 or reg.32 of the Universal Credit, Personal Independence Payment, Jobseeker's Allowance and Employment and Support Allowance (Decisions and Appeals) Regulations 2013) might have the same practical effect.

     RH v SSWP (DLA) [2018] UKUT 48 (AAC), mentioned in the main work on p.245, has been reported as [2018] AACR 33.

p.261, *annotation to the Social Security Act 1998 s.17 (Finality of decisions)*

4.006.1   By reg.3 of the Childcare Payments (Appeals) Regulations 2016, this section is applied with such substantial modifications (see Vol.IV of the main work) that one wonders why the Commissioners for Her Majesty's Revenue and Customs bothered, rather than making separate provision which would have been simpler for all concerned.

p.267, *annotation to the Social Security Act 1998 s.19(3) (Medical examination required by Secretary of State)*

Whereas reg.9(1) of the Social Security (Personal Independence Pay-   4.007
ment) Regulations 2013 provides that a claimant may be "required" to
attend for and participate in an examination, s.19(2) and (3) of the 1998
Act contemplate a mere "request". Whether this makes any difference in
practice is perhaps doubtful, because a person is likely to be able to show
good cause for failing to comply with a request that was not made in
terms that indicated the likely consequence of failing to attend. The
terms in which the request was made may, for that and other reasons, be
highly relevant to the question whether there was good cause for a failure
to attend and therefore a copy of the request should be provided with the
Secretary of State's response to an appeal, even if the claimant has not
expressly put its terms in issue, although a failure to do so will not
necessarily justify the First-tier Tribunal drawing inferences against the
Secretary of State (*SSWP v DC (JSA)* [2017] UKUT 464 (AAC);
[2018] AACR 16, where the question was whether the claimant had had
good cause for failing to participate in a back-to-work scheme). The
need to include a copy of the request in a response to an appeal does not
depend on there being any technical necessity to prove that the request
was put in terms of a "requirement", such as there was held to be in *MB
v SSWP (PIP)* [2018] UKUT 213 (AAC).

p.282, *annotation to the Social Security Act 1998 s.27(1) (Restrictions on entitlement to benefit in certain cases of error)*

ERRATUM: The Applicant in the case mentioned at the bottom of   4.008
the page was DS, rather than JS. Accordingly, the case should be cited as
R.(DS) v Secretary of State for Work and Pensions [2018] UKUT 270
(AAC).

p.343, *amendment to the Welfare Reform Act 2012 s.127 (Information-sharing between Secretary of State and HMRC)*

With effect from January 16, 2017, s.2(3) of, and para.17(8) of Sch.2   4.008.1
to, the Savings (Government Contributions) Act 2017 amend s.127 of
omitting the "or" at the end of para.(b) of the definition of "HMRC
function" in s.127(7) and inserting after para.(c) the following new
paragraph:

"(d) which is conferred by or under section 2 of, or Schedule 2 to, the
Savings (Government Contributions) Act 2017 (bonuses in respect of
savings in Help-to-Save accounts);"

p.504, *annotation to the Social Security (Claims and Payments)
Regulations 1987 (SI 1987/1968) reg.43 (Children)*

A child claimant of DLA will have had to have an appointee under this   4.009
regulation. On conversion to PIP, however, an appointee can only be

appointed under reg.57 of the Universal Credit etc. (Claims and Payments) Regulations 2013—there is no automatic conversion of the appointee who has acted for the child for DLA purposes: see *P v SSWP* [2018] UKUT 359 (AAC).

p.513, *amendments to the Social Security (Claims and Payments) Regulations 1987 (SI 1987/1968) Sch.4 (Prescribed times for claiming benefit)*

4.010   With effect from October 18, 2018, reg.2 of the Social Security (Claims and Payments) (Social Fund Maternity Grant) (Amendment) Regulations 2018 (SI 2018/989) substituted "6 months" for "3 months" in each of entries (a) to (f) of para.8 of Sch.4.

p.583, *annotation to the Universal Credit etc. (Claims and Payments) Regulations 2013 (SI 2013/380) reg.57 (Persons unable to act)*

4.011   A child claimant of DLA will have had to have an appointee under reg.43(1) of the Social Security (Claims and Payments) Regulations 1987. On conversion to PIP, an appointee can only be appointed under this regulation—there is no automatic conversion of the appointee who has acted for the child for DLA purposes: see *P v SSWP* [2018] UKUT 359 (AAC).

p.605, *Social Security and Child Support (Decisions and Appeals) Regulations 1999 (SI 1999/991 reg.1 (Citation, commencement, application and interpretation)*

4.011.1   ERRATUM: in the definition of "official error", the words "the Department or the [^{21}, the Commission] Inland Revenue" should read "the Department [^{21}[^{27} . . .]] or the Inland Revenue".

pp.637-639, *annotation to the Social Security and Child Support (Decisions and Appeals) Regulations 1999 (SI 1999/991) reg.3ZA (Consideration of revision before appeal)*

4.012   *R.(CJ) v Secretary of State for Work and Pensions* [2017] UKUT 324 (AAC) has been reported as [2018] AACR 5. *A fortiori*, if an application is made late under reg.3(1) or (3) but within the 13 month absolute time limit and the Secretary of State overlooks or fails to deal with the question of lateness and simply considers the merits of the application, the application has been "considered" (*AO v SSWP (CSM)* [2017] UKUT 499 (AAC)). In *PH v SSWP (DLA)* [2018] UKUT 404 (AAC), the Upper Tribunal has decided that, where an application for revision is made under reg.3(1) or (3) but was made more than 13 months after the original decision so that time could not be extended under reg.4, the Secretary of State will not have "considered" the application and so there is no right of appeal against the original decision. However, it was also pointed out that, where an application is made under reg.3(5)(a), on the ground of "official error", there is no time limit in the 1999 Regulations. The provision under which an application is made is to be determined by considering the substance of the application, rather than its form, so that a spurious allegation of "official error" will not assist a claimant. The Upper Tribunal recognised that the implication of this analysis is that, in a case where a decision is accompanied by a notice under reg.3ZA(1), a refusal to revise has the effect of extending the time for appealing against the decision when the ground of revision is "official error", contrary to the approach taken in *R(IS) 15/04*. This is because the time for appealing in a case where a notice has been issued under reg.3ZA(1) runs, under r.22(2)(d)(i) of the Tribunal Procedure (First-tier Tribunal) (Social Entitlement Chamber) 2008, from the date the "result of mandatory reconsideration" is issued. Because reg.3ZA(2) does not refer only to applications for revision within the scope of reg.3(1) or (3), the constraints imposed by the terms of para.5 of Sch.1 to the Rules, a predecessor of which was the provision considered in *R(IS) 15/04*, do not apply.

p.641, *annotation to the Social Security and Child Support (Decisions and Appeals) Regulations 1999 (SI 1999/991) reg.4 (Late application for revision)*

R.(CJ) v Secretary of State for Work and Pensions [2017] UKUT 324 (AAC) has been reported as [2018] AACR 5. In *PH v SSWP (DLA)* [2018] UKUT 404 (AAC), the Upper Tribunal has decided that, where an application for revision is made under reg.3(1) or (3) but was made more than 13 months after the original decision so that time could not be extended under reg.4, the Secretary of State will not have "considered" the application and so there is no right of appeal against the original decision.   4.013

pp.660-662, *annotation to the Social Security and Child Support (Decisions and Appeals) Regulations 1999 (SI 1999/991) reg.6(2)(r) (Supersession of decisions)*

There have been a number of cases that have considered the related issues of the relevance of evidence of previous awards, either of the same benefit or of other benefits, the duties of the Secretary of State to provide such evidence with responses to appeals or of the First-tier Tribunal to obtain it, and the duty of the First-tier Tribunal to provide reasons for rejecting arguments based on such previous awards. Unsurprisingly, the cases are all very fact-specific. The relevant issues have been most comprehensively considered in *CH v SSWP (PIP)* [2018] UKUT 330 (AAC). It is convenient to deal with all the more important cases here, in the context of supersessions following the receipt of medical evidence, although in fact the two cases considered together by the Upper Tribunal in *CH* were both initial claims for personal independence payment by claimants who were entitled to disability living allowance.   4.014

In *JC v DSD (IB)* [2011] NICom 177; [2014] AACR 30 and *FN v SSWP (ESA)* [2015] UKUT 670 (AAC); [2016] AACR 24, which are mentioned in the annotations in the main work to reg.6(2)(g) and (r) and also in the annotation to r.24 of the Tribunal Procedure (First-tier Tribunal) (Social Entitlement Chamber) Rules 2008, a Tribunal of Social Security Commissioners in Northern Ireland and a three-judge panel of the Upper Tribunal were concerned with the duties of the Secretary of State to provide, and of the First-tier Tribunal to obtain, evidence relating to earlier claims for benefit. In the former case, both claims were for incapacity benefit but in the latter case, the Upper Tribunal was concerned with earlier evidence relating to incapacity benefit in a case where the claimant's entitlement to employment and support allowance was in issue. Incapacity benefit was a predecessor of employment and support allowance and the three-judge panel considered that the evidence might be relevant, notwithstanding that the conditions of entitlement were different.

In *CH*, the Upper Tribunal applied the same approach to cases where a claimant's entitlement to personal independence payment was in issue and there was a question whether evidence relating to an earlier claim for disability living allowance might be relevant. The Upper Tribunal declined an invitation to specify areas of overlap, but did offer the following guidance—

"48. First, although in *FN* at [83] the Upper Tribunal said that overlap between the substantive criteria was only an example of when past evidence might be relevant, it is difficult to envisage in what other circumstances DLA evidence would be relevant. . . . .

49. Second, as is clear from the case law to which I have referred, DLA evidence will not be relevant where the claimant's condition has since improved.

50. Third, DLA evidence could not assist where the claimant's case in the PIP appeal is inconsistent with the particular PIP descriptor being applicable. Thus, where the evidence of the claimant in the example at paragraph 15 is that he or she is able to walk over 50 metres at 1.5 times normal walking speed, DLA evidence relating to a previous award of the HRMC will not be relevant.

51. Fourth, it is highly unlikely that evidence other than the medical evidence from the DLA claim could be relevant to a subsequent PIP claim. Other evidence, such as what the claimant said in the DLA claim form, can be repeated for the purpose of the PIP claim if thought relevant. Previous statements by the claimant are unlikely to assist as to credibility as such statements are just as likely to show consistent misrepresentation or exaggeration as they are to show truth or accuracy.

52. Fifth, the age of the evidence is likely to affect its relevance but on occasions even quite old evidence may assist, for example where there is reason to doubt the PIP evidence or it is incomplete. Older evidence may also assist where variability is in issue (see *JC* at [50(viii)]). It is not appropriate to specify a particular age beyond which DLA evidence will not assist although, in general, relevance is likely to decrease with age. Whether it does assist in any particular case is a matter for the First-tier Tribunal's judgment.

53. Sixth, an indefinite award of DLA would have been based on the prognosis given at that time but that prognosis is unlikely to provide assistance at the time of a PIP decision when there is a reliable up-to-date assessment of the claimant's actual condition.

54. Finally, PIP assessments may not be as reliable as the Secretary of State would like to have the Tribunal believe (see paragraphs 25-27). It is the tribunal's task to decide what weight to afford the PIP evidence. Medical evidence relating to a previous DLA award may assist in evaluating the quality of the PIP assessment."

As to the duty of the Secretary of State to attach evidence to responses, the Upper Tribunal noted that the Secretary of State's policy, which had not always been followed in practice, was that disability living allowance evidence would be included where the claimant has asked for it to be taken into account, but where the claimant has not asked, the appeal submission would inform the tribunal only of that fact and the level and date of the last disability living allowance award in a transfer case. The information provided to the tribunal did not state what disability living allowance evidence was in the Secretary of State's possession including whether there was an examining medical practitioner's report, nor were copies provided. The Judge said—

"57. . . . . In the light of the decisions in *JC* and *FN*, I consider that, even if the claimant does not ask for the DLA evidence to be taken into account, the Secretary of State's duty means that she should consider whether DLA evidence in her possession is relevant to the PIP appeal, taking into account the guidance in these Reasons, and should provide to the tribunal the relevant evidence which is in her possession. It would usually be sufficient for the Secretary of State to consider the medical evidence that was available for the most recent determination. I do not consider that it would be unduly onerous for the Secretary of State to do this. I acknowledge that it is not my role to mandate the Secretary of State's performance of her duties, but I note that the Secretary of State has indicated that she will be addressing her procedures in the light of this decision and so I suggest that as a matter of good practice she could consider taking on board my observations."

As to the First-tier Tribunal's duty to obtain evidence where the Secretary of State did not provide it, the Judge said—

"59. As was made clear in *JC* and *FN* the tribunal is not required as a matter of law to consider DLA evidence on a PIP appeal if the evidence is not relevant (*JC* at [50(vi)] and *FN* [79]). Moreover, a tribunal will not always err in law in determining an appeal without all relevant evidence (*FN* at [78] and [79]). The question is whether the evidence is necessary fairly to determine the appeal. Thus, at [84] the Upper Tribunal said:
'a First-tier Tribunal is entitled to call on what evidence it considers relevant to the proper determination of the issues arising in the appeal' (emphasis added)
60. In disability appeals there is frequently relevant evidence, such as GP records, which is not before the tribunal. There is no general

requirement on the tribunal to obtain such evidence. It is for the tribunal to decide whether it is proportionate to do so, consistently with the overriding objective. The position has been put succinctly by Judge Nicholas Paines QC in *GC v SSWP (ESA)* [2014] UKUT 174 (AAC):

'34. Tribunals are often faced with cases in which categories of information that might be helpful to the tribunal are not in their papers. For example, they may or may not have a claimant's GP records; the claimant may have been to a specialist for treatment, but the papers do not contain any report from the specialist; the claimant may not have been examined on behalf of the DWP by an examining medical practitioner; or, as here, an ability similar to the ability at issue before the tribunal may have been adjudicated on for the purposes of another social security benefit, but the papers are not before the tribunal. Other examples can no doubt be proffered. In all these situations, it seems to me, the tribunal has a discretion, to be exercised judicially, as to whether they adjourn with a view to obtaining the further material.

35. In exercising that discretion, the tribunal will balance the competing factors, which include: the wishes of the claimant, particularly if represented; the delay to the proceedings before it; the amplitude of the evidence already before it; the likely relevance or helpfulness, so far as it can be judged, of the missing material, etc.'

61. Ultimately it is for the First-tier Tribunal to make its own judgment whether DLA evidence may be relevant and whether to call for it in a PIP appeal. In accordance with the decisions in *JC* and *FN*, and without setting down any hard and fast rules, the following guidance should assist in deciding whether to call for the relevant evidence.

62. First and most obviously, it must reasonably be considered that the DLA evidence would be relevant to the PIP decision as discussed above. At a minimum this will depend on there being relevant overlapping criteria in issue and a plausible case that the claimant's condition has not improved.

63. Second, even if the DLA evidence is likely to be relevant on the above basis, the First-tier Tribunal will not be required to obtain that evidence if it is satisfied that the PIP evidence is reliable and sufficient to enable it to determine whether the PIP criteria which are in issue are satisfied.

64. Third, if the First-tier Tribunal considers that the PIP evidence is insufficient or if it has cause to doubt the reliability of the PIP evidence, it should consider obtaining potentially relevant DLA evidence.

65. Fourth, if the First-tier Tribunal decides that the appellant is not credible and so making false or exaggerated claims about their difficulties, that may make it unnecessary to call for the DLA evidence. However, the tribunal might also consider whether the DLA evidence could assist in assessing the appellant's credibility where that is called in to question.

66. Fifth, if the claimant relies on the DLA award, the tribunal must address the argument made—see the discussion in *KW* v *SSWP (ESA)* [2018] UKUT 216 (AAC)—but it is a matter for the tribunal to determine whether to obtain the DLA evidence.

67. If the DWP's processes work, the question whether the tribunal should obtain the DLA evidence should only arise where the claimant did not ask for it to be taken into account and the Secretary of State has decided that it is not relevant. It is not consistent with the tribunal's investigative and enabling role simply to leave matters there. The claimant may not have appreciated that DLA evidence may be relevant, and the Secretary of State does not have the last word on relevance. But how is the First-tier Tribunal to go about the task of deciding whether to call for the DLA evidence where it does not know what DLA evidence there is? In the light of what the tribunal knows about the level and date of the last DLA award, it will be able to make a judgment as to whether there is any question of DLA evidence being potentially relevant and, in particular, whether any overlapping criteria are likely to be in issue. If they are not, it need not consider further whether to obtain that evidence. But if there is a possibility of the DLA evidence being relevant, then the tribunal ought to consider whether to obtain it.

68. Where an appeal is determined in the absence of the claimant it would only be in very obvious cases that the tribunal might consider obtaining the DLA evidence, for instance where there is a clear and substantial inconsistency between the PIP assessment and a recent DLA award. If the claimant is present, the tribunal can explore matters further if it appears that the DLA evidence may be relevant. It could find out more about the basis for the award, whether there was a medical examination, what other medical evidence there was, and why the claimant did not ask for the DLA evidence to be taken into account. It is for the tribunal to decide what inquiries to make but I give these examples to show that they can be made quickly and easily at a hearing and do not impose an undue burden on the tribunal.

69. In summary, the tribunal need only consider whether to obtain the DLA evidence if it has decided that it is or may be relevant. There is no question of it being required to obtain it simply to see what else there is. Even where the tribunal decides that the DLA evidence would be relevant, it may decide to determine the appeal without obtaining it. But it must consider whether to do so and take into account the range of relevant considerations, as explained in *GC*, and with due regard to the restraint to be exercised as urged by the Upper Tribunal in *FN* at [80]. Finally, where the question whether to seek DLA evidence has arisen and the tribunal decides to proceed without it, the duty on the tribunal to act judicially means that an appropriate explanation should be given. In most cases a brief explanation will suffice."

As to the duty to provide reasons where a claimant relied on an earlier   **4.015**
award of benefit, the judge rejected an argument that *YM v SSWP (PIP)* [2018] UKUT 16 (AAC), mentioned in the annotation in the main work

to r.34 of the Tribunal Procedure (First-tier Tribunal) (Social Entitlement Chamber) Rules 2008, had been wrongly decided. Note, though, that the Secretary of State has appealed against *YM* and the appeal is pending.

Evidence of the Department for Work and Pensions' retention policy for documents in disability cases was recorded in *GD v SSWP (PIP)* [2017] UKUT 415 (AAC) as follows—

"a. PIP Reassessment Claimants are asked at outset if they want the DWP to include their DLA medical evidence when considering the PIP claim. Where DLA medical evidence is used, then that evidence will be attached to the claimants PIP file and marked as supporting that PIP decision. This will be kept for at least 2 years if the PIP decision was a disallowance, or longer if the decision was an award. If there has been no request from the claimant to use their DLA medical evidence for their PIP claim then the old DLA evidence will be destroyed 3 months after the DLA decision has terminated. The PIP retention period is 24 months if the evidence is no longer classified as supporting. Once the DLA evidence has been included as part of the PIP claim it will have the same retention as any other PIP supporting document.

b. There is a departmental policy regarding document and data retention. However, benefits decide what fits their circumstances as documents can be retained for longer/shorter if there is a valid business need e.g. DLA is roughly 14 months for documents but PIP is 24 months due to the potential linking provision of Regulation 15 of the Social Security (Personal Independence Payment) Regulations 2013, but is consistent within each benefit.

c. . . . .Normally the DLA File is destroyed 14 months after it ceases to support an existing award. This period starts from 7 months after termination of award. The computer record will keep for 7 months and then close. The paper file will then be destroyed 14 months after that. However if any of that DLA evidence has been considered within the PIP claim then that evidence will support the PIP decision and it will be kept for as long as the PIP decision is current and 2 years after the PIP is no longer current.

d. If the DLA medical evidence has been used to consider the PIP claim then this will be included in the evidence bundle sent to the tribunal."

There may be instances where evidence can be provided even though the retention policy suggests that the documents should have been destroyed, but generally regard should clearly be had to the policy when consideration is being given by the First-tier Tribunal to directing the Secretary of State to provide evidence relating to former claims.

On an appeal to the Upper Tribunal, the question is whether the Upper Tribunal erred in law in failing to adjourn to obtain further evidence or in failing to give reasons for not doing so. It will be apparent from what was said in *CH*, that it will be highly relevant how the case was argued before the First-tier Tribunal. This is particularly so in cases where the evidence said to be relevant relates to a different benefit, typically personal independence payment in employment and support allowance appeals and vice versa. In *AG v SSWP (ESA)* [2017] UKUT 413 (AAC), the judge said—

"7. . . . I see no reason why, generally speaking, a tribunal ought not to be able to rely upon the absence of an adjournment request in order for further evidence to be obtained where a claimant has an experienced representative in the field of welfare benefits law. But it may well be good practice for a tribunal, where it thinks such an application could reasonably and sensibly be made, to query with the representative whether or not doing so has been considered. . . . "

Referring to that decision did not assist the claimant in *MC v SSWP (ESA)* [2018] UKUT 391 (AAC), where an argument that the First-tier Tribunal, when considering an appeal in respect of employment and support allowance, should have adjourned of its own volition to obtain evidence relating to a successful claim for personal independence payment was rejected because the claimant's representatives had not asked the First-tier Tribunal to obtain the evidence. In *MH v SSWP (ESA)* [2018] UKUT 194 (AAC), the question of obtaining the evidence was raised in the proceedings before the First-tier Tribunal and the Upper Tribunal had no difficulty in deciding that the First-tier Tribunal had been entitled to decide not to adjourn given the other evidence that was before it.

Where the First-tier Tribunal rejects an argument that an earlier award of the same, or a different, benefit is relevant, it should give reasons for doing so (*KW v SSWP (PIP)* [2018] UKUT 216 (AAC)). However, even if it does not expressly address the argument, it will not err in law if, in a case where there was no evidence of the basis of the previous award, the necessary implication of its findings and reasoning is that either it disagreed with the previous assessment in the light of the evidence before it or it found that there had been a material improvement in the claimant's condition (*VH v SSWP (ESA)* [2018] UKUT 290 (AAC)).

pp.699-700, *annotation to the Social Security and Child Support (Decisions and Appeals) Regulations 1999 (SI 1999/991) reg.19 (Suspension and termination for failure to submit to medical examination)*

Regulation 19(1) provides that the Secretary of State may "require" a   **4.016** claimant to submit to a medical examination and, to that extent, the language is similar to the language in reg.9(1) of the Social Security (Personal Independence Payment) Regulations 2013 in the light of which, it was suggested in *OM v SSWP (PIP)* [2017] UKUT 458 (AAC), "something worded as a request rather than a creation of a legal obligation may not count". In contrast, s.19(2) of the Social Security Act 1998 contemplates a mere "request". It is arguable that there is no difference between a request and a requirement when the consequence of a failure to comply with either may be, but may only be, the termination of entitlement to benefit. In either case, a person is likely to be able to show good cause for failing to comply with the request or requirement if it was not made in terms that indicated the likely consequence of failing to attend. The terms in which the request or requirement was made may, for that and other reasons, be highly relevant to the question whether there was good cause for a failure to attend and submit to a medical examination and therefore a copy of the request or requirement should be provided with the Secretary of State's response to an appeal (*MB v SSWP (PIP)* [2018] UKUT 213 (AAC)), even if the claimant has not expressly put its terms in issue, although a failure to do so will not necessarily justify the First-tier Tribunal drawing inferences against the Secretary of State unless the Secretary of State has been given an opportunity to remedy the defect (see *SSWP v DC (JSA)* [2017] UKUT 464 (AAC); [2018] AACR 16, where the question was whether the claimant had had good cause for failing to participate in a back-to-work scheme and which was considered in *MB*).

p.716, *amendment to the Social Security and Child Support (Decisions and Appeals) Regulations 1999 (SI 1999/991) Sch.2 (Decisions against which no appeal lies)*

4.017   With effect from November 15, 2018, reg.16 of the Social Security (Updating of EU References) (Amendment) Regulations 2018 (SI 2018/1084) amended para.10 of Sch.2 to the 2013 Regulations by inserting ", as amended from time to time," after "1408/71".

p.722, *annotation to the Social Security and Child Support (Decisions and Appeals) Regulations 1999 (SI 1999/991) Sch.2 (Decisions against which no appeal lies)*

4.018   *RH v SSWP (DLA)* [2018] UKUT 48 (AAC) has been reported as [2018] AACR 33.

p.738, *annotation to the Universal Credit, Personal Independence Payment, Jobseeker's Allowance and Employment and Support Allowance (Decisions and Appeals) Regulations 2013 (SI 2013/381) reg.7 (Consideration of revision before appeal)*

4.019   See the supplementary annotation to reg.3ZA of the Social Security and Child Support (Decisions and Appeals) Regulations 1999 (above).

p.751, *annotation to the Universal Credit, Personal Independence Payment, Jobseeker's Allowance and Employment and Support Allowance (Decisions and Appeals) Regulations 2013 (SI 2013/381) reg.26 (Medical evidence and limited capability for work etc.)*

4.020   See the supplementary annotation to reg.6(2)(r) of the Social Security and Child Support (Decisions and Appeals) Regulations 1999 (above).

p.780, *amendment to the Universal Credit, Personal Independence Payment, Jobseeker's Allowance and Employment and Support Allowance (Decisions and Appeals) Regulations 2013 (SI 2013/381) Sch.3 (Decisions against which no appeal lies)*

With effect from November 15, 2018, reg.16 of the Social Security (Updating of EU References) (Amendment) Regulations 2018 (SI 2018/1084) amended para.17 of Sch.3 to the 2013 Regulations by inserting ", as amended from time to time" after "1408/71".   4.021

pp.798-799, *amendments to the Social Security (Information-sharing in relation to Welfare Services etc.) Regulations 2012 (SI 2012/1483) reg.9A (Using purposes connected with the healthy start scheme)*

With effect from April 11, 2018, para.21(p) of the Schedule to the Secretaries of State for Health and Social Care and for Housing, Communities and Local Government and Transfer of Functions (Commonhold Land) Order 2018 (SI 2018/378) added in reg.9A (1) and (4) after "for Health" in each place, the words "and Social Care".   4.022

p.800, *amendments to the Social Security (Information-sharing in relation to Welfare Services etc.) Regulations 2012 (SI 2012/1483) reg.10 (Qualifying persons)*

With effect from April 11, 2018, para.21(p) of the Schedule to the Secretaries of State for Health and Social Care and for Housing, Communities and Local Government and Transfer of Functions (Commonhold Land) Order 2018 (SI 2018/378) added in reg. 10(1)(c) and (2) after "for Health" in each place, the words "and Social Care".   4.023

p.858, *Social Security (Medical Evidence) Regulations 1976 (SI 1976/615) Sch.1*

ERRATUM: the reference in bold to "regulation 2(1)(a)" alongside the title of "Schedule 1" is incorrect; it should read "regulation 2(1)".   4.024

p.898, *amendments to the Social Security (Payments on Account, Overpayments and Recovery) Regulations 1988 (SI 1988/664) reg.8 (Duplication and prescribed payments)*

With effect from November 15, 2018, para.7 of the Schedule to the Social Security (Updating of EU References) (Amendment) Regulations 2018 (SI 2018/1084) amended para.1(g) of reg.8 so that it reads: 4.025

"(g) any payment of benefit under the legislation of any member State other than the United Kingdom concerning the branches of social security mentioned in Article 4(1) of Regulation (EEC) No.1408/71, as amended from time to time, on the application of social security schemes to employed persons, to self-employed persons and to members of their families moving within the Community, or in Article 3(1) of Regulation (EC) No.883/2004 of the European Parliament and of the Council of 29 April 2004, as amended from time to time, on the coordination of social security systems, whether or not the benefit has been acquired by virtue of the provisions of either regulation, as amended from time to time."

pp.991-992, *amendments to the Child Benefit and Guardian's Allowance (Administration) Regulations 2003 (SI 2003/492) reg.6 (Time within which claims to be made)*

4.026   With effect from July 20, 2018, reg.3 of the Child Benefit, Tax Credits and Childcare Payments (Section 67 Immigration Act 2016 Leave) (Amendment) Regulations 2018 (SI 2018/788) inserted the following provisions. After sub-paragraph (2)(d) was inserted:

"(e) a person who has been granted section 67 leave makes a claim for that benefit or allowance within three months of receiving notification from the Secretary of State of the grant of that leave."

In paragraph (3) after "(2)(d)" was inserted "or (2)(e)".
After paragraph (3) was inserted:

"(4) In this regulation "section 67 leave" means leave to remain in the United Kingdom granted by the Secretary of State to a person who has been relocated to the United Kingdom pursuant to arrangements made by the Secretary of State under section 67 of the Immigration Act 2016."

p.1055, *annotation to the European Communities Act 1972*

4.027   An agreement has been reached between the government of the United Kingdom and the European Union in relation to the UK's withdrawal from the EU: see *https://assets.publishing.service.gov.uk/government/uploads/system/uploads/attachment_data/file/759019/25_November_Agreement_on_the_withdrawal_of_the_United_Kingdom_of_Great_Britain_and_Northern_Ireland_from_the_European_Union_and_the_European_Atomic_Energy_Community.pdf* (accessed November 28, 2018). The document was endorsed by leaders at a special meeting of the European Council on November 25, 2018. Part 2 on Citizens' Rights, which deals both with rights of residence (as to which there will be relatively little change during the proposed transitional period—until December 2020) and the co-ordination of social security systems may be of particular interest to readers of this book, and reference may also be made to the "Common Provisions" in Part 1. It was rejected by the Parliament of the United Kingdom on 15 January 2019 and at the time of writing the position remains unclear.

Trials of an "EU Settlement scheme" have been underway, initially only on a limited basis, but have been extended more widely from 21 January 2019. See Appendix EU of the Immigration Rules.

The Immigration and Social Security Co-ordination (EU Withdrawal) Bill currently before Parliament will provide powers to modify EU-derived legislation in relation to free movement and social security co-ordination post-Brexit.

p.1082, *annotation to the Treaty on the Functioning of the European Union art.21*

For a discussion of the interplay between the rights created by *Banger* and the conditions in C-456/12 *O and B*, see *SSHD v Christy* [2018] EWCA Civ 2378. **4.028**

pp.1085–1086, *annotation to the Treaty on the Functioning of the European Union art.21*

On September 13, 2018, the Court gave its judgment in C-618/16 *Prefeta*, answering question (1) in the affirmative and so not needing to answer question (2). **4.029**

p.1097, *annotation to the Treaty on the Functioning of the European Union art.45*

On September 13, 2018, the Court gave its judgment in C-618/16 *Prefeta*: see para.3.73 **4.030**

p.1099, *annotation to the Treaty on the Functioning of the European Union art.49*

Hrabkova v SSWP is now reported as [2018] AACR 38. **4.031**

p.1099, *annotation to the Treaty on the Functioning of the European Union art.49*

The reference to the CJEU in *HMRC v HD (CHB)* is numbered C-544/18. **4.032**

p.1100, *annotation to the Treaty on the Functioning of the European Union art.56*

NB v HMRC (TC) is now reported as [2018] AACR 26. **4.033**

p.1130, *annotation to Regulation (EU) No 492/2011 art.7*

On September 13, 2018, the Court gave its judgment in C-618/16 *Prefeta*: see para.3.73. **4.034**

p.1135, *annotation to Regulation (EU) No 492/2011 art.10*

Bolton MBC v HY (HB) is now reported as [2018] AACR 31. **4.035**

p.1136, *annotation to Regulation (EU) No 492/2011 art.10*

Hrabkova v SSWP is now reported as [2018] AACR 38. **4.036**

p.1139, *annotation to Directive 2004/38/EC*

4.037   With effect from July 24, 2018, the Immigration (European Economic Area) Regulations 2016 have themselves been amended (subject to transitional and saving provisions) by the Immigration (European Economic Area) (Amendment) Regulations 2018 (SI 2018/801). See Volume II for details.

p.1145, *annotation to Directive 2004/38/EC art.2*

4.038   The question whether a child, who is in the permanent legal guardianship of a Union citizen or citizens under *'kefalah'*, or some equivalent arrangement provided for in the law of his or her country of origin, is a "direct descendant" within the meaning of art.2.2(c) is among the questions referred to the CJEU by the Supreme Court in *SM (Algeria) v Entry Clearance Officer* [2018] UKSC 9. (*Kefalah* had the effect under Algerian law of awarding the Union citizens legal custody and transferring parental responsibility to them.) The case has the reference C-129/18.

p.1147, *annotation to Directive 2004/38/EC art.2*

4.039   The same (now) Upper Tribunal Judge supplemented his decision in CIS/2100/2007 by making clear in *SSWP v MF (SPC)* [2018] UKUT 179 (AAC) that neither help with translation, nor the provision of emotional and social support, could contribute to "dependency".

p.1152, *annotation to Directive 2004/38/EC art.3*

4.040   In *SSHD v Christy* [2018] EWCA Civ 2378, the Court of Appeal rejected the Secretary of State's submission that an unmarried partner's right under art.3(2) required the conditions in C-456/12 *Minister voor Immigratie, Integratie en Asiel v O and S* (as to which, see generally para.3.81) to be fulfilled.

p.1156, *annotation to Directive 2004/38/EC art.7(1)(a)*

4.041   *Hrabkova v SSWP* is now reported as [2018] AACR 38.

p.1157, *annotation to Directive 2004/38/EC art.7*

4.042   On September 13, 2018, the Court gave its judgment in C-618/16 *Prefeta*: see para.3.73

p.1158, *annotation to Directive 2004/38/EC art.7*

4.043   The reference to the CJEU in *HMRC v HD (CHB)* is numbered C-544/18.

p.1159, *annotation to Directive 2004/38/EC art.7*

4.044   In *Tarola* (C-483/17), the Advocate General (opinion of November 15, 2018) suggests that art.7(3)(c) is not confined to fixed-term contracts, thus a person who has worked for two weeks before becoming involuntarily unemployed is protected.

p.1164, *annotation to Directive 2004/38/EC art.7(1)(b)*

AMS v SSWP (PC) [2017] UKUT 48 (AAC) and *AMS v SSWP (PC)* [2017] UKUT 381 (AAC) are together now reported as [2018] AACR 27.   **4.045**

p.1164, *annotation to Directive 2004/38/EC art.7(1)(b)*

A reference to the CJEU has been made by the Court of Appeal in Northern Ireland in C-93/18 *Bajratari*, asking the following questions: **4.046**

1. Can income from employment that is unlawful under national law establish, in whole or in part, the availability of sufficient resources under Article 7(1)(b) of the Citizens Directive?
2. If 'yes', can Article 7(1) (b) be satisfied where the employment is deemed precarious solely by reason of its unlawful character?

p.1207, *annotation to Regulation (EC) No 883/2004 art.1(i)*

HMRC v MB (CHB) is now reported as [2018] AACR 32.   **4.047**

p.1228, *annotation to Regulation (EC) No 883/2004 art.12*

Judgment in C-527/16 *Salzburger Gebietskrankenkasse* was given on September 6, 2018.   **4.048**

p.1274, *annotation to Regulation (EC) No 883/2004 art.67 (Members of the family residing in another Member State)*

HMRC v MB (CHB) is now reported as [2018] AACR 32.   **4.049**

p.1277, *annotation to Regulation (EC) No 883/2004 art.68 (Priority rules in the event of overlapping)*

The question of what is meant by the "basis" on which the benefit is payable, identified in the opening sentences of para.3.444 has been considered by Advocate General Mengozzi in an opinion delivered on October 4, 2018 in C-322/17 *Bogatu v Minister for Social Protection* and what is said in para.3.444 should now be considered in the light of it.   **4.050**

p.1366, *annotation to Regulation (EC) No 987/2009 art.19 (Provision of information to persons concerned and employers)*

Judgment in C-527/16 *Salzburger Gebietskrankenkasse* was given on September 6, 2018.   **4.051**

p.1435, *annotation to Council Directive 79/7/EEC art.4*

The decision of the CJEU in C-451/16 is now reported as [2018] AACR 37.   **4.052**

p.1458, *annotation to Human Rights Act 1998 s.3 (Interpretation of legislation)*

4.053   *SSWP v Carmichael and Sefton Council* was distinguished in *JT v First-tier Tribunal, Criminal Injuries Compensation Authority and Equality and Human Rights Commission* [2018] EWCA Civ 1735, holding in essence that the prohibition on disapplication identified in *Carmichael* related only to situations where it was not possible to identify a particular offending provision in the relevant secondary legislation.

The Upper Tribunal has issued a leap-frog certificate under ss.14A to 14C of the Tribunals, Courts and Enforcement Act 2007 (see paras. 5.87–5.90) in *Secretary of State for Work and Pensions v (1) DL and (2) RR (HB)* [2018] UKUT 355 (AAC), a case in which the Upper Tribunal was bound by *Carmichael*. It will now be for the Supreme Court to decide whether or not to grant any application made to it for permission to appeal.

p.1502, *annotation to Human Rights Act 1998 Sch.1–art.14 (Prohibition of discrimination)*

4.054   *Stevenson v SSWP* is now reported as [2018] AACR 17.

p.1509, *annotation to Human Rights Act 1998 Sch.1–art.14 (Prohibition of discrimination)*

4.055   The appeals in *R(DA)* and *R(DS)* were heard on July 17-19, 2018. Judgment is awaited at the time of writing.

p.1509, *annotation to Human Rights Act 1998 Sch.1–art.14 (Prohibition of discrimination)*

4.056   On August 30, 2018 the Supreme Court gave judgment in *Siobhan McLoughlin* [2018] UKSC 48. The difference in treatment between unmarried and married partners was held to be lacking in justification, Lady Hale, giving the majority judgment, observing at [39] that:

> "The allowance exists because of the responsibilities of the deceased and the survivor towards their children. Those responsibilities are the same whether or not they are married to or in a civil partnership with one another. The purpose of the allowance is to diminish the financial loss caused to families with children by the death of a parent. That loss is the same whether or not the parents are married to or in a civil partnership with one another."

p.1510, *annotation to Human Rights Act 1998 Sch.1–art.14 (Prohibition of discrimination)*

4.057   In *R(TP and AR) v SSWP* [2018] EWHC 1474 (Admin) the failure of the universal credit legislation to make provision for the needs of those who under predecessor benefits would have qualified for the severe disability and enhanced disability premiums was held not to involve differential treatment or, if it did, it was justified. A claim of discrimination as between those who had carers and those who did not was rejected on the ground that the treatment was justified. However, the operation of the transitional arrangements, under which a person formerly entitled to those premiums would have to apply for universal credit if he or she moved to a new housing authority area (when those moving within the same housing authority area would not) and on doing so would not receive any transitional protection to compensate for the loss of income to which the loss of the premiums significantly contributed, was held (para 88) to be manifestly without reasonable foundation and not to strike a fair balance.

p.1511, *annotation to Human Rights Act 1998 Sch.1–art.14 (Prohibition of discrimination)*

The Supreme Court has given judgment in *Siobhan McLaughlin* [2018] UKSC 48. See para.4.126. 4.058

p.1545, *annotation to the Tribunals, Courts and Enforcement Act 2007 s.7 (Chambers: jurisdiction and Presidents)*

With effect from January 1, 2019, Mrs Justice Farbey is Chamber President of the Administrative Appeals Chamber of the Upper Tribunal. 4.058.1

p.1552, *amendment to the Tribunals, Courts and Enforcement Act 2007 s.11 (Right to appeal to Upper Tribunal)*

With effect from May 25, 2018, s.211 of, and paras. 130 and 131 of Sch.19 to, the Data Protection Act 2018 amended s.11(5)(b) of the 2007 Act by substituting "section 27(3) or (5), 79(5) or (7) or 111(3) or (5) of the Data Protection Act 2018" for "section 28(4) or (6) of the Data Protection Act 1998". 4.059

p.1562, *annotation to the Tribunals, Courts and Enforcement Act 2007 s.11 (Right to appeal to Upper Tribunal)*

Broughal v Walsh Brothers Builders Ltd [2018] EWCA Civ 1610 has been reported at [2018] 1 W.L.R. 5781. 4.059.1

pp.1569-1575, *annotation to the Tribunals, Courts and Enforcement Act 2007 s.12 (Proceedings on appeal to Upper Tribunal)*

The correct neutral citation number for *LS v HMRC (TC)* is [2017] UKUT 257 (AAC) and the decision has been reported as [2018] AACR 2. 4.060

In *R.(JT) v First-tier Tribunal* [2018] EWCA Civ 1735, Leggatt LJ, with whom Sir Terence Etherton MR and Sharpe LJ agreed, distinguished *Secretary of State for Work and Pensions v Carmichael* [2018] EWCA Civ 548; [2018] 1 W.L.R. 3429 (mentioned in the main work) on the ground that in *JT* it was possible simply to treat the discriminatory provision as invalid and disapply it, rather than rewriting it. That approach was not open to the Upper Tribunal in *SSWP v DL (HB)* [2018] UKUT 355 (AAC) and so the Upper Tribunal followed *Carmichael* but, on October 5, 2018, granted a "leapfrog" certificate under s.14A of the 2007 Act, thus enabling the claimant to apply to the Supreme Court for permission to appeal under s.14B with a view to challenging the decision in *Carmichael*.

p.1576, *amendment to the Tribunals, Courts and Enforcement Act 2007 s.13 (Right to appeal to Court of Appeal etc.)*

4.061   With effect from May 25, 2018, s.211 of, and paras. 130 and 132 of Sch.19 to, the Data Protection Act 2018 amended s.13(8)(a) of the 2007 Act by substituting "section 27(3) or (5), 79(5) or (7) or 111(3) or (5) of the Data Protection Act 2018" for "section 28(4) or (6) of the Data Protection Act 1998".

p.1585, *annotation to the Tribunals, Courts and Enforcement Act 2007 s.13 (Right to appeal to Court of Appeal etc.)*

4.061.1   The problem with the drafting of Chapter 41 of the Rules of the Court of Session that is noted in the last paragraph of the annotation in the main work was considered in *Hakim: re Application for Leave to Appeal* [2001] ScotCS 59; 2001 SC 789 in the context of an application for permission to appeal against a decision of the Immigration Appeal Tribunal. The Court of Session took a pragmatic approach and held that, although it involved "a somewhat forced reading of the statutory provisions and the rules", "the period of 42 days should be taken to run from the date of the refusal of leave to appeal by the Immigration Appeal Tribunal".

p.1591, *annotation to the Tribunals, Courts and Enforcement Act 2007 s.15 (Upper Tribunal's "judicial review" jurisdiction)*

4.061.2   A case is one "arising under the law of England and Wales" if an application for judicial review is made to the Upper Tribunal on the basis that the High Court of England and Wales would have jurisdiction but for sections 15 to 18 of the 2007 Act. The Upper Tribunal can have no greater jurisdiction than the High Court would have had (*R. (CICA) v First-tier Tribunal (CIC)* [2018] UKUT 439 (AAC), where the Upper Tribunal struck out an application for judicial review seeking a quashing order in respect of a decision of the First-tier Tribunal that had been made in Scotland in a case where all the material events had occurred in Scotland).

p.1599, *annotation to the Tribunals, Courts and Enforcement Act 2007 s.20 (Transfer of judicial review applications from the Court of Session)*

4.061.3   The cases of *MB* and *NF*, mentioned in the main work, were considered in *R. (CICA) v First-tier Tribunal (CIC)* [2018] UKUT 439

(AAC), where the Upper Tribunal gave guidance as to the circumstances in which it would accept jurisdiction in a case with more connection with Scotland than with England and Wales.

p.1624, *amendment to the First-tier Tribunal and Upper Tribunal (Composition of Tribunal) Order 2008 art.2 (Number of members of the First-tier Tribunal)*

As mentioned in the annotation in the main work, a new art.2 was substituted for the old one with effect from May 18, 2018. As at December 10, 2018, no practice direction had been issued under the substituted article.   4.062

p.1630, *amendment to the First-tier Tribunal and Upper Tribunal (Composition of Tribunal) Order 2008 (SI 2008/2835) art.3 (Number of members of the Upper Tribunal)*

As mentioned in the annotation in the main work, art.3 was amended with effect from May 18, 2018. As at December 10, 2018, no practice direction had been issued under the amended article.   4.063

pp.1640-1641, *annotation to the Tribunal Procedure (First-tier Tribunal) (Social Entitlement Chamber) Rules 2008 (SI 2008/2685) r.4 (Delegation to staff)*

A registrar's failure to give adequate reasons for refusing a postponement led to the decision of the First-tier Tribunal being set aside in *JC v SSWP (PIP)* [2018] UKUT 110 (AAC) because the judge presiding at the hearing did not consider afresh whether there should be a postponement.   4.064

pp.1645-1648, *annotation to the Tribunal Procedure (First-tier Tribunal) (Social Entitlement Chamber) Rules 2008 (SI 2008/2685) r.5(3)(h) (Case management powers)*

In *JC v SSWP (PIP)* [2018] UKUT 110 (AAC), a welfare rights representative applied for a postponement because she had been double booked. A registrar refused the application simply on the ground that the hearing had been listed to the exclusion of other claimants and the claimant could bring a family member or friend to support her. When the hearing took place, the presiding judge did not consider afresh whether there should be a postponement. The Upper Tribunal set aside the First-tier Tribunal's decision on the substantive appeal, saying that—   4.065

"9. . . . the registrar's reasons as recorded were clearly inadequate to justify her decision. It amounts to saying that any case that has been listed cannot be postponed because inevitably another case was deprived of the slot allocated to the claimant. That cannot be right. The loss of the right to be represented and the delay in having a case come before the tribunal are not directly comparable such that the latter always trumps the former. . . . "

p.1656, *annotation to the Tribunal Procedure (First-tier Tribunal) (Social Entitlement Chamber) Rules 2008 (SI 2008/2685) r.8 (Striking out a party's case)*

4.066   The correct neutral citation number for *LS v HMRC (TC)* is [2017] UKUT 257 (AAC) and the decision has been reported as [2018] AACR 2.

p.1683, *amendment to the Tribunal Procedure (First-tier Tribunal) (Social Entitlement Chamber) Rules 2008 (SI 2008/2685) r.23 (Cases in which the notice of appeal is to be sent to the decision maker)*

4.067   With effect from October 13, 2018, r.2 of the Tribunal Procedure (Amendment No.2) Rules 2018 (SI 2018/1053) amended rule 23(2) by omitting "no later than the latest of" after "so that it is received" and then in sub-paragraph (2)(a), inserting ", no later than the latest of" after "in a housing benefit or council tax benefit case".

This corrects the drafting error mentioned in the annotation in the main work.

pp.1686-1689, *annotation to the Tribunal Procedure (First-tier Tribunal) (Social Entitlement Chamber) Rules 2008 (SI 2008/2685) r.24(1)-(5) (Responses and replies)*

4.068   In *FI v HMRC (CHB)* [2018] UKUT 226 (AAC), HMRC failed to include with its response copies of letters sent by the claimant on the ground that, although they indicated that the claimant might be self-employed they did not, in its view, show on the balance of probabilities that she was. The First-tier Tribunal set aside the First-tier Tribunal's decision on the ground that the letters should have been included because they were relevant and it was not for HMRC to usurp the role of the tribunal. The Upper Tribunal held that that was so notwithstanding that the claimant could have provided the documents and that in *FN v SSWP (ESA)* [2015] UKUT 670 (AAC); [2016] AACR 24, mentioned in the annotation to r.24 in the main work, it had been held that not every breach of r.24 would result in a decision of the First-tier Tribunal being held to be wrong in law.

See also the supplementary annotation to reg.6(2)(r) of the Social Security and Child Support (Decisions and Appeals) Regulations 1999 (above).

pp.1693-1702, *annotation to the Tribunal Procedure (First-tier Tribunal) (Social Entitlement Chamber) Rules 2008 (SI 2008/2685) r.27 (Decision with or without a hearing)*

4.069   See the supplementary annotation to r.34 of the Tribunal Procedure (Upper Tribunal) Rules 2008 (below).

p.1702, *annotation to the Tribunal Procedure (First-tier Tribunal) (Social Entitlement Chamber) Rules 2008 (SI 2008/2685) r.28 (Entitlement to attend a hearing)*

In *TA v SSWP (PIP)* [2018] UKUT 26 (AAC), the decision of the 4.070 First-tier Tribunal was set aside where the hearing had taken place 90 miles from the appellant's home. She had originally asked for the decision to be made on the papers and the case had, perfectly properly, been listed at a distant venue rather than the one nearest her home because of that request. However, the First-tier Tribunal adjourned so that she could attend but then, unaccountably, listed the case for hearing at the same venue. When the claimant protested, it listed the case even further away from her home. The Upper Tribunal pointed out that, although the claimant had asked for her case to be decided on the papers, she was entitled to change her mind in the light of the First-tier Tribunal's adjournment, which had been given for precisely that purpose. Something very similar happened in *TB v SSD (WP)* [2014] UKUT 357 (AAC). In neither case did the panel deciding the case consider the case's history before deciding to proceed in the appellant's absence.

p.1720, *annotation to the Tribunal Procedure (First-tier Tribunal) (Social Entitlement Chamber) Rules 2008 (SI 2008/2685) r.34 (Reasons for decisions)*

In *CH v SSWP (PIP)* [2018] UKUT 330 (AAC), discussed in detail 4.071 in the supplementary annotation to reg.6(2)(r) of the Social Security and Child Support (Decisions and Appeals) Regulations 1999 (above), the Upper Tribunal rejected an argument that *YM v SSWP (PIP)* [2018] UKUT 16 (AAC), mentioned in the annotation to r.34 in the main work, had been wrongly decided. Note, though, that the Secretary of State has appealed against *YM* and the appeal is pending before the Court of Appeal.

Where the First-tier Tribunal rejects an argument that an earlier award of the same, or a different, benefit is relevant to the case under consideration, it should give reasons for doing so (*KW v SSWP (PIP)* [2018] UKUT 216 (AAC)). However, even if it does not expressly address the argument, it will not err in law if, in a case where there was no evidence of the basis of the previous award, the necessary implication of its findings and reasoning is that either it disagreed with the previous assessment in the light of the evidence before it or it found that there had been a material improvement in the claimant's condition (*VH v SSWP (ESA)* [2018] UKUT 290 (AAC)).

pp.1731-1732, *annotation to the Tribunal Procedure (First-tier Tribunal) (Social Entitlement Chamber) Rules 2008 (SI 2008/2685) r.39 (Tribunal's consideration of application for permission to appeal)*

A judge giving permission to appeal on limited grounds must say so 4.071.1 clearly in the decision itself and not merely in the reasons for the decision; otherwise there is a risk that the decision will be treated by the

Upper Tribunal as a grant of unlimited permission (*Safi v Secretary of State for the Home Department* [2018] UKUT 388 (IAC)).

pp.1741-1745, *amendments to the Tribunal Procedure (Upper Tribunal) Rules 2008 (SI 2008/2698) r.1 (Citation, commencement, application and interpretation)*

4.072   ERRATUM: In r.1(2), "Lords" should read "Lands".

With effect from October 13, 2018, r.3(1) and (2) of the Tribunal Procedure (Amendment No.2) Rules 2018 (SI 2018/1053) amended two definitions in r.1(3) of the 2008 Rules. Neither amendment affects social security cases. In the definition of "national security certificate appeal", the words ", sections 27, 79 or 111 of the Data Protection Act 2018" were inserted after "Data Protection Act 1998". In the definition of "respondent", there was substituted for sub-paragraph (b)—

"(b) in any other any other application for permission to appeal, or any other appeal except a road transport case, the person who made the decision that has been challenged;".

p.1756, *annotation to the Tribunal Procedure (Upper Tribunal) Rules 2008 (SI 2008/2698) r.8 (Striking out a party's case)*

4.073   The correct neutral citation number for *LS v HMRC (TC)* is [2017] UKUT 257 (AAC) and the decision has been reported as [2018] AACR 2.

pp.1759-1761, *annotation to the Tribunal Procedure (Upper Tribunal) Rules 2008 (SI 2008/2698) r.10 (Orders for costs)*

4.073.1   Rule 10 does not contain provisions analogous to CPR r.36 and so the Upper Tribunal is not obliged to award costs on an indemnity basis in circumstances where a party has failed to "better" an offer of settlement and a court would award costs on such a basis (*Mann v Transport for London* [2018] EWCA Civ 1520; [2018] 1 W.L.R. 5104).

pp.1793-1794, *annotation to the Tribunal Procedure (Upper Tribunal) Rules 2008 (SI 2008/2698) r.34 (Decision with or without a hearing)*

4.074   In *CH v SSWP (JSA) (No.2)* [2018] UKUT 320 (AAC), the Upper Tribunal made adjustments to its normal procedure to meet the reasonable needs of an appellant with reading (and related difficulties with memory, concentration and information processing) and difficulties with interpersonal interactions. These were allowing a 15-minute break after each 45 minutes, allowing the appellant to record the proceedings (subject to the usual condition that the recording not be published in any format), allowing another person to read parts of the appellant's speaking note and switching off all fluorescent ceiling lighting. The judge gave detailed reasons for making these adjustments.

p.1811, *annotation to Practice Directions*

4.075   ERRATUM: the correct reference in the General Note should be to the *Practice Direction (Audio Recordings of Proceedings: Access)*.

PART V

UPDATING MATERIAL:
VOLUME IV

TAX CREDITS AND HMRC-ADMINISTERED SOCIAL SECURITY BENEFITS

Commentary by

Nick Wikeley

Edward Mitchell

Ian Hooker

p.22, *amendment to the Taxes Management Act 1970 s.118 (Interpretation)*

After the definition of "NRCGT return" insert the definition as fol- 5.001
lows: ""partner" is to be construed in accordance with section
12AA(10B) of this Act;".

p.107, *annotation to Social Security (Contributions and Benefits Act 1992 (1992 c.4 Sch 10) (Priority between persons entitled to Child Benefit)*

In *GC v SSWP and DC (CHB)* [2018] UKUT 223 (AAC) Judge 5.002
Wikeley has dealt again with the matter of competing claims by sepa-
rated parents and the confusion arising from their dealings with HMRC.
In this case their child began living with his mother, but after about 5
years his father claimed that his son had chosen to move to live with him,
and he made a competing claim for Child Benefit. The decision records
a sorry account of conflicting decisions that then followed by HMRC
and two separate appeals to the FTT. Judge Wikeley found that both
FTTs had made the same mistake in failing to recognise that natural
justice, and the requirements of a fair hearing, required that each parent
should have been made a party to the other's appeal. He set aside the
decisions of both FTT and having joined the father as a party to the
mother's appeal, and giving him leave for a late appeal, directed a new
hearing before a fresh FTT.

p.147, *annotation to the Tax Credits Act 2002 s.3 (Claims)*

Arthur v HMRC [2017] EWCA Civ 1756 is now reported as [2018] 5.003
AACR 10.

p.169, *annotation to the Tax Credits Act 2002 s.12 (Child care element)*

NB v HMRC (TC) [2016] NI Com 47 is now reported as [2018] 5.004
AACR 26.

p.170, *annotation to the Tax Credits Act 2002 s.14 (Initial decisions)*

LS and RS v HMRC (TC) [2017] UKUT 257 (AAC) is now reported 5.005
as [2018] AACR 2.

p.173, *annotation to the Tax Credits Act 2002 s.15 (Revised decisions after notifications)*

LS and RS v HMRC (TC) [2017] UKUT 257 (AAC) is now reported 5.006
as [2018] AACR 2.

p.177, *annotation to the Tax Credits Act 2002 s.16 (Other revised decisions)*

LS and RS v HMRC (TC) [2017] UKUT 257 (AAC) is now reported 5.007
as [2018] AACR 2.

p.178, *annotation to the Tax Credits Act 2002 s.16 (Other revised decisions)*

5.008   The reference to David Gaulke MP should read David Gauke MP.

p.260, *amendment to the Income Tax (Earnings and Pensions) Act 2003 s.7 (Meaning of "employment income", "general earnings" and "specific employment income")*

5.009   Delete "or" at the end of s.7(5)(c), and after paragraph (c) insert:

"(ca) section 402B (termination payments, and other benefits, that cannot benefit from section 403 threshold), or".

p.386, *amendment to Income Tax (Trading and Other Income) Act 2005 Chapter 5 (Settlements: Amounts treated as income of settlor)*

5.010   In the heading for Chapter 5, after "OF SETTLOR", insert "OR FAMILY".

p.386, *amendment to Income Tax (Trading and Other Income) Act 2005 s.619 (Charge to tax under Chapter 5)*

5.011   Delete "and" at the end od subs.(1)(c) and insert after subs.(1)(d) the following:

"(e) benefits whose amount or value is treated as income of the settlor or a close family member as a result of section 643A (benefits provided out of protected foreign-source income), and
(f) amounts treated as income of the settlor or a close family member by section 643J or 643L (gifts provided out of benefits)."

p.427, *annotation to the Welfare Reform Act 2012 Sch.6 (Migration to universal credit)*

5.012   For a discussion of departmental practice, including the use of 'stop notices' given to HMRC by the DWP, intended to give effect to reg.8, see *HMRC v LH (TC)* [2018] UKUT 306 (AAC). The 'stop notice' in that case resulted in HMRC deciding that the appellant's tax credit award had terminated under reg.8. This caused obvious difficulties for the claimant because the reg.8 process was initiated following her mistaken claim for universal credit, which resulted in no award of that benefit. Upper Tribunal Judge Jacobs observed that there was no evidence that the basic conditions for universal credit in s.4 of the Welfare Reform Act 2012 were met (see Volume 5 of this work for details of the basis conditions), and satisfaction of those conditions is a pre-condition to the operation of reg.8. Upper Tribunal Judge Jacobs rejected HMRC's argument that the mere existence of the 'stop notice' was sufficient to trigger termination of the claimant's tax credit award under reg.8. The First-tier Tribunal "needed some evidence to link the stop notice itself to the Secretary of State being satisfied about the basic conditions" and the tribunal erred in law by failing to take steps to require the supply of such evidence.

p.528, *annotation to the Working Tax Credit (Entitlement and Maximum Rate) Regulations 2002 (SI 2002/2005) reg.9 (Disability element and workers who are to be treated as at a disadvantage in getting a job)*

The reference to para.(5) in the note under the heading *First disability condition* should read para.(9).   5.013

p.529, *annotation to the Working Tax Credit (Entitlement and Maximum Rate) Regulations 2002 (SI 2002/2005) reg.9 (Disability element and workers who are to be treated as at a disadvantage in getting a job) Case G*

In *ABM v HMRC (TC)* [2018] UKUT 317 (AAC), Upper Tribunal   5.014
Judge West held that the amendment of Case G in 2003 so as to substitute "entitled" for "qualified" did not remove "the link between what a recipient's entitlement should have been, if determined correctly, in tax year one and his entitlement in tax year two" and the definition of "entitled" in the second paragraph of Case G was intended to clarify, rather than alter, meaning. In simple terms, "entitled" means "correctly entitled" and the purpose of that second paragraph is to:

> "provide certainty in those cases where the entitlement conditions have been found to have been satisfied for a particular year, but no disability element has actually been paid, or was due in that year as a result of the level of the claimant's income ... [and] Case G was intended to support recipients with the continuation of an entitlement, but for one year alone, following a decision, particularly since the decision on entitlement was made after the end of the tax year to which it related and in which the tax credits were received [given the distinction drawn by the Tax Credits Act 2002 between the award of tax credit for a tax year and entitlement for that year, which is fixed by a decision under section 18 typically following the end of the tax year in question]".

In addition, after the note to Case G insert the following new commentary before the paragraph beginning "There are special rules ... ":
   In *ABM v HMRC (TC)* [2018] UKUT 317 (AAC), Judge West held that the First-tier Tribunal erred in law by failing to consider whether an appellant satisfied any of the Cases. Instead, the tribunal's consideration was limited solely to Case C, which had been the focus of HMRC's appeal submission.

p.534, *the Working Tax Credit (Entitlement and Maximum Rate) Regulations 2002 (SI 2002/2005) reg.13(7) (Entitlement to child care element of working tax credit)*

The figure "1" in the second line of subs.(7) as printed is a reference   5.015
to the first amendment in the list of amendments on p.535.

p.541, *annotation to the Working Tax Credit (Entitlement and Maximum Rate) Regulations 2002 (SI 2002/2005) reg.14 (Entitlement to child care element of working tax credit)*

5.016   *NB v HMRC (TC)* [2016] NI Com 47 is now reported as [2018] AACR 26.

p.603, *annotation to the Tax Credits (Definition and Calculation of Income) Regulations 2002 (SI 2002/2006) reg.19*

5.017   With effect from April 11, 2018, Art.15 of, and para.21(g) of the Schedule to, The Secretaries of State for Health and Social Care and for Housing, Communities and Local Government and Transfer of Functions (Commonhold Land) Order 2018 (SI 2018/378) inserted "and Social Care" after "for Health" in item 12(e) in table 6 in reg.19

pp.620-621, *annotation to the Child Tax Credit Regulations 2002 (SI 2002/2007) reg.3 (Circumstances in which a person is or is not responsible for a child or qualifying young person)*

5.018   As regards the commentary in the first paragraph of para.2.202, as Upper Tribunal Judge Wikeley said in *AG v HMRC & AG (TC)* [2018] UKUT 318 (AAC), "the language of Rule 2.2 is mandatory" and "not making a decision as to the issue of main responsibility is not an option", where the Judge followed *PG v HMRC and NG (TC)* [2016] AACR 45. It is not permissible to determine the main responsibility test according to which if the competing claimants made the first claim (*AG v HMRC & AG (TC)* [2018] UKUT 318 (AAC)).

p.630, *heading to the Child Tax Credit Regulations 2002 (SI 2002/2006) reg.9 (Exception to the purpose of regulation 7(2A)(b))*

5.019   The heading in bold font should be justified to the left hand margin.

p.630, *amendment to the Child Tax Credit Regulations 2002 (SI 2002/2006) reg.9(1) (Exception to the purpose of regulation 7(2A)(b))*

5.020   With effect from November 28, 2018, reg.3(a) of the Child Tax Credit (Amendment) Regulations 2018 (SI 2018/1130) substituted a new para.(1) as follows:

"(1) For the purposes of regulation 7(2A)(b), an exception applies in relation to A if—
(a) A is (in accordance with paragraphs (5) and (6)) the third or subsequent child or qualifying young person for whom the claimant, or either or both of the joint claimants, is or are responsible and either—
(i) any of regulations 10 to 14 applies in relation to A; or
(ii) all, or all but one, of the other children or qualifying young persons ("AA") for whom the claimant, or either or both of

the joint claimants, is or are responsible are adopted within the meaning given by regulation 11 or cared for under a non-parental caring arrangement within the meaning given by regulation 12 (reading references to "A" in those regulations as if they were references to "AA"); or

(b) A is (in accordance with paragraphs (5) and (6)) the first or second child or qualifying young person for whom the claimant, or either or both of the joint claimants, is or are responsible."

pp.630-632, *amendments to the Child Tax Credit Regulations 2002 (SI 2002/2006) reg.9(2),(4)-(6) and (8) (Exception to the purpose of regulation 7(2A)(b))*

With effect from November 28, 2018, reg.3(a) of the Child Tax Credit (Amendment) Regulations 2018 (SI 2018/1130) omitted paras.(2) and (4), substituted "this regulation", for "paragraphs (1) and (2)" in para.(5), omitted para.(8) and substituted for para.(6) the following new paragraph: **5.021**

"(6) In a case where the date determined under paragraph (5) is the same in respect of two or more members, their order (as between themselves only) is to be such as the Board determines to be appropriate to ensure that the individual element of child tax credit is included in respect of the greatest number of members.",

pp.632-633, *annotation to the Child Tax Credit Regulations 2002 (SI 2002/2006) reg.9 (Exception to the purpose of regulation 7(2A)(b))*

Delete the existing commentary (paras 2.225-2.226) and replace with the following: **5.022**

"Regulation 9 contains exceptions to the general rule in reg.7(2A) that child tax credit must not include an element for third or subsequent children born on or after April 6, 2017. According to the Explanatory Memorandum to SI 2017/387, which added reg.9 to the Child Tax Credit Regulations 2002, these exceptions are designed for cases where claimants are "not fully able to make choices" about the numbers of children in their families. Below, references to child should be read as including a qualifying young person and a reference to claimant being responsible for a child as a reference, in the case of joint claimants, to either or both of the claimants being responsible for the child.

In seeking to understand this complex regulation, the legal mechanism by which reg.7(2) excludes a child from attracting a child element should be borne in mind. The general rule is that a child (referred to by the Regulations as 'A') born on or after April 6, 2017 is excluded unless a claimant is claiming the child element for only one other child. This Regulation sets out when 'A' is to attract a child element even though s/he was born on or after April 6, 2017 and the claimant is already claiming the child element for at least two children.

The first exception, in reg.9(1)(a)(i) applies where A is the third or subsequent child for whom a claimant is responsible and any of regulations 10 to 14 apply to A (those regulations are concerned with multiple births, adoption, non-parental caring arrangements (sometimes referred to as kinship care) and non-consensual conception). Accordingly, a child born on or after April 6, 2017 to whom any of regs.10 to 14 apply will always attract a child element in a tax credit award.

The second exception, in reg.9(1)(a)(ii), works in a different way. While its purpose is to identify when A (i.e. a child born on or after April 6, 2017 who is the third or subsequent child for whom a claimant is responsible) attracts a child element, it does so not by reference to A's circumstances but by reference to the circumstances of the other children for whom a claimant is responsible. Where all, or all but one, of these other children are adopted or cared for under a non-parental caring arrangement, A attracts a child element even though the claimant is already receiving a child element for at least two children. This exception was added by SI 2018/1130, at least in part, in response to the High Court's decision in *SC & Others v Secretary of State for Work & Pensions* [2018] EWHC 864 (Admin) and is intended to ensure that adoptive parents and non-parental carers are not prejudiced by the order in which adopted children, or children cared for under non-parental arrangement, join a claimant's household, as could happen under the original version of reg.9.

In *SC* Ouseley J. held that the general two-child limit was not, in its entirety, contrary to the rights protected by the European Convention on Human Rights. The Judge appeared to accept that it is "inevitable that, if child–related benefits, paid to a parent and used by the household, are reduced or not made available for a third or further child, that that will affect more women, because of the higher proportion of single-parent households which they make up". On that basis, the introduction of the general two-child limit could be considered to indirectly discriminate against women for the purposes of Article 14 of the European Convention on Human Rights (the Convention's anti-discrimination provision) when taken with Article 8 (right to respect for private and family life). However, Ouseley J. went on to hold that the general two-child limit was justified and not therefore discriminatory. While it was likely to create a "perverse incentive not to form households", the general two-child limit was not manifestly without reasonable foundation taking into account the aim of limiting government spending and the other sources of support available to single-parent households.

5.023   However, in *SC* Ouseley J. went on to hold that one feature of the original two-child limit legislative scheme, as provided for in the amended Child Tax Credit Regulations 2002, was irrational on traditional domestic judicial review principles and therefore not authorised by primary legislation. The scheme's defect concerned its original provisions about the order in which a claimant is treated as becoming responsible for a child. The Judge held:

> "215. The issue here relates to the . . . Regulations and not to the primary legislation: Mr Drabble [for the applicants] contends that the exception in relation to a child cared for by the family is perverse because the availability of CTC for a third child depends on whether the third child was born before or after the family began to care for the

second child. Mr Higlett [for the Secretary of State] suggests the justification that, because the cared for child is not to be treated as of any less value than a natural child of the family, and the family, caring for a child, should face the same choice about a third child as would a family not in receipt of CTC, the sequencing provision is rational and justifiable in domestic public law terms.

216. I do not accept that. I do not think that in so far as it was seriously considered, there is any rational justification for a parent's decision, about whether to have a child of their own, to be affected by whether that decision was made before or after another decision, as to whether they should care for someone else's child, which could need to be made quite independently of a decision about having their own children. The purpose of the exception is to encourage, or at least to avoid discouraging, a family from looking after a child who would otherwise be in local authority care, with the disadvantages to the child over family care which that can entail, and the public expenditure it can require. The choice which the family is being asked to make has a very different and indeed opposite purpose in relation to public expenditure, from that which is part of the principal thinking behind the two child provision. It is not rationally connected to the purposes of the legislation, and indeed it is in conflict with them. The perversity of the provision is well-illustrated by CC's evidence that HMRC advised her that a device was at hand whereby the two child provision could be circumvented, and in a way which CC and CD rejected, in the best interests of the cared for child. HMRC disputes giving any such advice, though seemingly not that the device would work.

217. It is not the exception itself which is unlawful but the sequencing or ordering part of it . . . "

The third exception, in reg.9(1)(b) applies where A is, in accordance with reg.9(5) and (6), the first or second child for whom the claimant is responsible. Its purpose is not immediately obvious since the general rule in reg.7(2A) only operates to exclude a child born on or after April 6, 2017 if the claimant is already claiming the child element for two or more children. However, it does make sense if one considers the various ways in which a claimant might become responsible for children. Take for example, the case of a claimant who is claiming the child tax element for two natural children, one of whom was born after April 6, 2017. If the claimant then adopted a child born before April 6, 2017, without reg.9(1)(b) the claimant would lose the child element for the second natural child if the child element were claimed for the adopted child. Regulation 7(2A) would apply to the second natural child since s/he would be a child born on or after 2017 and the person responsible for the child would be claiming the child element for two other children. Regulation 9(1)(b) prevents this from happening since, under the sequence of responsibility rules in reg.9(5), the second natural child would be the second child for whom the claimant was responsible.

The fourth exception, in reg.9(3), only comes into play where an exception has already been established for A. It creates a further exception for a child born on or after April 6, 2017 where (a) the general two-child rule in reg.7(2A) would ordinarily require the child to be ignored, and (b) the claimant was already responsible for the child before the date on which the claimant became responsible for A. For example, it would apply to a claimant whose natural child was born on or after April 6, 2017 and who subsequently adopted a child born on or after that date. The adoption would not displace entitlement to the child element for the claimant's natural child.

Regulations 9(5) and (6) contains rules for determining whether a child is the first, second, third etc. child for whom a claimant is responsible. In the case of children claimed for by natural or step-parents, the sequence of responsibility is determined by the child's date of birth. In other cases, the sequence of responsibility order is determined by the date on which a claimant became responsible for a child. For example, take a claimant with two natural children born in April 2015 and September 2017 who in 2018 adopts a child born in July 2017. The sequence of responsibility is: (1) natural child born in April 2015; (2) natural child born in September 2017; (3) child adopted in 2018. Where the rules operate so that a claimant became responsible for two or more children on the same date, reg.9(6) provides that the order of responsibility is to be such as HMRC determines appropriate to ensure that the individual element of child tax credit is included in respect of the greatest number of members. Such a determination might need to be made where a claimant adopts two or more children on the same date."

p.635, *amendment to the Child Tax Credit Regulations 2002 (SI 2002/2006) reg.12 (Non-parental caring arrangements)*

5.024   With effect from November 28, 2018, reg.4 of the Child Tax Credit (Amendment) Regulations 2018 (SI 2018/1130) substituted "the Children (Scotland) Act 1995" for "that Act" in reg.12(3)(f).

pp.638-639, *amendment to the Child Tax Credit Regulations 2002 (SI 2002/2006) reg.14 (Continuation of certain exceptions)*

5.025   With effect from November 28, 2018, reg.5 of the Child Tax Credit (Amendment) Regulations 2018 (SI 2018/1130) omitted "by virtue of regulation 10, 11 or 13 applying"
In both para.(2)(b) and para.(4)(b).

p.640, *annotation to the Child Tax Credit Regulations 2002 (SI 2002/2006) reg.14 (Continuation of certain exceptions)*

5.026   Delete the existing General Note at para.2.236 and replace with the following text:

"This regulation provides for continuation, in certain circumstances, of the exceptions relating to multiple births, adoption and non-consensual conception but only in the case of step-parents who, on their own account, cannot take advantage of one of the specific exceptions to the general two-child rule in reg.7(2A). For example, reg.14 would apply where, under a joint child tax credit claim, a mother's circumstances fell within reg.13 (non-consensual conception). If the mother then died, the step-parent could not take advantage of reg.13. Similarly, a joint-claiming step-parent would not come within the multiple births exception in reg.10 if the natural parent, and other joint claimant, abandoned the family. To prevent this, reg.14 provides for the relevant exception to continue to apply. However, the step-parent will lose the benefit of the exception if s/he ceases to be entitled to child tax credit for six months or more (reg.14(7))."

pp.658-659, *annotation to the Tax Credits (Claims and Notifications) Regulations 2002 (SI 2002/2014) reg.5 (Manner in which claims to be made)*

The issue in *MK v HMRC (TC)* [2018] UKUT 238 (AAC) was whether a claimant's telephone call to HMRC about tax credits amounted a claim for tax credits for the purposes of reg.2(5). Regulation 5(2)(a) enacts the general rule that a claim for tax credit is to be made in writing on a form approved or authorised by HMRC for the purposes of the claim. Regulation 5(2)(b), however, permits a claim to be made in such other manner as HMRC may decide "having regard to all the circumstances". Upper Tribunal Judge Wikeley noted that, in principle, reg.5(2)(b) could permit a claim to be made orally. However, the question whether HMRC should have allowed an oral claim was not within the First-tier Tribunal's jurisdiction (*CTC/31/2006*). Moreover, the telephone call made by the appellant could not reasonably be construed as a claim. It was a request for a claim form. **5.027**

p.713, *amendment to the Tax Credits (Immigration) Regulations 2003 (SI 2003/653) reg.3 (Exclusion of persons subject to immigration control from entitlement to tax credits)*

With effect from July 20, 2018, reg.5(2) of the Child Benefit, Tax Credits and Childcare Payments (Section 67 Immigration Act 2016 Leave) (Amendment) Regulations 2018 (SI 2018/788) inserted "or has been granted section 67 leave" after "refugee" in para.(5)(a) and inserted after para.(9) the following new paragraph: **5.028**

"(10) In this regulation "section 67 leave" means leave to remain in the United Kingdom granted by the Secretary of State to a person who has been relocated to the United Kingdom pursuant to arrangements made by the Secretary of State under section 67 of the Immigration Act 2016.".

p.715, *annotation to the Tax Credits (Immigration) Regulations 2003 (SI 2003/653) reg.3(4)-(9) (Exclusion of persons subject to immigration control from entitlement to tax credits)*

In para.2.425 of the commentary, delete the three sentences from "However," (in the fourth line of the note) and ending with "reg.21ZB)." and replace with the following text: **5.029**

"However, if the claimant is notified that s/he has been granted refugee status, or granted section 67 leave, the claimant may claim tax credits retrospectively (para. (5)(a)). "Section 67 leave" means leave to remain in the UK granted to a person who has been relocated to the UK pursuant to arrangements made by the Secretary of State under section 67 of the immigration Act 2016, those arrangements being for the purpose of relocating to the UK unaccompanied refugee children from other countries in Europe (paragraph (10). Any such claim must be made within one month of the notification of refugee status or section 67 leave (para. 5(b))."

Also in para.2.425 of the commentary, delete the sentence "In the event of a successful application for asylum, the claim for tax credits is treated as having been made on the date of the submission of the claim for asylum" and replace with "In the event of the grant of refugee status or section 67 leave, the tax credits claim is treated as having been made on the date of the asylum claim".

After the first paragraph in para.2.425 of the commentary insert:

The issue in *MK v HMRC (TC)* [2018] UKUT 238 (AAC) was whether a claimant's telephone call to HMRC about tax credits, made within one month of the date on which he was granted refugee status, amounted to a claim for tax credits for the purposes of reg.2(5). The telephone call was made on December 1, 2016 but a written claim form was not received by HMRC until February 9, 2017. If the claim was not made until the later date, the claimant's entitlement would commence from January 9, 2017 (one month before the claim was made). If the telephone call amounted to a claim, entitlement would commence from July 24, 2014 being the date on which the claimant first claimed asylum. The appeal turned on the provisions of reg.5(2) of the Tax Credits (Claims and Notifications) Regulations 2002. Regulation 5(2)(a) enacts the general rule that a claim for tax credit is to be made in writing on a form approved or authorised by HMRC for the purposes of the claim. Regulation 5(2)(b), however, permits a claim to be made in such other manner as HMRC may decide "having regard to all the circumstances". Upper Tribunal Judge Wikeley noted that, in principle, reg.5(2)(b) could permit a claim to be made orally. However, the question whether HMRC should have allowed an oral claim was not within the First-tier Tribunal's jurisdiction (*CTC/31/2006*). Moreover, the telephone call of December 1, 2016 could not reasonably be construed as a claim. It was a request for a claim form. Judge Wikeley held that the First-tier Tribunal correctly dismissed the appellant's appeal against HMRC's decision that his tax credit entitlement commenced from January 9, 2017.

p.720, *amendment to the Tax Credits (Residence) Regulations 2003 (SI 2003/654) reg.3 (Circumstances in which a person is treated as not being in the United Kingdom)*

5.030 With effect from July 20, 2018, reg.4(2)(a) of the Child Benefit, Tax Credits and Childcare Payments (Section 67 Immigration Act 2016

Leave) (Amendment) Regulations 2018 (SI 2018/788) inserted after para.(7)(m) the following new subparagraph:

"(n) has been granted section 67 leave."

p.720, *amendment to the Tax Credits (Residence) Regulations 2003 (SI 2003/654) reg.3 (Circumstances in which a person is treated as not being in the United Kingdom)*

With effect from July 20, 2018, reg.4(2)(b) of the Child Benefit, Tax Credits and Childcare Payments (Section 67 Immigration Act 2016 Leave) (Amendment) Regulations 2018 (SI 2018/788) inserted after para.(9) the following new paragraph: **5.031**

"(10) In this regulation "section 67 leave" means leave to remain in the United Kingdom granted by the Secretary of State to a person who has been relocated to the United Kingdom pursuant to arrangements made by the Secretary of State under section 67 of the Immigration Act 2016.".

p.722, *annotation to the Tax Credits (Residence) Regulations 2003 (SI 2003/654) reg.3 (Circumstances in which a person is treated as not being in the United Kingdom)*

Arthur v HMRC [2017] EWCA Civ 1756 is now reported as [2018] AACR 10. **5.032**

p.735, *amendment to the Tax Credit (Polygamous Marriages) Regulations 2003 (SI 2003/742) reg.25A (Amendments to the Child Tax Credit Regulations 2002)*

With effect from November 28, 2018, reg.6 of the Child Tax Credit (Amendment) Regulations 2018 (SI 2018/1130) substituted "paragraph (1)(a) and (b) for "either or both"" for "paragraphs (1) to (5) for "either or both" (in each place they appear)" in para.(a) of reg.25A (which modifies regulation 9 of the Child Tax Credit Regulations 2002). **5.033**

p.759, *amendment to the Child Benefit (General) Regulations 2006 (SI 2006/223) reg.1 (Citation, commencement and interpretation)*

With effect from July 20, 2018, reg.2(2) of the Child Benefit, Tax Credits and Childcare Payments (Section 67 Immigration Act 2016 Leave) (Amendment) Regulations 2018 (SI 2018/788) amended reg.1 by inserting after the definition of "remunerative work" the following the following new definition: **5.034**

""section 67 leave" means leave to remain in the United Kingdom granted by the Secretary of State to a person who has been relocated to the United Kingdom pursuant to arrangements made by the Secretary of State under section 67 of the Immigration Act 2016.".

p.775, *amendment to the Child Benefit (General) Regulations 2006 (SI 2006/223) reg.23(6) (Circumstances in which person treated as not being in Great Britain)*

5.035   With effect from July 20, 2018, reg.2(3) of the Child Benefit, Tax Credits and Childcare Payments (Section 67 Immigration Act 2016 Leave) (Amendment) Regulations 2018 (SI 2018/788) amended reg. 23 by inserting after para. (6)(m) the following new subparagraph:

"(n) has been granted section 67 leave.".

p.779, *amendment to the Child Benefit (General) Regulations 2006 (SI 2006/223) reg.27(5) (Circumstances in which person treated as not being in Northern Ireland)*

5.036   With effect from July 20, 2018, reg.2(4) of the Child Benefit, Tax Credits and Childcare Payments (Section 67 Immigration Act 2016 Leave) (Amendment) Regulations 2018 (SI 2018/788) amended reg. 27 by inserting after para. (5)(m) the following new subparagraph:

"(n) has been granted section 67 leave.".

p.826, *amendment to the Statutory Sick Pay (Mariners, Airmen and Persons Abroad) Regulations 1982 (SI 1982/1349) reg.5 (Persons in other member States–meaning of "employee")*

5.037   With effect from November 15, 2018, reg.4 of, and para.2 of the Schedule to, the Social Security (Updating of EU References) (Amendment) Regulations 2018 (SI 2018/1084) inserted ", as amended from time to time, or Regulation EC No. 883/2004 of the European Parliament and of the Council of 29 April 2004, as amended from time to time, on the coordination of social security systems" after "1408/71" in para.(b).

p.869, *amendment to the Statutory Maternity Pay (Persons Abroad and Mariners) Regulations 1987 (SI 1987/418) reg.2 (Persons in other member States—meaning of "employee")*

5.038   With effect from November 15, 2018, reg.4 of, and para.5 of the Schedule to, the Social Security (Updating of EU References) (Amendment) Regulations 2018 (SI 2018/1084) inserted ", as amended from time to time, or Regulation (EC) No. 883/2004 of the European Parliament and of the Council of 29 April 2004, as amended from time to time, on the coordination of social security systems" after "1408/71" in para.(b).

p.1141, *amendment to the Childcare Payments (Eligibility) Regulations 2015 (SI 2015/448) reg.8 (Persons treated as being, or not being, in the United Kingdom)*

5.039   With effect from July 20, 2018, reg.6(2) of the Child Benefit, Tax Credits and Childcare Payments (Section 67 Immigration Act 2016

Leave) (Amendment) Regulations 2018 (SI 2018/788) inserted "(1)" after "8" and before "The", omitted "or" at the end of sub-para.(c) and inserted at the end of sub-para.(d) but before the full stop the following:

"; or
(e) a person who has been granted section 67 leave.
(2) In this regulation "section 67 leave" means leave to remain in the United Kingdom granted by the Secretary of State to a person who has been relocated to the United Kingdom pursuant to arrangements made by the Secretary of State under section 67 of the Immigration Act 2016.".

PART VI

UPDATING MATERIAL: VOLUME V

UNIVERSAL CREDIT

Commentary by

John Mesher

Richard Poynter

Nick Wikeley

pp.7-8, *Universal Credit—An Introduction (Introduction of universal credit)*

The process of "de-gatewayfication" described in the main work (i.e.,   6.001
the progressive removal of the gateway conditions in "live service" areas,
thereby turning them into full/digital service areas in which everyone of
working age who wishes to claim a means-tested benefit must claim
universal credit) was completed on December 12, 2018 (see the final
entry in the Schedule to the Welfare Reform Act 2012 (Commencement
No. 17, 19, 22, 23 and 24 and Transitional and Transitory Provisions
(Modification) (No. 2)) Order 2018 (SI 2018/881)). From that date,
with a few limited exceptions, every person of working age who wishes to
claim a non-contributory, means-tested, benefit has had to claim universal credit, rather than an "existing" benefit.

The exceptions were:

- claimants who are responsible for three or more children (this
  exception will come to an end with effect from February 1,
  2019);
- some claimants in "specified accommodation" (broadly, supported
  accommodation) and temporary accommodation, who can still
  claim housing benefit;
- some claims for housing benefit and tax credits made by members
  of "mixed-age" couples (*i.e.,* where one member of the couple has
  attained the qualifying age for state pension credit—currently
  65—but the other has not. This is due to change with effect from
  May 15, 2019, from which date it is intended that such couples
  should be required to claim universal credit, rather than state pension credit.
- some tax credit claimants. (Note, however, that tax credits were
  abolished with effect from February 1, 2019 except for people who
  had tax credit award for a period that included January 31, 2019
  and in certain other cases: see s.33(1)(f) WRA 2012 (at para.1.122
  of Vol.V of the main work) and the Welfare Reform Act 2012
  (Commencement No. 32 and Savings and Transitional Provisions)
  Order 2019 (SI 2019/167).)

In addition, a new exception was introduced with effect from January
16, 2019 by the UC (Transitional Provisions) (SDP Gateway) Amendment Regulations 2019 (SI 2019/10), which introduced a new gateway
condition that prevents people who are, or have been, entitled to an
existing benefit which includes the severe disability premium (SDP)
from claiming universal credit.

The next stage is that some claimants of existing benefits will undergo
a process of "managed migration" to universal credit. It is intended that
this process will begin in July 2019 and will stop once 10,000 awards of
universal credit have been made. New draft regulations governing that
process (the draft Universal Credit (Managed Migration Pilot and Miscellaneous Amendments) Regulations 2019) have been published and
are available online at *http://www.legislation.gov.uk/ukdsi/2019/9780111
178317*

p.60, *annotation to the Welfare Reform Act 2012 s.14 (Claimant commitment)*

6.002   *JB v SSWP (UC)* [2018] UKUT 360 (AAC) was one of the Scottish cases referred to in the text of the main volume. The claimant was made subject to a sanction under s.27(2)(a) of the WRA 2012 for failing for no good reason to comply with a work-related requirement under s.15 (work-focused interview requirement). He had failed to attend an appointment with an adviser on January 12, 2017, saying later that he had thought that the appointment was for the next day and later still that he did not attend because of health issues.

The First-tier Tribunal found that the claimant had signed and agreed a claimant commitment on October 27, 2016 that included a requirement to attend and take part in appointments with advisers when required and had been notified at a previous appointment of the requirement to attend on January 12, 2017. It rejected his argument that he had had good reason for failing to attend. However, the claimant commitment supplied in evidence by the Department was not signed or dated and contained a provision for action to be taken by September 20, 2016. It was therefore improbable that the document in the papers had been notified to the claimant on October 27, 2016 and the SSWP had not supplied any other evidence of what claimant commitment had been accepted and what requirements might have been notified in it. Accordingly, although the unrepresented claimant had not raised the issue of whether he had been properly notified of the requirement to attend the appointment on January 12, 2017, the tribunal went wrong in law by proceeding on the basis that a claimant commitment agreed by the claimant on October 27, 2016 imposed a work-related requirement to attend a work-focused interview. Nor had the SSWP put forward coherent evidence of what had been said at an earlier appointment. The written submission relied on an attendance on June 1, 2016, which did not work because the universal credit claim began on September 7, 2016. The appointment history showed a "work-focused review" on December 21, 2016, but there was no evidence of any notification then of a future appointment. There could be no reliance on any presumption of regularity because there was no evidence of a general practice or "script" of what claimants are told at appointments about the need to attend work-focused interviews. Although it was implicit in the claimant's position that he knew of the appointment on January 12, 2017, a sanction could only be imposed if there had been proper notification of the requirement in question and the SSWP had failed to show that. The case was remitted to a new tribunal for rehearing, as it was fair (the issue not having been raised until the Upper Tribunal judge gave permission to appeal), to allow the DWP an opportunity to produce further evidence.

Judge Poole QC therefore did not need to decide whether the terms of the claimant commitment in the papers in themselves were capable of constituting a notification of a requirement to participate in work-focused interviews when notified of appointments. However, she did make interesting observations on that and other wider issues. The SSWP had submitted that the standard terms of claimant commitment were prepared so that claimants could understand them, but were clear and imperative, and that in the context of a system including sanctions claimants and advisers knew that when they were requested to attend interviews it was obligatory to turn up. Judge Poole did not in so many words either accept or reject that submission, but her observations indicate that it could only be accepted subject to heavy qualifications.

In her introductory discussion of the legal principles the judge stressed that while the universal credit legislation gave the SSWP considerable flexibility, the flip side of that was that in sanctions cases the SSWP had to be able to evidence the imposition of the requirement in question. The more informal the means of communication to a claimant the more efficient its recording systems will have to be, so that copies can be produced in cases of appeal. Her opinions on the wider issues were set out as follows in para.29: **6.003**

> "29.1 The UC legislation is deliberately drafted to leave a degree of flexibility for the SSWP, and permits multiple methods of communication to claimants (paragraphs 16 and 17 above). There is a flexibility in the manner and means of notification. Given this legislative intention, it would be inappropriate for the Upper Tribunal to set out particular requirements for wording of notifications, or the means by which this is done.
>
> 29.2 In cases where the issue arises, the key matter for tribunals to consider is whether fair notice has been given, having regard to all the communications between the SSWP and the claimant (paragraphs 18-20 above). What tribunals need to do is look at the evidence produced by the SSWP, in the context in which it arises, together with any evidence taken from the claimant, and ask the question: does the evidence show that the substance of the relevant requirement and consequences of non-compliance were notified to the claimant? The answer to this question will turn on the particular circumstances of a case.
>
> 29.3 There is a virtue in plain English, and in couching notifications about what a claimant has to do in terms that claimants can readily understand. The Upper Tribunal Judge who granted permission raised the issue of whether requirements should be spelled out expressly and not left to implication. In my view it is not necessary that there is reproduction of statutory wording or reference to particular section or regulation numbers, or indeed any prescribed form of wording. What is important is the substance. In this case the question was whether it could fairly be said, on the totality of the evidence, that the claimant had been notified of an obligation to attend a work-focused interview and the consequences of non-compliance.
>
> 29.4 Unless the only evidence bearing on the imposition of a requirement in a sanctions case is the claimant commitment, it is artificial to focus on the sufficiency of the precise terms of the claimant commitment. This is because requirements can be imposed in various ways, including by a combination of documents (paragraph 20 above).

Indeed, in this case the SSWP does not maintain that the wording in the claimant commitment of itself imposed a work-related requirement to attend a work-focused interview on 12 January 2017. Where a claimant commitment is part of the evidence, general reference to 'appointments' in the claimant commitment seems to me to be a sensible shorthand way of conveying a need to attend meetings but leaving flexibility to impose requirements at a later stage under either Section 15 or Section 23 of the 2012 Act. I also consider the passages set out in paragraph 26 above about sanctions for not meeting requirements, giving detail of how payments are cut, and sanctions for not meeting requirements. So where the claimant commitment has been notified, then those requirements have to be considered in conjunction with other evidence before the tribunal bearing on communication to the claimant of requirements and consequences of non-compliance. This can include, for example, later appointment cards, texts about appointments, and verbal communications at interview. It seems to me that when considering the efficacy of verbal communication, although the SSWP's record keeping will be key, it is permissible to take into account a regular pattern of interviews. For example, a claimant may have been asked at interview to come back for the same sort of interview two weeks later. The claimant's experience from earlier interviews may be relevant to whether they have been informed of the substance of a requirement and consequences of non-compliance. Further, while intimation of date, time and place of appointment is a necessary component of intimation, that will be insufficient of itself unless linked in some way to notification to a claimant of a requirement to attend and consequences of non-compliance. The overall point is that tribunals have to consider not only the wording of the claimant commitment, but of all the evidence bearing on whether the substance of the relevant requirement and consequences of non-compliance were notified to the claimant.

29.5 [Deals with some of the consequences of the differences between the powers in s.15 and s.23]."

That overall approach may not be too difficult to apply if the Department takes on board at all levels the lessons of *JB*, not to mention its own existing guidance, and routinely maintains and provides to tribunals clear and consistent records of the requirements imposed on claimants. However, if the familiar lazy assumptions exemplified in *JB* continue (or appear in older cases from before a hoped-for change of practice), a sharper focus may be necessary on how to resolve the tensions between some of the principles canvassed in para.29 in the circumstances of individual cases. For instance, at a broad level it might continue wrongly to be assumed that, if what is done (e.g. in the drafting of the standard form of terms in claimant commitments) is sensible in policy terms, the actual terms of the relevant legislation have been complied with. At a more grassroots level, there might well continue to be a failure to realise the need to provide tribunals with copies of all the evidence beyond the claimant commitment necessary to show the imposition of the requirement in question. In either case, it might become necessary to address directly the effect of the standard form of terms in the claimant commitment, as in the examples given in the main volume. It is submitted that the principle expressed at the end of para.29.3 (and in earlier paragraphs) of *JB* that the test is whether the evidence shows that the claimant has been notified of an obligation becomes primary and that there is a fundamental difference between a commitment being undertaken by a claimant and a requirement being imposed by the SSWP.

In para.34 of *JB*, Judge Poole mentions two documents produced to the Upper Tribunal by the SSWP, of potential relevance in the rehearing. One was a computer printout recording the signing, acceptance and issue of a claimant commitment on September 13, 2016, together with something called a "claimant pack". The other was a standard form document headed "Your meeting plan" with spaces for entering dates, times and contacts of next meeting, with a warning on the back that missing meetings without rearranging in advance risks a sanction. According to the SSWP, the meeting plan document is issued with the "commitment pack", which the judge noted might or might not be the same thing as the "claimant pack". Such documents, in particular a complete copy of the claimant or commitment pack, might well be relevant in future cases, but only if properly put into evidence before tribunals.

p.63, *annotation to the Welfare Reform Act 2012 s.15 (Work-focused interview requirement)*

See *SN v SSWP (JSA)* [2018] UKUT 279 (AAC), detailed in the entry for pp.121-2 of Vol.II, for discussion of what might amount to a failure to participate (in that case in a mandatory work activity scheme) and the expression of some doubt about the result in *SA v SSWP (JSA)* [2015] UKUT 454 (AAC). 6.004

p.75, *annotation to the Welfare Reform Act 2012 s.22 (Claimants subject to all work-related requirements)*

See *JB v SSWP (UC)* [2018] UKUT 360 (AAC), detailed in the entry for p.60, for discussion of the effect of the standard terms of claimant commitments and the notification of the imposition of requirements by other means. 6.005

p.76, *annotation to the Welfare Reform Act 2012 s.23 (Connected requirements)*

See *SN v SSWP (JSA)* [2018] UKUT 279 (AAC), detailed in the entry for pp.121-2 of Vol.II, for discussion of what might amount to a failure to participate (in that case in a mandatory work activity scheme) and the expression of some doubt about the result in *SA v SSWP (JSA)* [2015] UKUT 454 (AAC). 6.006

p.79, *annotation to the Welfare Reform Act 2012 s.24(4) (Imposition of requirements)*

6.007   See *JB v SSWP (UC)* [2018] UKUT 360 (AAC), detailed in the entry for p.60, for discussion of the effect of the standard terms of claimant commitments and the notification of the imposition of requirements by other means.

p.87, *annotation to the Welfare Reform Act 2012 s.26(2)(b) (Higher-level sanctions)*

6.008   See *SN v SSWP (JSA)* [2018] UKUT 279 (AAC), detailed in the entry for pp.121-2 of Vol.II, for discussion of what might amount to a failure to participate (in that case in a mandatory work activity scheme) and the expression of some doubt about the result in *SA v SSWP (JSA)* [2015] UKUT 454 (AAC).

p.92, *annotation to the Welfare Reform Act 2012 s.27 (Other sanctions)*

6.009   See *SN v SSWP (JSA)* [2018] UKUT 279 (AAC), detailed in the entry for pp.121-2 of Vol.II, for discussion of what might amount to a failure to participate (in that case in a mandatory work activity scheme) and the expression of some doubt about the result in *SA v SSWP (JSA)* [2015] UKUT 454 (AAC).

p.116, *amendment to the State Pension Credit Act 2002 s.3A (Housing credit) as inserted by the Welfare Reform Act 2012 Sch.4 para 4*

6.010   With effect from April 6, 2018 s.20(8) of the Welfare Reform and Work Act 2016 amended s.3A of the State Pension Credit Act 2002 by omitting the words from "(and," to "payments)"in subs.(5)(a). However, note that s.3A of the 2002 Act itself has yet to be brought into force. It is anticipated it will only come into effect when the roll out of universal credit is complete.

p.176, *amendment to the Universal Credit Regulations 2013 (SI 2013/376) reg.24A (Availability of the child element where maximum exceeded)*

6.011   With effect from November 28, 2018, reg.3(1) and (3) of the Universal Credit and Jobseeker's Allowance (Miscellaneous Amendments) Regulations 2018 (SI 2018/1129) amended reg.24A by inserting a new sub-para.(za) before para.(1)(a) as follows:

"(za) any child or qualifying young person in relation to whom an exception applies in the circumstances set out in—
    (i) paragraph 3 (adoptions) or paragraph 4 (non-parental caring arrangements) of Schedule 12; or
    (ii) paragraph 6 of Schedule 12 by virtue of an exception under paragraph 3 of that Schedule having applied in relation to a previous award;",

by inserting the following after the word "person" in subpara.(1)
(b)(ii):

"in the circumstances set out in paragraph 2 (multiple births), paragraph 5 (non-consensual conception) or, except where sub-paragraph
(za)(ii) applies, paragraph 6 (continuation of existing exception in a
subsequent award) of Schedule 12",

and by omitting para.(4).

p.180, *amendment to the Universal Credit Regulations 2013
(SI 2013/376) reg.24B (Order of children and qualifying young persons)*

With effect from November 28, 2018, reg.3(1) and (4) of the Univer-   6.012
sal Credit and Jobseeker's Allowance (Miscellaneous Amendments)
Regulations 2018 (SI 2018/1129) amended reg.24B to read as follows:

"Order of children and qualifying young persons
24B.—(1) Subject to [paragraphs (2) and (2A)], the order of children
or qualifying young persons in a claimant's household is to be determined by reference to the [the date of birth of each child or qualifying
young person for whom the claimant is responsible, taking the earliest
date first.]
    (2) In a case where—
    (a) the date in relation to two or more children or qualifying young
        persons for whom the claimant is responsible (as determined
        under paragraph (1)) is the same date; [. . .]
    (b) [. . .]
the order of those children or qualifying young persons (as between
themselves only) in the claimant's household is the order determined
by the Secretary of State that ensures that the amount mentioned in
section 10(1) of the Act is available in respect of the greatest number
of children or qualifying young persons.
    [(2A) Any child or qualifying young person to whom regulation
24A(1)(za) applies is to be disregarded when determining the order of
children and qualifying young persons under this regulation.]
    (3) In this regulation and Schedule 12, "claimant" means a single
claimant or either of joint claimants."

p.218, *annotation to the Universal Credit Regulations 2013 (SI
2013/376) reg.54 (Calculation of earned income—general principles)*

A judicial review challenge to the inflexibility of the structure of   6.013
assessment periods and the attribution of earned income actually
received in each period (or information received from HMRC under the
real time information provisions of reg.61), which, as operated by the
DWP, could easily lead to two regular monthly payments being counted
in one assessment period and none in another, was heard in the Administrative Court in November 2018. However, the Court decided that it
did not need to address the issues of irrationality, breach of art.14 of the

ECHR and breach of the Equality Act 2010 that had been raised originally. That was because it concluded that the DWP had been interpreting regs 54 and 61 wrongly and that the correct interpretation
removed the claimants' problems (*R. (on the application of Johnson) v
Secretary of State for Work and Pensions* [2019] EWHC 23 (Admin)). It is
understood that at the further hearing on February 26, 2019 no further
remedy was laid down by the court than that the Secretary of State was
to make decisions in accordance with the judgment. The Secretary of
State was refused permission to appeal, but may of course renew the
application before the Court of Appeal.

The claimants were all single parents of youngish children and were in
employment and paid monthly either on the last working day or the last
banking day of the month. Their universal credit assessment periods ran
either from the 30th of one month to the 29th of the next or from the
28th to the 27th. To take the facts of Ms Johnson's case, she was paid her
salary for November 2017 on November 30, 2017 and her salary for
December 2017 on December 29, 2017. Her employer was a Real Time
Information (RTI) employer and it appears (though it is not explicit in
the judgment) that the pay information was received by the Secretary of
State from HMRC on the dates of payment. Because her assessment
period was 30–29, the Department took the view that reg.61 required it
to calculate her earned income in respect of the assessment period
ending on December 29, 2017 as including both the payment made on
November 30, 2017 and that made on December 29, 2017, with the
result that 63% of the excess of the two payments (after the deductions
required by reg.55(5)) over her work allowance of £192 was deducted
from the maximum amount of universal credit. It was the decision to
that effect on January 6, 2018 that was challenged in the application for
judicial review. It was accepted that, on that basis, the claimant's earned
income in respect of the assessment period ending on January 29, 2018
would be nil, so that there would be no deduction from the maximum
amount of universal credit for that period, but the claimant would have
been deprived of the benefit of the £192 work allowance in relation to
that assessment period, as well as suffering the cash flow difficulties of
being faced with a severely reduced payment of universal credit not
followed by an increased amount until a month later. The other three
claimants were affected in essentially the same way. The Court did not
state whether or not the decisions in their cases were made in reliance on
reg.61, but since most employers are RTI employers it seems likely that
they were. That is important in the assessment of the correctness or
otherwise of the decision in *Johnson*.

The judges considered mainly the proper construction of reg.54(1)
and the general principle set out there. They concluded that in both
reg.54(1) and 61 the use of the formula that the amount of earned
income in respect of an assessment period is to be "based on" the actual
amounts received in that period, or the HMRC information received by
the Secretary of State in that period, meant that there was "intended to
be some other factor, not the mere mechanical addition of monies
received in a particular period, which the calculation has to address"
(para.51). They continued in para.52:

"That other factor is the period in respect of which the earned income is earned. It is the earned income in respect of the period of time included within the assessment period that is to be calculated. That is to be based on the actual amounts received in the assessment period. There may, however, need to be an adjustment where it is clear that the amounts received in an assessment period do not, in fact, reflect the amounts of earned income received in respect of the period of time included within that assessment period."

That construction was said to accord with the reality of the underlying situation of monthly paid employees and to avoid nonsensical conclusions such as that a claimant had no earned income during a period when she was clearly working and being paid. It was said also to be consistent with the wider context of the 2013 Regulations and in particular reg.22, which uses the terms of earned income "in respect of" the assessment period, and in particular of the aim of the work allowance in reflecting the living costs involved in each assessment period.

In dealing with some specific submissions made for the Secretary of State, the Court recognised (para.57) that outside the situation of monthly salary payments, for instance where hours varied from month to month or bonuses or commissions were paid, there might be no reason to depart from the starting point of actual amounts received in each assessment period.

Despite the Court's focus on the precise words of reg.54(1) and the evident truth that the draftsman could easily have put the matter beyond doubt by the use of different language, there are cogent arguments against the Court's construction that were not addressed in the decision. First, the formula "is, unless otherwise provided in this Chapter, to be based on the actual amounts received" in the assessment period in question might be argued equally naturally to mean that the calculation had to be made by taking the actual amounts received except in so far as any other provision required otherwise, leaving no room for the implication of any other factor. The use of the word "actual" could be said to support that approach. The Court's construction gives no force to that word and indeed leaves regulation 54(1) with little practical content, since few calculations could fail to be based, in the sense only of a starting point, on the actual amounts received in the assessment period. The phrase "in respect of" in reg.22 appears neutral in itself. The Court also leaves in doubt when factors beyond the terms of reg.54(1) should be applied outside cases of regular monthly salary payments. For instance, could claimants not argue that an annual bonus should be attributed over a year and not taken into account entirely in the assessment period of receipt (and, if so, how might the surplus earnings rules in the post-April 2018 reg.54A apply)?

Second, the examination of the wider context of the 2013 Regulations failed to get to grips with the precise words of reg.61. Although reg.61(2)(a) does use the phrase "based on", para.(2)(b) does not. It simply provides that that for an assessment period in which no information is received by the Secretary of State from HMRC the amount of earned income is to be taken as nil. And the provisions in para.(5) about the powers of the Secretary of State when making a decision in one of the para.(3) circumstances in which para.(2) does not apply would not have been necessary if there was a general power to take account of other factors.

Those points are particularly important since Ms Johnson's case, and very probably the other three, fell within reg.61, not 54(1). Although strictly concerned only with the decisions about the assessment periods in which two sets of HMRC pay information were received, it was an essential part of the Court's reasoning that in the following assessment period, in which no pay information was received, the claimants should be treated as having received their regular monthly salary and have their work allowance credited. However, that conclusion runs directly counter to the terms of reg.61(2)(b), in which there is no potential get-out phrase like "based on". Nor could para.(2) be disapplied under para.(3), because so far as one can tell all of the HMRC information was perfectly accurate and timely in reporting pay on the day on which it was paid. The information could not be said to fail to reflect the definition of employed earnings in reg.55 (para.(3)(b)(ii)), because reg.55 is only concerned with what sorts of payments count as employed earnings, not with attribution to particular assessment periods.

pp.246–250, *annotation to the Universal Credit Regulations 2013 (SI 2013/376) reg.61 (Information for calculating earned income—real time information etc.)*

6.014   See para.6.013 for discussion of the effect of the decision in *R (on the application of Johnson) v Secretary of State for Work and Pensions* [2019] EWHC 23 (Admin) on the interpretation of reg.61, in particular in circumstances in which two reports of the payment of regular monthly salaries are received by the SSWP from HMRC in the same assessment period.

p.272, *amendment to the Universal Credit Regulations 2013 (SI 2013/376) reg.77(5) (Company analogous to a partnership or one person business)*

6.015   With effect from November 5, 2018, reg.3(5) of the Universal Credit and Jobseeker's Allowance (Miscellaneous Amendments) Regulations 2018 (SI 2018/1129) amended reg.77(5) by substituting the words ", Chapter 9 (managed service companies) or Chapter 10 (workers' services provided through intermediaries) of Part 2 of ITEPA and that income is derived from activities that are the person's main employment" for the words from "or Chapter 9" to the end of para.(5).

The amendment first up-dates the references to ITEPA in extending the exclusion of the operation of reg.77 to arrangements under Chapter 10, as well as Chapters 8 and 9. Then it narrows the exclusion to circumstances where the activities under the arrangement in question are the claimant's main employment.

p.369, *amendment to the Universal Credit Regulations 2013 (SI 2013/376) Sch.4 para.29 (Housing costs element for renters—Renters excepted from shared accommodation)*

With effect from November 28, 2018, reg.3(1) and (6)(d) of the   **6.016** Universal Credit and Jobseeker's Allowance (Miscellaneous Amendments) Regulations 2018 (SI 2018/1129) amended Sch.4, para 29 by substituting "(9A)" for "(9)" in sub-para.(1) and inserting the following sub-paragraph after sub-para (9):

"(9A) E is under 35 years old and satisfies the foster parent condition (within the meaning of paragraph 12(4)).".

pp.375-377, *annotation to the Universal Credit Regulations 2013 (SI 2013/376) Sch.4 (Housing costs element for renters) paras.8-12 and 26-29*

Delete the final three paragraphs of the commentary on p.376 and the   **6.017** first four lines on p.347 which are redundant following the decision of the Supreme Court in *R (Carmichael and Rourke) (formerly known as MA and others) v Secretary of State for Work and Pensions* [2016] UKSC 58, which is noted on p.375.

p.396, *amendment to the Universal Credit Regulations 2013 (SI 2013/376) Sch.10 (Capital to be disregarded)*

With effect from December 10, 2018, art.11 of the Social Security   **6.018** (Scotland) Act 2018 (Best Start Grants) (Consequential Modifications and Saving) Order 2018 (SI 2018/1138) added the following after para.20 of Sch.10:

"**21.** Any early years assistance given within the past 12 months in accordance with section 32 of the Social Security (Scotland) Act 2018."

The restriction of this disregard to receipts within the previous 12 months does not apply to other means-tested benefits. Early years assistance is not listed in reg.66 of the Universal Credit Regulations 2013, so cannot count as unearned income.

p.399, *annotation to the Universal Credit Regulations 2013 (SI 2013/376) Sch.10 para.18 (Capital to be disregarded—arrears of benefit)*

See the new reg.10A of the Universal Credit (Transitional Provisions)   **6.019** Regulations 2014, inserted with effect from September 11, 2018 by reg.8 of the Social Security (Treatment of Arrears of Benefit) Regulations 2018 (SI 2018/932) (entry for p.498).

p.488, *annotation to the Universal Credit (Transitional Provisions) Regulations 2014 (SI 2014/1230) reg.5 (Exclusion of entitlement to certain benefits)*

The implementation arrangements for universal credit were the sub-   **6.020** ject of judicial review in *R (TP and AR) v Secretary of State for Work and*

Pensions [2018] EWHC 1474 (Admin). The High Court (Lewis J.) held that the implementation arrangements were discriminatory because disability premiums would be lost if a claimant moved from one local authority to another (thus triggering a requirement to claim universal credit) but not if the claimant moved within the same local authority (and so was not required to claim universal credit). Lewis J. summarised the background as follows:

"1. These are two claims challenging aspects of the regulations creating and implementing the system of universal credit, which is intended to replace the existing system of welfare benefits. The claimants are both individuals who, under the previous system governing welfare benefits, had been in receipt of an income related employment and support allowance ("the basic allowance"). In addition, as they met certain additional criteria, they had been in receipt of certain additional premiums (known as Severely Disability Premium ("SDP") and Enhanced Disability Premium ("EDP")).

2. On moving to a new local housing authority area, the claimants had to apply for universal credit which replaced both housing benefit and the former income related benefits (including the basic allowance, and SDP and EDP) which the claimants had been receiving. The amount of the standard allowance payable as part of universal credit was higher than the basic allowance formerly payable but as universal credit does not include the additional disability premiums (the SDP and EDP) the total cash payment received by way of income related support under universal credit was less than the income related support that the claimants had been receiving under the former system. The claimants received over £170 a month less as a result of the transfer to universal credit."

The claimants challenged the universal credit regime in two principal respects. First, they challenged the Universal Credit Regulations 2013, contending that the absence of any additional payments for those who previously were eligible to claim SDP and EDP constituted unlawful discrimination contrary to Article 14, read with Article 1 of the First Protocol to the ECHR. Secondly, the claimants challenged the absence of any element of transitional protection as part of the implementation arrangements contending that this, too, constituted unlawful discrimination on the same basis. Lewis J. dismissed the first challenge but upheld the second (a further challenge based on the public sector equality duty was rejected). The High Court expressed its conclusions as follows:

"113. The 2013 Regulations establishing universal credit do not involve discrimination contrary to Article 14 ECHR in so far as they do not include any element which corresponds to the additional disability premiums payable under the previous regime. Any differential treatment between different groups is objectively justifiable.

114. The implementing arrangements do at present give rise to unlawful discrimination contrary to Article 14 ECHR read with Article 1 of the First Protocol to the ECHR. There is differential treatment

between the group of persons who were in receipt of additional disability premiums (the SDP and EDP) and who transferred to universal credit on moving to a different local housing authority area and so receive less money by way of income related support than they previously received and the group of persons in receipt of SDP and EDP and who move house within the same local housing authority area but are not required to transfer to universal credit and continue to receive the basic allowance and SDP and EDP and suffer no loss of income. That differential treatment is based on status. That differential treatment has not been objectively justified at present. A declaration will be granted that there is unlawful discrimination. The defendant will then be able to determine how to rectify the unlawful discrimination."

At the time the claim was brought in *R (TP and AR) v Secretary of State for Work and Pensions*, the Government was not planning to make provision for transitional protection payments in the universal credit scheme until July 2019 at the earliest. However, on June 7, 2018, shortly before the High Court's judgment was handed down, the then Secretary of State for Work and Pensions announced measures to commence before July 2019 to provide transitional protection for some claimants, including those in receipt of the SDP, who would otherwise lose out on migration to universal credit. The relevant part of the written statement (HCWS745) read as follows:

" . . . The Government has already made a commitment that anyone who is moved to Universal Credit without a change of circumstance will not lose out in cash terms. Transitional protection will be provided to eligible claimants to safeguard their existing benefit entitlement until their circumstances change.

Today I am announcing four additions to these rules to ensure that Universal Credit supports people into work, protects vulnerable claimants and is targeted at those who need it.

In order to support the transition for those individuals who live alone with substantial care needs and receive the Severe Disability Premium, we are changing the system so that these claimants will not be moved to Universal Credit until they qualify for transitional protection. In addition, we will provide both an on-going payment to claimants who have already lost this Premium as a consequence of moving to Universal Credit and an additional payment to cover the period since they moved.

Second, we will increase the incentives for parents to take short-term or temporary work and increase their earnings by ensuring that the award of, or increase in, support for childcare costs will not erode transitional protection.

Third, we propose to re-award claimants' transitional protection that has ceased owing to short-term increases in earnings within an assessment period, if they make a new claim to UC within three months of when they received the additional payment.

Finally, individuals with capital in excess of £16,000 are not eligible for Universal Credit. However, for Tax Credit claimants in this situation, we will now disregard any capital in excess of £16,000 for 12 months from the point at which they are moved to Universal Credit. Normal benefit rules apply after this time in order to strike the right balance between keeping incentives for saving and asking people to support themselves.

The process of migrating claimants on legacy benefits will begin in July 2019 as previously announced. In order to make the changes to the system it will be necessary to extend the completion of UC to March 2023. As throughout UC roll out, we will keep the exact timetable under review to do what is sensible from a delivery and fiscal perspective.

These changes will form part of the Universal Credit Managed Migration and Transitional Protection Regulations which we intend to bring forward in the Autumn.

This Government is committed to delivering a welfare system that supports claimants and is fair to taxpayers."

In November 2018 SSAC published its report *The Draft Universal Credit (Managed Migration) Regulations 2018 (SI 2018/****)*. Most, but not all, of SSAC's recommendations were accepted, or 'accepted in principle', and a revised set of the draft regulations was published alongside the government's response. However, in further correspondence with the Secretary of State, the Chair of SSAC has indicated that the Committee "remains concerned" about the government's expectation that everyone must make a claim to universal credit under managed migration. SSAC has also raised several other matters which it still wishes to see addressed. In December 2018 the House of Commons Work and Pensions Select Committee wrote to the Secretary of State calling on the draft regulations to be withdrawn.

p.498, *amendment to the Universal Credit (Transitional Provisions) Regulations 2014 (SI 2014/1230), insertion of new reg.10 (Arrears of benefit disregarded as capital)*

6.021   With effect from September 11, 2018, reg.8 of the Social Security (Treatment of Arrears of Benefit) Regulations 2018 (SI 2018/932) inserted the following new regulation after reg.10:

"**Arrears of benefit disregarded as capital**
10A.—(1) This regulation applies in relation to the calculation of an award of universal credit (the "current award") where the claimant has received a payment of arrears of benefit, or a payment made to compensate for arrears due to the non-payment of benefit, of £5,000 or more, and the following conditions are met—
  (a) the payment—
    (i) is received during the current award; or
    (ii) was received during an award of an existing benefit or state pension credit (the "earlier award") and the claimant became entitled to the current award within one month of the date of termination of the earlier award;
  (b) in the case of a payment falling within sub-paragraph (a)(i), it would be disregarded from the calculation of the claimant's

capital if the claimant were entitled to an existing benefit or state pension credit;

(c) in the case of a payment falling within sub-paragraph (a)(ii), it was disregarded from the calculation of the claimant's capital for the purposes of the earlier award; and

(d)
the period of entitlement to benefit to which the payment relates commences before the first date on which, by virtue of section 33 of the Act (abolition of benefits), no claimant is entitled to an existing benefit.

(2) Where this regulation applies, notwithstanding anything in the Universal Credit Regulations, the payment is to be disregarded from the calculation of the claimant's capital for 12 months from the date of receipt of the payment, or until the termination of the current award (if later)."

pp.904-905, *annotation to the Universal Credit (Decisions and Appeals) Regulations 2013 (SI 2013/381) reg.3 (Service of documents)*

In *SP v SSWP (UC)* [2018] UKUT 227 (AAC) the Upper Tribunal 6.022 (Judge Jacobs) held that the words "under any provision of these Regulations" in paras.(1) and (2) have the effect that reg.3 does not apply to notices given or sent under the 2012 Act or the Universal Credit Regulations 2013.

PART VII

SCOTLAND:
LEGISLATION CONCERNING
DEVOLVED MATTERS

Social Security (Scotland) Act 2018

(2018 asp 9)

CONTENTS

PART 1

TENETS AND OVERSIGHT

7.001

PART 2

GIVING OF ASSISTANCE BY SCOTTISH MINISTERS

CHAPTER 1

ASSISTANCE TO BE GIVEN ACCORDING TO DETERMINATION OF ENTITLEMENT

CHAPTER 2

TYPES OF ASSISTANCE TO BE GIVEN

CHAPTER 3

DETERMINING ENTITLEMENT

CHAPTER 4

FURTHER PROVISION ABOUT DETERMINING ENTITLEMENT

CHAPTER 5

RECOVERY OF VALUE OF ASSISTANCE

Assistance given in error

Funeral expense assistance

CHAPTER 6

OFFENCES AND INVESTIGATIONS

CHAPTER 7

UPRATING FOR INFLATION

PART 3

SUPPLEMENTING ASSISTANCE UNDER OTHER ENACTMENTS

Top up of reserved benefits

Carer's allowance: temporary provision

PART 4

FURTHER PROVISION IN CONNECTION WITH PARTS 2 AND 3

PART 5

DISCRETIONARY HOUSING PAYMENTS

PART 6

UNIVERSAL CREDIT: PAYMENT TO JOINT CLAIMANTS

PART 7

FINAL PROVISIONS

The Bill for this Act of the Scottish Parliament was passed by the Parliament on 25th April 2018 and received Royal Assent on 1st June 2018
An Act of the Scottish Parliament making provision about social security.

PART 1

TENETS AND OVERSIGHT

1. to 9. *Omitted.*   7.002
10. to 14. *Not yet in force.*
15. to 20. *Omitted.*
21. to 22. *Not yet in force.*
23. *Omitted.*

PART 2

GIVING OF ASSISTANCE BY SCOTTISH MINISTERS

CHAPTER 1

ASSISTANCE TO BE GIVEN ACCORDING TO
DETERMINATION OF ENTITLEMENT

Duty to give assistance

24.—The Scottish Ministers must give an individual whatever assis-   7.003
tance of a type described in Chapter 2 the individual is entitled to be

given under a determination of the individual's entitlement to assistance.

Meaning of "determination of entitlement"

7.004   **25.**—(1) References in this Part to a determination of an individual's entitlement to assistance are to a determination made—
(a) by the Scottish Ministers—
    (i) under section 37, or
    (ii) (following a request for a re-determination) under section 43,
(b) by the First-tier Tribunal for Scotland—
    (i) under section 49 in an appeal against a determination made by the Scottish Ministers, or
    (ii) (subsequent to such an appeal) under its Tribunals Act powers,
(c) by the Upper Tribunal for Scotland under its Tribunals Act powers (subsequent to an appeal against, or following a review of, a decision of the First-tier Tribunal),
(d) by the Court of Session under its Tribunals Act powers (in an appeal against a decision of the Upper Tribunal), or
(e) by the Supreme Court of the United Kingdom—
    (i) in an appeal under section 40 of the Court of Session Act 1988 against a decision of the Court of Session, or
    (ii) on a reference made by the Court of Session under schedule 6 of the Scotland Act 1998.

(2) In this section, "Tribunals Act powers" means powers under Part 6 (review or appeal of decisions) of the Tribunals (Scotland) Act 2014.

Individual's right to stop receiving assistance

7.005   **26.**—(1) An individual may request that the Scottish Ministers cancel a determination of the individual's entitlement to assistance.

(2) On being requested to do so under subsection (1), the Scottish Ministers must cancel a determination—
(a) with immediate effect, or
(b) with effect from a later date specified in the request.

(3) An individual is not entitled, and is not to become entitled, to be given assistance by a determination after it has been cancelled.

(4) A request under subsection (1) must be made in such form as the Scottish Ministers require.

(5) The Scottish Ministers must publicise any requirements for the time being set under subsection (4).

Later determination supersedes earlier

7.006   **27.**—(1) The latest determination of an individual's entitlement to a particular type of assistance in respect of a given period or event supersedes any earlier determination insofar as it deals with the individual's entitlement to that type of assistance in respect of the same period or event.

150

(2) Accordingly the individual is not entitled, and is not to become entitled, to be given any assistance in respect of that period or event by the earlier determination insofar as it has been superseded.

CHAPTER 2

TYPES OF ASSISTANCE TO BE GIVEN

28. to 31. *Not yet in force.*   7.007

Early years assistance

32.—(1) Early years assistance is assistance (which may or may not   7.008
take the form of money) given by the Scottish Ministers under section 24 to help towards meeting some of the costs associated with having, or expecting to have, a child in the family.

(2) The Scottish Minsters are to make regulations prescribing—

(a) the eligibility rules that are to be applied to determine whether an individual is entitled to early years assistance, and

(b) what early years assistance an individual who is entitled to it is to be given.

(3) Schedule 6 makes provision about the exercise of the power conferred by subsection (2).

GENERAL NOTE

This section came into force on December 10, 2018 (see the Social Security   7.009
(Scotland) Act 2018 (Commencement No.3) Regulations 2018 (SSI 2018/357), reg.2). As yet, the only form of assistance available under this Act, apart from the supplement to carer's allowance payable under s.81, is early years assistance in the form of a pregnancy and baby grant payable under the Early Years Assistance (Best Start Grants) (Scotland) Regulations 2018, which Regulations are made partly under subs.(2).

33. to 36. *Not yet in force.*

CHAPTER 3

DETERMINING ENTITLEMENT

Determination by the Scottish Ministers

Duty to make determination

37.—The Scottish Ministers are to make a determination of an indi-   7.010
vidual's entitlement to a type of assistance described in Chapter 2—

(a) on receiving an application for that type of assistance from the individual, or

(b) when required to do so by regulations under section 52.

Application for assistance

7.011   **38.**—(1) An application for assistance must be—

(a) made to the Scottish Ministers in such form, and

(b) accompanied by such evidence,

as the Scottish Ministers require.

(2) The Scottish Ministers must publicise any requirements for the time being set under subsection (1).

(3) Once—

(a) an individual has applied for a particular type of assistance in respect of a period or (as the case may be) event, and

(b) the Scottish Minsters have made a determination of the individual's entitlement to that type of assistance in respect of the period or event,

the individual cannot make another application for that type of assistance in respect of the period or event.

(4) Despite subsection (3), an individual may make another application for a particular type of assistance in respect of an event if the latest determination of the individual's entitlement to that type of assistance in respect of the event states that the individual may make another application.

(5) If the Scottish Ministers reject something purporting to be an application for assistance, they must inform the individual concerned of—

(a) the decision to do that,

(b) the reasons for it, and

(c) the individual's right to appeal under section 61.

Withdrawal of application

7.012   **39.**—(1) An individual who has made an application for assistance may request that the Scottish Ministers disregard it.

(2) If an individual requests that an application be disregarded—

(a) the Scottish Ministers are not to make a determination of the individual's entitlement to any type of assistance on the basis of the application, and

(b) accordingly, their duty to do so under section 37 ceases to apply.

(3) A request under subsection (1) must be made in such form as the Scottish Ministers require.

(4) The Scottish Ministers must publicise any requirements for the time being set under subsection (3).

Notice of determination

7.013   **40.**—(1) Having made a determination under section 37 of an individual's entitlement to assistance, the Scottish Ministers must inform the individual—

(a) of the determination,

(b) of the reasons for it,

(c) of the individual's right under section 41 to request that the Scottish Ministers re-determine the individual's entitlement to the assistance,

(d) that the individual will have the right under section 46 to appeal to the First-tier Tribunal against the determination should the Scottish Ministers fail to deal with a request for a re-determination within the period allowed for re-determination, and

(e) if relevant, that the individual has the right to request a copy of an assessment report under section 60.

(2) The Scottish Ministers must fulfil their duty under subsection (1) in a way that leaves the individual with a record of the information which the individual can show to, or otherwise share with, others.

Re-determination by the Scottish Ministers

Right to request re-determination

41.—(1) An individual may request that the Scottish Ministers re-determine the individual's entitlement to a particular type of assistance after being informed (in accordance with section 40) of a determination by the Ministers of the individual's entitlement to that type of assistance. 7.014

(2) A request for a re-determination is valid only if the conditions set out in the following subsections are satisfied—

(a) subsection (3), and

(b) subsection (4).

(3) The condition referred to in subsection (2)(a) is satisfied if the request is made in such form as the Scottish Ministers require.

(4) The condition referred to in subsection (2)(b) is satisfied if—

(a) the request is made before the end of the period prescribed by the Scottish Ministers in regulations, or

(b) in a case where the request is made after that period has ended—

　(i) the individual has a good reason for not requesting a re-determination sooner (see section 42), and

　(ii) the request is made before the end of the day that falls one year after the day on which the individual is informed (in accordance with section 40) of the determination.

(5) The Scottish Ministers must publicise any requirements for the time being set under subsection (3).

(6) If the Scottish Ministers decide that something purporting to be a request for a re-determination does not satisfy the condition in subsection (3), they must inform the individual concerned of—

(a) the decision,

(b) the reasons for it, and

(c) the individual's right to appeal under section 61.

7.014.1 *Subsection (4)*

The period prescribed for requesting a re-determination of entitlement to early years assistance is 31 days beginning with the day that the claimant is informed of the right to make the request (Early Years Assistance (Best Start Grants) (Scotland) Regulations 2018 Sch.1 para.1).

Late request for re-determination

7.015 **42.**—(1) It is for—

(a) the Scottish Ministers, or

(b) on appeal under section 61, the First-tier Tribunal for Scotland, to decide whether, for the purpose of section 41(4)(b), an individual has a good reason for not requesting a re-determination sooner.

(2) Having made a decision under subsection (1), the Scottish Ministers must inform the individual concerned—

(a) of the decision, and

(b) if the decision is that the individual has no good reason for not requesting a re-determination sooner, of—

(i) the reasons for the decision, and

(ii) the individual's right to appeal under section 61.

Duty to re-determine

7.016 **43.**—(1) On being requested under section 41 to re-determine an individual's entitlement to a particular type of assistance, the Scottish Ministers are to make a determination of the individual's entitlement to that type of assistance.

(2) The Scottish Ministers must aim to make the determination within the period allowed for re-determination.

(3) If the Scottish Ministers fail to make the determination within the period allowed for re-determination—

(a) their duty to make the determination ends (but they may still make it), and

(b) section 45 applies.

(4) If the Scottish Ministers make the determination (whether or not within the period allowed for re-determination), section 44 applies.

(5) The period allowed for re-determination is to be prescribed by the Scottish Ministers in regulations.

(6) The reference in subsection (1) to a request under section 41 is to a request that is valid according to subsection (2) of that section.

GENERAL NOTE

7.016.1 *Subsection (2)*

In relation to determining entitlement to early years assistance, the period allowed for re-determination is 16 working days beginning with the day that the request for a re-determination is received by the Scottish Ministers (Early Years Assistance (Best Start Grants) (Scotland) Regulations 2018 Sch 1 para.2).

Notice of re-determination

44.—(1) Having made a determination under section 43 of an individ-   7.017
ual's entitlement to a particular type of assistance, the Scottish Ministers
must—
(a) inform the individual—
   (i) of the determination,
   (ii) of the reasons for it,
   (iii) of the individual's right to appeal to the First-tier Tribunal
      under section 46 against the determination,
   (iv) if relevant, that the individual has the right to request a copy
      of an assessment report under section 60, and
(b) provide the individual with a form that the individual can complete and submit to the Scottish Ministers in order to bring an
   appeal against the determination.
(2) The Scottish Ministers must fulfil their duty under subsection
(1)(a) in a way that leaves the individual with a record of the information
which the individual can show to, or otherwise share with, others.

Notice where re-determination not made timeously

45.—(1) Having failed to make a determination under section 43 of an   7.018
individual's entitlement to a particular type of assistance within the
period allowed for re-determination, the Scottish Ministers must—
(a) inform the individual—
   (i) that the individual's request for a re-determination has not
      been dealt with within the period allowed, and
   (ii) that the individual therefore has the right to appeal to the
      First-tier Tribunal against the determination under section
      37 which prompted the request for a re-determination, and
(b) provide the individual with a form that the individual can complete and submit to the Scottish Ministers in order to bring an
   appeal against the determination.
(2) The Scottish Ministers must fulfil their duty under subsection
(1)(a) in a way that leaves the individual with a record of the information
which the individual can show to, or otherwise share with, others.

Appeal against the Scottish Ministers' determination

Right to appeal to First-tier Tribunal against determination

46.—(1) An individual may appeal to the First-tier Tribunal for   7.019
Scotland—
(a) against a determination under section 43 of the individual's entitlement to assistance, or
(b) in a case where subsection (2) applies, against the determination
   under section 37 referred to in that subsection.
(2) This subsection applies where—

    (a) having been informed of a determination under section 37 of the individual's entitlement to assistance, the individual has made a request for a re-determination under section 41, and

    (b) the Scottish Ministers have failed to make a determination under section 43 in consequence of that request within the period allowed for re-determination.

GENERAL NOTE

7.019.1   The First-tier Tribunal for Scotland is established under s.1 of the Tribunals (Scotland) Act 2014. See the annotation to that provision (below) and, for procedure in social security cases, see the First-tier Tribunal for Scotland Social Security Chamber (Procedure) Regulations 2018 (also below).

    Note that separate, and more limited, provision is made by s.61 for appeals against process decisions.

Initiating an appeal

7.020   **47.**—(1) In order to bring an appeal under section 46 against a determination, an individual must submit to the Scottish Ministers the form provided under section 44 or (as the case may be) 45 in relation to the determination.

(2) On receiving a form that they provided under section 44 or 45, the Scottish Ministers must send—

    (a) the form, and

    (b) the information held by them that they used to make the determination in question, to the First-tier Tribunal.

(3) Having complied with subsection (2), the Scottish Ministers must inform the individual to whom the determination in question relates that they have done so.

(4) In this section, references to a form include a copy of a form.

(5) For the avoidance of doubt, the form that the Scottish Ministers provide under section 44 or 45 need not be a physical form.

(6) Scottish Tribunal Rules providing for the form and manner in which an appeal under section 46 is to be brought may not displace the effect of subsection (1), but this section is otherwise without prejudice to what may be provided under any power to make Scottish Tribunal Rules.

Deadline for appealing

7.021   **48.**—(1) An appeal under section 46—

    (a) may be brought without the First-tier Tribunal's permission if an appeal application is made within the period of 31 days beginning with the day the relevant event occurred,

    (b) may be brought only with the First-tier Tribunal's permission if an appeal application is made after the period mentioned in paragraph (a),

    (c) may not be brought if an appeal application has not been made within the period of one year beginning with the day the relevant event occurred.

(2) In subsection (1)—

(a) "the relevant event" means—
  (i) in the case of an appeal against a determination under section 43, the individual to whom the determination relates being informed of it in accordance with section 44,
  (ii) in the case of an appeal against a determination under section 37, the individual to whom the determination relates being informed (in accordance with section 45) that the individual has the right to appeal against it,
(b) an appeal application is made when a form, that relates to the determination in question and has been completed to the extent that Scottish Tribunal Rules require, is received by the Scottish Ministers having been submitted in accordance with section 47(1).

(3) The First-tier Tribunal may give permission under subsection (1)(b) for an appeal to be brought only if it is satisfied that there is a good reason for the application not having been made sooner.

First-tier Tribunal's power to determine entitlement

49.—In an appeal under section 46 against a determination of an individual's entitlement to a particular type of assistance, the First-tier Tribunal may—   7.022
(a) uphold the determination, or
(b) make its own determination of the individual's entitlement to the type of assistance in question.

The determination of entitlement

Decisions comprising determination

50.—(1) A determination of an individual's entitlement to a particular type of assistance consists of—   7.023
(a) a decision about whether or not the eligibility rules prescribed in the applicable regulations are satisfied in the individual's case,
(b) if those rules are satisfied, a decision (taken in accordance with the applicable regulations) about what assistance of the type in question the individual is entitled to be given,
(c) if the determination is to be made on the basis that the individual has ongoing entitlement to the type of assistance in question (see section 51), a decision about what assistance of the type in question the determination is to entitle the individual to be given in the future, and
(d) if the determination is of an individual's entitlement to assistance in respect of an event, a decision about whether the individual's application for assistance in respect of the event is possibly premature.

(2) If it is decided under subsection (1)(d) that an individual's application for assistance in respect of an event is possibly premature, the

determination must include a statement that the individual may make another application for assistance in respect of the event.

(3) An individual's application for assistance in respect of an event is possibly premature for the purpose of subsection (1)(d) if—

(a) the decision under subsection (1)(a) is that the eligibility rules prescribed in the applicable regulations are not satisfied in the individual's case, and

(b) it is possible that circumstances may change so that, in relation to the event in question, those rules will be satisfied in the individual's case.

(4) In this section, "the applicable regulations" means the regulations made under the section in Chapter 2 that describes the type of assistance in question.

Determination on basis of ongoing entitlement

7.024   **51.**—(1) The Scottish Ministers may by regulations—

(a) provide that a determination of an individual's entitlement to a specified type of assistance is to be made on the basis that the individual has ongoing entitlement to that type of assistance, and

(b) provide for exceptions to any provision made by virtue of paragraph (a).

(2) Regulations making provision by virtue of subsection (1)(a) are also to—

(a) prescribe the time, or times, at which an individual is to become entitled to be given assistance under a determination made on the basis that the individual has ongoing entitlement, and

(b) provide that a decision about what assistance the individual is to become entitled to be given under such a determination in respect of any future period is to be taken in accordance with the applicable regulations on the strength of such assumptions as are specified.

(3) Without prejudice to the generality of subsection (2)(b), the assumptions that may be specified include an assumption that the eligibility rules prescribed in the applicable regulations will continue to be satisfied in an individual's case for a specified duration or indefinitely.

(4) In this section—

"the applicable regulations" means the regulations made under the section in Chapter 2 that describes the type of assistance in question,

"specified" means specified by regulations under this section.

Determination without application

7.025   **52.**—(1) The Scottish Ministers may by regulations provide that, in such circumstances as the regulations specify, the Scottish Ministers are to make a determination of an individual's entitlement to a particular type of assistance without receiving an application.

(2) The Scottish Ministers may by regulations make provision about the information that is to be used, and the assumptions that are to be

made, in making a determination when required to do so by regulations under subsection (1).

GENERAL NOTE

For regulations made under this section, see para.2 of sch.1 to the Early Years   7.025.1
Assistance (Best Start Grants) (Scotland) Regulations 2018, which enables a determination to be made without a second application where an application has been made for early years assistance in respect of one child and the applicant is expected to become eligible for early years assistance in respect of another child within ten days after the application was made.

It is apparent from s.37 that "application" in this section means an application for assistance. These powers to make regulations therefore appear to enable Scottish Ministers not only to make provision for assistance to be awarded without an application but also to provide for determinations that have the effect of superseding earlier determinations (see s.27). However, partly because the only form of assistance currently available are Best Start Grants, which are one-off payments so that changes of circumstances are irrelevant, and partly because a new "determination" does not appear to be necessary when deciding whether there a person is liable to repay an overpayment (see s.63), the grounds upon which a determination may be made without receiving an application need not yet be extensive. On the other hand, one effect of the current limited provision is that the only ways of correcting a wrongful refusal of a grant are by making a request under s.41 for a re-determination or appealing under s.46, both of which are subject to time limits. (Making a further application is generally precluded by s.38(3).) Thus, there is no equivalent of revision on the grounds of "official error" under, say, reg.3(5)(a) of the Social Security and Child Support (Decisions and Appeals) Regulations 1999 (see Vol III of the main work). It remains to be seen what provision will be made when more complicated forms of assistance are introduced.

CHAPTER 4

FURTHER PROVISION ABOUT DETERMINING ENTITLEMENT

Identifying possible eligibility

Duty to inform about possible eligibility

53.—(1) Subsection (2) applies if, in the course of their making a   7.026
determination of an individual's entitlement to assistance, it appears to the Scottish Ministers that the individual may be eligible for other assistance.

(2) The Scottish Ministers must—

(a) inform the individual that the individual may be eligible for the other assistance, and

(b) either—

(i) provide the individual with information about how to apply for it, or

(ii) if regulations under section 52 so allow, ask the individual whether they should proceed with making a determination of the individual's entitlement to the other assistance without receiving an application.

(3) Subsection (2)(b)(ii) does not preclude the Scottish Ministers from requesting further information under section 54(1) for the purpose of determining the individual's entitlement to the other assistance.

(4) In this section, "other assistance" means—

(a) a different type of assistance described in Chapter 2 from the type of assistance that the determination mentioned in subsection (1) relates to, or

(b) the same type of assistance as that determination relates to, but in respect of a different period or (as the case may be) event.

Obtaining information to make determination

Obligation to provide information on request

7.027   **54.**—(1) When—

(a) the Scottish Ministers are determining an individual's entitlement to assistance (whether under section 37 or 43), and

(b) they require further information in order to satisfy themselves about any matter material to the making of the determination, they may request that the individual provide them with the information within such period as they specify.

(2) If the individual fails to provide the requested information by the end of the specified period the Scottish Ministers may, without further consideration, proceed to make the determination on the basis that the eligibility rules prescribed in the applicable regulations are not satisfied in the individual's case (see section 50).

(3) For the avoidance of doubt, the information which the Scottish Ministers may request an individual to provide under subsection (1) includes the results of an assessment, including one which the individual has not undergone at the time the request is made.

7.028   **55.** *Not yet in force.*

Duty to notify change of circumstances

7.029   **56.**—(1) The Scottish Ministers may place a duty to notify them about a change in circumstances on a person to whom subsection (3), (4) or (5) applies.

(2) The Scottish Ministers place a duty under subsection (1) on a person by informing the person—

(a) of the changes in circumstances which the person has a duty to notify them about,

(b) of the way in which the person is to notify them, and

(c) that failing to notify them about a change in any of those circumstances in that way may be an offence under section 72.

(3) This subsection applies to an individual who is to be given assistance under section 24 under a determination made on the basis that the individual has ongoing entitlement to the type of assistance in question.

(4) This subsection applies to a person acting on behalf of an individual to whom subsection (3) applies in relation to any application for the assistance or the determination of the individual's entitlement.

(5) This subsection applies to a person to whom payments are to be made under section 24 by way of assistance to another person under a determination made on the basis that that other person has ongoing entitlement to the type of assistance in question.

Lifting of duty to notify change of circumstances

57.—(1) A duty to notify the Scottish Ministers about a change of   7.030
circumstances placed on a person under section 56 ceases to apply
when—

(a) it is lifted under subsection (2), or

(b) it stops being the case that a change in any of the circumstances to which the duty relates can affect someone's entitlement to be given assistance under section 24.

(2) The Scottish Ministers may lift a duty placed on a person under section 56 by informing the person that the duty is lifted.

(3) Under subsection (2), the Scottish Ministers may lift a duty as it relates to some or all of the changes in circumstances which the person has a duty to notify them about.

Appointees

Appointment of person to act on behalf of individual

58.—(1) The Scottish Ministers may appoint a person (an   7.031
"appointee")—

(a) to act on behalf of an individual in connection with the determination of the individual's entitlement to assistance under section 24, and

(b) to receive such assistance on the individual's behalf.

(2) The Scottish Ministers may only appoint an appointee if it appears to them that either subsection (3) or (4) applies.

(3) This subsection applies if—

(a) the individual is deceased, and

(b) there is no executor appointed on the individual's estate.

(4) This subsection applies if, in relation to the matters mentioned in subsection (1)—

(a) the individual is incapable within the meaning of the Adults with Incapacity (Scotland) Act 2000,

(b) there is no guardian acting or appointed under that Act,

(c) the individual's estate is not being administered by a judicial factor, and

(d) there is no other person who has authority to act on behalf of the individual and is willing to do so.

(5) An individual who is under 16 years may not be appointed as an appointee.

(6) Where an appointee is appointed in relation to an individual—

(a) the appointee can do anything that the individual could do in connection with the determination of the individual's entitlement to assistance (including making an application for assistance),

(b) the Scottish Ministers may request that the appointee provide them with information that they may otherwise request the individual to provide under section 54 (and subsections (2) and (3) of that section apply to that request as they apply to a request made to the individual),

(c)

any information that would be given to the individual under or by virtue of this Part must be given to the appointee instead.

(7) The Scottish Ministers may terminate an appointment under this section at any time.

Support during discussions and assessments

Right to support

7.032   **59.**—(1) The Scottish Ministers must comply with an individual's wish to have another person ("a supporter") present during any discussion or assessment relating to the individual's entitlement to a type of assistance described in Chapter 2, unless the wish is unreasonable.

(2) The Scottish Ministers' duty under subsection (1) includes ensuring that any person acting on their behalf complies with such a wish, unless the wish is unreasonable.

(3) The role of a supporter is to support the individual in question during the discussion or (as the case may be) assessment, and includes making representations on the individual's behalf.

(4) Nothing in this section is to be read as requiring the Scottish Ministers to provide or pay for a supporter.

Access to reports

7.033   **60.** *Not yet in force.*

Right to appeal Scottish Ministers' process decisions

Appeal to First-tier Tribunal against process decisions

61.—(1) An individual may appeal to the First-tier Tribunal for Scot- 7.034
land against a decision by the Scottish Ministers—
   (a) to reject something purporting to be an application for assistance
       (see section 38),
   (b) that something purporting to be a request for a re-determination
       does not satisfy the condition in section 41(3),
   (c) that an individual has no good reason for not requesting a re-
       determination sooner (see section 42).
   (2) An appeal under this section—
   (a) may be brought without the First-tier Tribunal's permission
       within the period of 31 days beginning with the day the individual
       was informed of the decision in accordance with this Act,
   (b) may be brought only with the First-tier Tribunal's permission
       after the period mentioned in paragraph (a),
   (c) may not be brought after the end of the period of one year
       beginning with the day the individual was informed of the decision
       in accordance with this Act.
   (3) The First-tier Tribunal may give permission under subsection
(2)(b) for an appeal to be made only if it is satisfied that there is a good
reason for the appeal not having been made sooner.
   (4) A decision by the First-tier Tribunal about—
   (a) the outcome of an appeal under this section, or
   (b) whether to give permission under subsection (2)(b) for an appeal
       to be brought, is final.
   (5) Accordingly (and without prejudice to the generality of subsection
(4)), any such decision by the First-tier Tribunal may be neither—
   (a) reviewed under section 43 of the Tribunals (Scotland) Act 2014,
       nor
   (b) appealed against under section 46 of that Act.

Presumption about when information is received

Presumption for purposes of sections 41, 48 and 61

62.—(1) Subsection (2) applies in relation to the references in sections 7.035
41, 48 and 61 to someone being informed of something by the Scottish
Ministers in accordance with a provision of this Act.
   (2) Where, in order to fulfil their duty to inform an individual of
something, the Scottish Ministers send information—
   (a) through the postal service to the last known address the Scottish
       Ministers have for the individual, or
   (b) by email to the email address most recently provided to the
       Scottish Ministers by the individual for the purposes of this Act,
the individual is to be taken to have received the information 48 hours
after it is sent by the Scottish Ministers unless the contrary is shown.

CHAPTER 5

RECOVERY OF VALUE OF ASSISTANCE

Assistance given in error

Liability for assistance given in error

7.036   **63.**—(1) An individual is liable to pay the Scottish Ministers the value of any assistance that was given to the individual due to an error (but see section 64).

(2) For the avoidance of doubt, the individual's liability under subsection (1) is limited to the difference in value between—

(a) the assistance that was given, and

(b) the assistance (if any) that would have been given had the error not been made.

(3) If the assistance was given in a form other than money, its value for the purposes of this section is what giving it cost the Scottish Ministers (excluding any administration costs).

(4) In this section and section 64, references to an error are to—

(a) an error in the performance of a function conferred by virtue of this Part, including a decision under section 50(1) being made—

  (i) wrongly, or

  (ii) correctly but on the basis of—

    (A) incorrect information, or

    (B) an assumption which proves to be wrong,

(b) a new decision under section 50(1) not being made after an assumption on the basis of which an earlier decision was made has proved to be wrong.

Exclusion from liability

7.037   **64.**—(1) An individual has no liability under section 63(1) in respect of assistance given due to an error if the error is neither—

(a) the individual's fault, nor

(b) the kind of error that an individual could reasonably be expected to notice.

(2) For the purpose of this section, an error is an individual's fault if it is caused or contributed to by the individual—

(a) providing false or misleading information,

(b) failing to notify the Scottish Ministers about a change in circumstances in breach of a duty to do so under section 56, or

(c) causing another person to do either of those things.

(3) In considering whether an error is of a kind that an individual could reasonably be expected to notice, the following are amongst the matters to which regard is to be had—

(a) the extent to which the value of the assistance given in error exceeds the value of the assistance that would have been given (if any) had the error not been made,

(b) whether any information given to the individual by the Scottish Ministers prior to, or immediately after, the assistance being given would have alerted a reasonable person to the fact that a decision had been, or was to be, made on the basis of incorrect information or a wrong assumption.

(4) In—

(a) subsection (2)(a), the reference to providing information includes making a statement,

(b) subsection (3)(b), the reference to information given to the individual by the Scottish Ministers does not include information explaining why the Ministers consider the assistance to have been given in error.

Consideration for debtor's circumstances

65.—(1) This section applies to decisions of the Scottish Ministers about—   7.038

(a) whether to seek to recover money owed under section 63, and

(b) the method by which money owed under that section is to be recovered.

(2) In making a decision to which this section applies, the Scottish Ministers must have regard to the financial circumstances of the individual who owes the money (so far as those circumstances are known to the Ministers).

66. *Omitted.*   7.039

Exclusion of other rights of recovery

67.—(1) An individual given assistance in error has no non-statutory   7.040 obligation based on redress of unjustified enrichment to pay the value of that assistance to the Scottish Ministers.

(2) In subsection (1)—

(a) "non-statutory obligation" means an obligation that arises from a rule of law rather than an enactment,

(b) the reference to assistance being given in error is to be construed in accordance with section 63(4).

First-tier Tribunal's jurisdiction

68.—The Scottish Ministers may by regulations transfer to the First-   7.041 tier Tribunal for Scotland some or all of the competence and jurisdiction that a sheriff has in relation to the recovery of money owed under section 63.

Liability where assistance given for period after death

69.—(1) An individual's estate is liable to pay the Scottish Ministers   7.042 the value of any assistance that was given to the individual under section 24 in respect of a period after the individual's death.

(2)For the avoidance of doubt, assistance may be regarded as having been given to an individual for the purposes of this section despite being given after the individual's death.

Funeral expense assistance

7.043   **70.** *Not yet in force.*

CHAPTER 6

OFFENCES AND INVESTIGATIONS

7.044   **71. to 76.** *Omitted*

CHAPTER 7

UPRATING FOR INFLATION

7.045   **77. to 78.** *Not yet in force*

PART 3

SUPPLEMENTING ASSISTANCE UNDER OTHER ENACTMENTS

Top up of reserved benefits

7.046   **79. to 80.** *Not yet in force.*

Carer's allowance: temporary provision

Carer's allowance supplement

7.047   **81.**—(1) The Scottish Ministers must make a payment (a "carer's allowance supplement") to qualifying individuals in respect of each of the following periods of each financial year—
    (a) 1 April to 30 September, and

166

(b) 1 October to 31 March.

(2) A qualifying individual is an individual who, on the qualifying date, was—

(a) in receipt of a carer's allowance under section 70 of the Social Security Contributions and Benefits Act 1992, and

(b) resident in Scotland.

(3) The qualifying date is a date determined by the Scottish Ministers falling within the period to which the payment relates.

(4) The amount of a carer's allowance supplement is to be calculated according to the following formula—

$$(JSA - CA) \times 26$$

where—

JSA is whichever is the higher of—

(a) the weekly amount specified in regulation 79(1)(c) of the Jobseeker's Allowance Regulations 1996 (S.I. 1996/207) as it has effect on the qualifying date, and

(b) that amount as it would have effect on the qualifying date if it were adjusted for inflation in accordance with subsection (5), and

CA is the weekly rate of carer's allowance specified in Part 3 of schedule 4 of the Social Security Contributions and Benefits Act 1992 as it has effect in Scotland on the qualifying date.

(5) The Scottish Ministers must, before the start of each new tax year, beginning with the first new tax year beginning after this section comes into force—

(a) calculate what the weekly amount specified in regulation 79(1)(c) of the Jobseeker's Allowance Regulations 1996 ("the JSA Regulations") would be if it were adjusted for inflation,

(b) publish a statement explaining how they have calculated inflation for this purpose.

(6) In calculating the amount for the purpose of subsection (5)(a), the Scottish Ministers may take account of any change in the weekly amount specified in regulation 79(1)(c) of the JSA Regulations since this section came into force.

(7) For the purposes of subsection (5), a tax year means a period beginning with 6 April in one year and ending with 5 April in the next.

(8) The Scottish Ministers may by regulations modify this section so as to modify who is a qualifying individual for the purposes of this section.

GENERAL NOTE

This section came into force on September 3, 2018 (see Social Security **7.048** (Scotland) Act 2018 (Commencement No.1) Regulations 2018 (SSI 2018/250), regs.2(1) and 3). It gives effect to the Scottish government's intention to provide carers with a supplement, so that the amount of carer's allowance that a person in Scotland receives on an annual basis will effectively be the same as the person would receive had they been in receipt of uprated JSA. Section 81 thus imposes a statutory duty on the Scottish Ministers to pay a supplement on a twice-yearly basis to persons who receive carer's allowance in Scotland (subs.(1)). Ministers are to determine a "qualifying date" in each half of the financial year (subs.(3)), and persons who are receiving carer's allowance on that date, and who are resident in Scotland, will receive the supplement (subs.(2)). Ministers are given the power to modify these two latter criteria (subs.(8)).

The section provides for calculation of the supplement (subs.(4)), which is designed to reflect the difference between the rate at which carer's allowance is paid and the rate of JSA, adjusted for inflation as described in subs.(5) (and if necessary by uprating: subs.(6)). At the time of writing the rate of JSA is not being uprated annually for inflation by the UK Government. Subsection (5) requires the Scottish Ministers to publish an uprated figure before the start of each tax year (defined by subs.(7)). Each payment will be the equivalent of 26 times the difference between the two figures (carer's allowance and uprated JSA) on the qualifying date (subs.(4)) – this is currently £221 each 6 months, and so £442 annually. In 2018/19 the first tranche of payments was made in September/ October 2018 (in effect backdated to April 2018) and the second in December 2018.

Payments of the carer's supplement are made automatically without the need for an individual claim. The Scottish Government has agreed with HMRC that the supplement will not count as income for tax credit purposes. However, carers who have an underlying entitlement to carer's allowance, and so do not receive a payment because they are in receipt of another benefit at the same or higher rate, do not qualify for the supplement.

The Scottish Government's long-term plan is to introduce a new benefit in Scotland, carer's assistance under s.28 of this Act, which will be paid at the same rate as JSA and income support. Once that new benefit is in place, the need for this supplement will disappear (hence s.82 below).

Power to repeal temporary provision

7.049   **82.**—(1) The Scottish Ministers may by regulations—
(a) repeal section 81 and revoke any regulations made under it, and
(b) repeal this section.

GENERAL NOTE

7.050   This section enables the Scottish Ministers to repeal the duty under s.81 above to pay the carer's allowance supplement and revoke any regulations made under it. This will enable the statute book to be 'tidied up' by the removal of the carer's allowance supplement provisions at the point when the supplement is no longer needed (as a result of the planned new Scottish benefit, carer's assistance, going live when s.28 is brought into force).

PART 4

FURTHER PROVISION IN CONNECTION WITH PARTS 2 AND 3

7.051   **83. to 85.** *Omitted.*
86. *Not yet in force.*
87. *Omitted.*

PART 5

DISCRETIONARY HOUSING PAYMENTS

88. to 93. *Not yet in force.*   7.052

PART 6

UNIVERSAL CREDIT: PAYMENT TO JOINT CLAIMANTS

94. *Not yet in force.*   7.053

PART 7

FINAL PROVISIONS

Ancillary provision

95.—The Scottish Ministers may by regulations make any incidental,   7.054
supplementary, consequential, transitional, transitory or saving provision they consider appropriate for the purposes of, or in connection with,
or for giving full effect to this Act or any provision made under it.

Regulation-making powers

96.—(1) A power to make regulations conferred by this Act includes   7.055
the power to make different provision for different purposes and areas.

(2) Regulations under any of the following provisions are subject to the
affirmative procedure: sections 11, 13, 22(1)(e), any section in Chapter
2 of Part 2 and sections 51, 52, 68, 75, 79, 81(8), 82, 85(2)(g) and (5),
86 and 93 and paragraph 4(2)(c) of schedule 1.

(3) Regulations under any of the following provisions are subject to the
negative procedure: sections 41(4)(a) and 43(5) and paragraph 13(2) of
schedule 1.

(4) Regulations under section 95—

(a) are subject to the affirmative procedure if they add to, replace or
    omit any part of the text of an Act (including this Act), but

(b) otherwise are subject to the negative procedure.

(5) Regulations under section 22(1)(e), which modify the functions of
the Scottish Commission on Social Security, may not be made after the
Commission is established unless the Scottish Ministers have consulted
the Commission about the modification.

97. to 98. *Omitted.*   7.056

Commencement

7.057   **99.**—(1) The following provisions come into force on the day after Royal Assent: this section and sections 95, 96, 97, 98 and 100.

(2) The other provisions of this Act come into force on such day as the Scottish Ministers may by regulations appoint.

(3) The power conferred by subsection (2) includes the power to make transitional, transitory or saving provision.

Short title

7.058   **100.**—The short title of this Act is the Social Security (Scotland) Act 2018.

7.059   **Schedules 1 to 5** *Not yet in force.*

SCHEDULE 6

(introduced by section 32)

EARLY YEARS ASSISTANCE REGULATIONS

PART 1

ELIGIBILITY

CHAPTER 1

ELIGIBILITY IS TO DEPEND ON HAVING, OR EXPECTING TO HAVE, RESPONSIBILITY FOR A CHILD

7.060   1 (1) The regulations must be framed so that an individual's eligibility depends on the individual satisfying one of the primary eligibility criteria.

(2) The primary eligibility criteria are that the individual—

(a) is, or has been, more than a specified number of weeks pregnant,

(b) has a relationship of a specified kind to another individual who is, or has been, more than a specified number of weeks pregnant,

(c) is to, or has, become responsible for a child within a specified period of the child's birth,

(d) is responsible for a child when a specified event in the child's life occurs or has become responsible for the child within a specified period of the event.

(3) The regulations are to define what being responsible for a child means for the purpose of determining entitlement to early years assistance.

CHAPTER 2

FURTHER CRITERIA

Limit to number of people entitled

7.061   2 The regulations may provide that an individual is not eligible, despite satisfying one of the primary eligibility criteria, on account of one of those criteria being satisfied in respect of the same child by someone else.

Residence and presence

3 The regulations may make an individual's eligibility depend on the individual being resident and present in a particular place.

Financial circumstances

4 The regulations may make an individual's eligibility depend on the individual's financial circumstances.

Receipt of, or eligibility for, other types of State assistance

5 The regulations may make an individual's eligibility depend on the individual—

(a) being, or not being, in receipt of another type of assistance (whether under this Act or another enactment),

(b) being, or not being, eligible or entitled to receive such assistance.

Application within specified period
6 The regulations may provide that an individual ceases to be eligible on account of satisfying a primary eligibility criteria unless, by a deadline specified in the regulations—
(a) the individual has applied for early years assistance, or
(b) the Scottish Ministers have become required to make a determination of the individual's entitlement to early years assistance by regulations under section 35.

PART 2

ASSISTANCE TO BE GIVEN

Restriction on giving assistance in a form other than money
7(1) The regulations may allow early years assistance to be given to an individual in a form other than money only if the individual (or a person acting on the individual's behalf) has agreed to the assistance being given in that form.   **7.062**

(2) If the regulations include provision of the kind mentioned in sub-paragraph (1), they must allow an individual (or a person acting on the individual's behalf) to withdraw agreement to being given early years assistance in a form other than money at any time.

PART 3

FINAL PROVISIONS

Generality of enabling power unaffected
8 Nothing in this schedule, apart from the following provisions, is to be taken to limit what may be prescribed in the regulations—   **7.063**
(a) Chapter 1 of Part 1,
(b) Part 2.

Interpretation
9 In this schedule—
"eligibility" means eligibility for early years assistance and "eligible" means eligible for early years assistance,
"the regulations" means regulations under section 32(2),
"specified" means specified in the regulations.

Schedules 7 to 10 *Not yet in force.*   **7.064**

The Early Years Assistance (Best Start Grants) (Scotland) Regulations 2018

(SSI 2018/370)

Made	*9th December 2018*
Coming into force	*10th December 2018*

7.065 The Scottish Ministers make the following Regulations in exercise of the powers conferred by sections 32(2), 41(4)(a), 43(5) and 52 of the Social Security (Scotland) Act 2018 and all other powers enabling them to do so.

In accordance with section 96 of that Act, a draft of these Regulations has been laid before and approved by resolution of the Scottish Parliament.

PART 1

INTRODUCTION

Citation

7.066   **1.** These Regulations may be cited as the Early Years Assistance (Best Start Grants) (Scotland) Regulations 2018.

Commencement

7.067   **2.** These Regulations come into force on the day after the day they are made.

Overview

7.068   **3.**—(1) Part 2 makes provision about the interpretation of these Regulations.

(2) Schedule 1 makes provision about matters of procedure for determining entitlement to early years assistance.

(3) Schedule 2 makes provision about the early years assistance that is to be given in connection with having, or expecting to have, a new baby in the family (referred to in these Regulations as "pregnancy and baby grant").

PART 2

INTERPRETATION

Expressions about time and timing

When an application is to be treated as made

7.069   **4.**—(1) An application is to be treated as made—

(a) on the day it is received by the Scottish Ministers; or

(b) if applicable, on—
    (i) the day chosen by the Scottish Ministers in accordance with paragraph(3); or
    (ii) the day the applicant nominates (or is deemed to have nominated) under regulation5.

(2) In a case where a determination is to be, or has been, made without an application (see Part 2 of schedule 1) references in these Regulations to the day the application is made are to be read as references to the day the determination is made.

(3) If, before making a determination on the basis of an application, the Scottish Ministers consider that the applicant—

(a) would not be eligible for the assistance applied for if the application were treated as made on the day they received it; and

(b) would be eligible for the assistance if the application were treated as made on a day falling within the period of 10 days beginning with the day they received it,

the Scottish Ministers may choose the day within that 10 day period on which the application is to be treated as made.

(4) For the avoidance of doubt, a thing that purports to be an application is not an application unless it is—

(a) made in the form; and

(b) accompanied by the evidence,

required under section 38 of the Social Security (Scotland) Act 2018.

Late application: nomination of date

5.—(1) An applicant may nominate the date on which an application will be treated as made by virtue of regulation 4(1)(b)(ii) if—   7.070

(a) the award of universal credit or assistance of a kind specified in regulation 11 that the applicant is relying on to meet the relevant eligibility condition is a backdated award;

(b) the backdated award is an award of assistance for—
    (i) a day that falls within the application window; or
    (ii) a period that includes at least 1 day that falls within the application window; and

(c) the application is received by the Scottish Ministers—
    (i) not more than 20 working days after the last day of the application window; and
    (ii) within 3 months of the applicant being informed of the backdated award by or on behalf of the public authority who made it.

(2) If the backdated award is for—

(a) 1 day only; or

(b) a period and only 1 day of it falls within the application window,

the applicant may only nominate that day under this regulation.

(3) If—

(a) the backdated award is for a period; and

(b) more than 1 day of the period falls within the application window, the applicant may nominate any of those days under this regulation.

(4) If the applicant is entitled to nominate a day under this regulation but has not done so, the applicant is to be deemed to have nominated—

(a) the only day the applicant could have nominated in accordance with paragraph (2); or

(b) the latest day the applicant could have nominated in accordance with paragraph (3).

(5) In this regulation—

"application window" means—

(a) in relation to an application for a pregnancy and baby grant, the period that—

(i) begins on the day the child in question is born; and

(ii) ends with the deadline set by paragraph 2 of schedule 2;

"backdated award" means an award of assistance for a day, or a period that begins on a day, that falls before the day the decision to make the award was taken;

"the relevant eligibility condition" means—

(a) in relation to an application for a pregnancy and baby grant, the eligibility condition in paragraph 1(e) of schedule 2;

"working day" means a day other than—

(a) a Saturday;

(b) a Sunday; or

(c) a bank holiday in Scotland under the Banking and Financial Dealings Act 1971.

Meaning of "birthday", for children born on 29th February

7.071   **6.** In a non-leap year, the birthday of a child born on 29th February is to be taken to be 28th February.

Calculations involving months

7.072   **7.**—(1) Where a day ("day 1") is described as falling a specified number of months before or after another day ("day 2"), the date of day 1 is to be determined as follows.

(2) Count backwards or forwards (as the case may be) the specified number of months from the month in which day 2 falls.

(3) If the month arrived at in accordance with paragraph (2) has a day corresponding to day 2, day 1 is that day of the month arrived at.

(4) If the month arrived at in accordance with paragraph (2) has too few days to have a day corresponding to day 2, day 1 is the last day of the month arrived at.

GENERAL NOTE

7.073   In the Queen's Printer's copy of the Regulations, a footnote to reg.7(4) says—

"For example, if a child is born on 31st August, the day falling 6 months after the day the child is born is 28th February (or 29th February in a leap year)."

174

Expressions about inter-personal relationships

Meaning of "partner"

8. An individual is to be regarded as the partner of another individual 7.074
on a day only if, on that day, the two individuals would be regarded as a
couple for the purposes of Part 1 of the Welfare Reform Act 2012 (see
section 39 of that Act).

Meaning of being responsible for a child

9.—(1) An individual is to be regarded as responsible for a child on a 7.075
day only if at least one of the following statements is true:—
  (a) the child is a dependant of the individual on the day in ques-
      tion;
  (b) the individual is one of the child's parents and, on the day in
      question—
      (i) normally lives with the child;
      (ii) is under 20 years of age; and
      (iii) is a dependant of another individual;
  (c) the child is, on the day in question, treated in law as the child of
      the individual by virtue of an order under section 54 of the
      Human Fertilisation and Embryology Act 2008;
  (d) the child is, on the day in question, treated in law as the child of
      the individual by reason of an adoption either—
      (i) effected under the law of Scotland; or
      (ii) effected under the law of another country or jurisdiction and
           recognised by the law of Scotland;
  (e) the child is, on the day in question, placed with the individual by
      an adoption agency;
  (f) the individual is, on the day in question, a guardian of the child
      appointed by deed, will or by a court;
  (g) the individual is, on the day in question, a kinship carer for the
      child.
  (2) In paragraph (1)(e), "adoption agency" means—
  (a) a local authority acting in its capacity as an adoption service
      provider under section 1 of the Adoption and Children (Scotland)
      Act 2007;
  (b) an adoption service provided as mentioned in paragraph 8(1)(b)
      of schedule 12 of the Public Services Reform (Scotland) Act 2010
      and registered under Part 5 of that Act;
  (c) an adoption agency within the meaning of section 2(1) of the
      Adoption and Children Act 2002;
  (d) an adoption agency within the meaning of article 3 of the Adop-
      tion (Northern Ireland) Order 1987.
  (3) For the purpose of paragraph (1)(g), an individual is a kinship
carer for a child on a day if—
  (a) the individual is a qualifying person in relation to the child within
      the meaning of section 72(2) of the Children and Young People
      (Scotland) Act 2014, and

(b) on the day in question, the child lives with the individual (exclusively or predominantly) under the terms of—
    (i) a kinship care order as defined in section 72(1) of the Children and Young People (Scotland) Act 2014, or
    (ii) an agreement between the individual, the individual's partner or both of them and—
        (aa) a local authority by which the child is looked after within the meaning of section 17(6) of the Children (Scotland) Act 1995;
        (bb) a local authority in England or Wales by which the child is looked after within the meaning of section 105(4) of the Children Act 1989; or
        (cc) an authority in Northern Ireland by which the child is looked after within the meaning of article 25 of the Children (Northern Ireland) Order 1995.

Meaning of "dependant"

7.076   **10.**—(1) An individual ("person A") is to be regarded as the dependant of another individual ("person B") on a day only if—
    (a) person B has been awarded—
        (i) child tax credit or child benefit for the day in question (or for a period that includes that day); or
        (ii) universal credit for—
            (aa) the assessment period that includes the day in question; or
            (bb) the assessment period that ended immediately before the assessment period mentioned in paragraph (aa) started; and
    (b) person A is recognised to be a dependant of person B in the terms of that award of assistance.

(2) It is immaterial for the purpose of this regulation that the award of assistance to person B does not include any amount in respect of person A due to a rule that restricts the number of dependants in respect of whom person B can be given that type of assistance.

Expressions about social security assistance

Meaning of references to specified kinds of assistance

7.077   **11.** References in these Regulations to a kind of assistance specified in this regulation are to the following:—
    (a) child tax credit;
    (b) housing benefit;
    (c) income-based jobseeker's allowance;
    (d) income-related employment and support allowance;
    (e) income support;
    (f) state pension credit;
    (g) working tax credit.

Meaning of references to assistance being awarded

12.—(1) An individual is not to be regarded as having been awarded   7.078
a kind of assistance for a day or a period if—
    (a) the award was made in error (whether or not induced by the
        individual); or
    (b) the sum awarded to the individual for the day or the period is
        £0.

(2) In sub-paragraph (1)(b), the reference to "the sum awarded"
means, in a case where a deduction has been made—
    (a) in respect of any liability the individual has to another person;
        or
    (b) by way of a sanction,
the sum that would have been awarded had the deduction not been
made.

(3) For the avoidance of doubt, in sub-paragraph (1) "kind of assistance" includes universal credit as well as the kinds of assistance specified in regulation 11.

Meaning of "assessment period" in relation to universal credit

13. "Assessment period" means a period in respect of which universal   7.079
credit may be payable to the individual in question in accordance with
section 7 of the Welfare Reform Act 2012.

Regulation 3(2)

SCHEDULE 1

Procedural matters

PART 1

Re-determination timescales

Deadline for requesting re-determination
1. The period for requesting a re-determination of entitlement to early years assistance   7.080
under section 41 of the Social Security (Scotland) Act 2018 is 31 days beginning with the
day that the individual is informed, in accordance with section 40 of that Act, of the right
to make the request.

Period allowed for re-determination
2.—(1) In relation to determining entitlement to early years assistance, the period
allowed for re-determination (within the meaning of section 43 of the Social Security
(Scotland) Act 2018) is 16 working days beginning with the day that the request for a
re-determination is received by the Scottish Ministers.
    (2) For the purpose of this paragraph, a "working day" is a day other than—
    (a) a Saturday;
    (b) a Sunday; or
    (c) a bank holiday in Scotland under the Banking and Financial Dealings Act 1971.

PART 2

Determination without application

Determination following application in connection with another child
3.—(1) The Scottish Ministers are to make a determination of an individual's entitle-   7.081
ment to early years assistance in connection with a child (without receiving an application)
in the circumstances described in sub-paragraph (2).

(2) The circumstance referred to in sub-paragraph (1) is that—

(a) the individual has applied for early years assistance in respect of a child; and

(b) it appears to the Scottish Ministers from the available information that, unless circumstances change, the individual will become eligible for early years assistance in respect of another child within the period—

  (i) beginning on the day the application is made; and

  (ii) ending at the end of the day that falls 10 days later.

(3) The determination that sub-paragraph (1) requires to be made is to be made on, or as soon as reasonably practicable after, the day that the Scottish Ministers anticipate will be the day on which the individual first becomes eligible for early years assistance in respect of the child as mentioned in sub-paragraph (2)(b).

(4) The determination that sub-paragraph (1) requires to be made is to be made (subject to sub-paragraph (5)) on the basis that whatever can be discerned from the available information to have been the case on the day the application mentioned in sub-paragraph (2)(a) was made remains the case on the day the determination is made.

(5) A determination is not to be made on the basis of the assumption set out in sub-paragraph (4) if, and to the extent that, the Scottish Ministers have information suggesting the assumption is unsound.

(6) In this paragraph, "the available information" means—

(a) the information provided in the application referred to in sub-paragraph (2)(a); and

(b) any other information obtained by the Scottish Ministers in connection with that application.

Regulation 3(3)

SCHEDULE 2

Pregnancy and baby grant

PART 1

Eligibility

Eligibility

7.082   **1.** An individual is eligible for a pregnancy and baby grant in respect of a child if—

(a) the individual's application for the grant is made before the deadline set by paragraph 2 (see regulation 4 in relation to when an application is to be treated as made);

(b) no-one else has received, or is due to receive, a pregnancy and baby grant or sure start maternity grant in respect of the child (but see paragraph 3);

(c) on the day the application is made the individual satisfies the residence requirement set by paragraph 4;

(d) at least one of these statements is true on the day the application is made—

  (i) the individual is the person who—

    (aa) is, or has been, more than 24 weeks pregnant with the child; or

    (bb) gave birth to the child before or during the 24th week of the pregnancy;

  (ii) the individual is the partner of the person described by head (i);

  (iii) the person described by head (i) is a dependant of the individual or the individual's partner (or both of them);

  (iv) either the individual or the individual's partner is (or both of them are) responsible for the child on the day the application is made;

(e) at least one of these statements is true—

  (i) the individual or the individual's partner has (or both of them have) been awarded, for the day the application is made (or for a period which includes that day), assistance of a kind specified in regulation 11;

  (ii) the individual or the individual's partner has (or both of them have) been awarded universal credit for—

    (aa) the assessment period that includes the day the application is made; or

    (bb) the assessment period that ended immediately before the assessment period mentioned in sub-head (aa) started;

    (iii) on the day the application is made the individual is under 18 years of age;

    (iv) on the day the application is made the individual is—

        (aa) 18 or 19 years of age; and

        (bb) a dependant of another individual; and

(f) the child is not, on the day the application is made, living in a residential establishment as defined in section 202(1) of the Children's Hearings (Scotland) Act 2011.

Deadline for applying

2.—(1) The deadline for an individual to apply for a pregnancy and baby grant in respect of a child is—   **7.083**

  (a) the end of the day that falls 6 months after the day the child is born if sub-paragraph (2) applies to the individual;

  (b) the end of the day before the child's first birthday if sub-paragraph (2) does not apply to the individual.

(2) This sub-paragraph applies to—

  (a) the person who is, or has been, pregnant with the child; and

  (b) any individual who is, or has been during the period described by sub-paragraph (3)—

    (i) the partner of the person referred to in paragraph (a); or

    (ii) an individual, or the partner of an individual, for whom the person referred to in paragraph (a) is a dependant.

(3) The period referred to in sub-paragraph (2)(b)—

    (i) begins on the first day of the 24th week of the pregnancy that resulted, or is to result, in the child's birth; and

    (ii) ends at the end of the day that falls 6 months after the day the child is born.

Exception to paragraph 1(b)

3.—(1) For the purpose of determining the entitlement of the individual referred to in this paragraph as the applicant, the eligibility condition in paragraph 1(b) is to be ignored in the circumstance described by sub-paragraphs (2) to (5).   **7.084**

(2) An individual ("the first grant recipient") has been, or is due to be, given in respect of the child—

  (a) a pregnancy and baby grant; or

  (b) a sure start maternity grant.

(3) Another individual ("the applicant") first came to be responsible for the child after—

  (a) the first grant recipient applied for a pregnancy and baby grant or a sure start maternity grant in respect of the child; or

  (b) a decision about the first grant recipient's entitlement to such a grant was taken by, or on behalf of, the public authority responsible for giving them (despite no application for a grant having been made).

(4) Since first coming to be responsible for the child, the applicant has not been—

  (a) the partner of the first grant recipient;

  (b) a dependant of the first grant recipient; or

  (c) an individual, or the partner of an individual, for whom the first grant recipient is a dependant.

(5) On the day the applicant's application for a pregnancy and baby grant in respect of the child is made, no-one other than the first grant recipient has been, or is due to be, given a pregnancy and baby grant or a sure start maternity grant in respect of that child.

Residence requirement

4.—(1) The residence requirement referred to in paragraph 1(c) is satisfied by an individual on a day if, on that day—   **7.085**

  (a) the individual is ordinarily resident in Scotland; and

  (b) in a case where neither the individual nor the individual's partner has been awarded assistance as mentioned in paragraph 1(e)(i) or (ii), the condition set by sub-paragraph (2) is also met.

(2) The condition referred to in sub-paragraph (1)(b) is met on any day that the individual is—

  (a) habitually resident in the European Economic Area or Switzerland;

(b) a refugee within the definition in Article 1 of the Convention relating to the status of refugees done at Geneva on 28th July 1951, as extended by article 1(2) of the Protocol relating to the status of refugees done at New York on 31st January 1967;

(c) a person who has been granted, or who is deemed to have been granted, leave outside the rules made under section 3(2) of the Immigration Act 1971, where that leave is—

(i) discretionary leave to enter or remain in the United Kingdom;

(ii) leave to remain under the destitution domestic violence concession; or

(iii) leave deemed to have been granted by virtue of regulation 3 of the Displaced Persons (Temporary Protection) Regulations 2005;

(d) a person who has humanitarian protection granted under the rules made under section 3(2) of the Immigration Act 1971; or

(e) a person who—

(i) is not subject to immigration control within the meaning of section 115(9) of the Immigration and Asylum Act 1999; and

(ii) is in the United Kingdom as a result of deportation, expulsion or other removal by compulsion of law from another country to the United Kingdom.

PART 2

ASSISTANCE TO BE GIVEN

Value of grant

7.086 **5.** The value of a pregnancy and baby grant is—

(a) the basic amount determined in accordance with paragraph 6; and

(b) any amount that falls to be added to the basic amount by way of a multiple pregnancy supplement (see paragraph 7).

The basic amount

7.087 **6.**—(1) The basic amount is—

(a) £600 if sub-paragraph (2) applies in relation to the child in respect of whom the grant is to be given; or

(b) £300 if it does not.

(2) This sub-paragraph applies in relation to the child (subject to sub-paragraph (3)) if, on the day the application for the grant is made—

(a) there is no-one under 16 years of age living in the same household as the individual to whom the grant is to be given; or

(b) if there is, that person is (or all of those persons are) one of the following—

(i) the child;

(ii) a sibling of the child born as a result of the same pregnancy that resulted in the child's birth;

(iii) a parent of the child;

(iv) a sibling of a parent of the child;

(v) a child for whom the individual is not responsible.

(3) Where more than one child is born, or is to be born, as a result of the same pregnancy—

(a) sub-paragraph (2) applies in relation to only one of the children; and

(b) it is for the Scottish Ministers to decide which.

Multiple pregnancy supplement

7.088 **7.**—(1) Subject to sub-paragraphs (2) and (3) a supplement of £300 is to be added to the basic amount in respect of a child born, or to be born, as a result of a multiple pregnancy.

(2) The supplement is to be added to the grant in respect of only one of the children born, or to be born, as a result of the pregnancy, and it is for the Scottish Ministers to decide which child's grant to supplement.

(3) No supplement is to be added if the individual to whom the grant is to be given—

(a) has not applied for a pregnancy and baby grant in respect of all of the children born, or to be born, as a result of the pregnancy; or

(b) is not eligible for a pregnancy and baby grant in respect of any of those children.

Form in which grant is given

8.—(1) Subject to sub-paragraph (2), a pregnancy and baby grant is to be given as money.   **7.089**

(2) If—

(a) the Scottish Ministers offer to give an individual some or all of the value of a pregnancy and baby grant in a form other than money; and

(b) the individual agrees to be given the grant in that form,

the grant is to be given in that form, unless the individual withdraws agreement before the grant is given.

PART 3

INTERPRETATION

Meaning of "child", "birth" and "born"

9.—(1) In this schedule, except in paragraph 1(d)(i)(bb)—   **7.090**

"child" includes still-born child;

"birth" includes still-birth and "born" is to be construed accordingly;

"still-born child" and "still-birth" have the meanings given in section 56(1) of the Registration of Births, Deaths and Marriages (Scotland) Act 1965.

(2) Sub-paragraph (1) also applies for the purpose of interpreting—

(a) the definition of "application window" in regulation 5(5) (which relates to the nomination of a date on which an application for assistance is to be treated as having been made); and

(b) paragraph 3 of schedule 1 (which describes circumstances in which a determination of entitlement is to be made by the Scottish Ministers without an application).

Meaning of "sure start maternity grant"

10. In this schedule, "sure start maternity grant" means a payment under—   **7.091**

(a) regulation 5(1) of the Social Fund Maternity and Funeral Expenses (General) Regulations 2005; or

(b) regulation 5(1) of the Social Fund Maternity and Funeral Expenses (General) Regulations (Northern Ireland) 2005.

Tribunals (Scotland) Act 2014

(2014 asp 10)

CONTENTS

PART 1

THE SCOTTISH TRIBUNALS

CHAPTER 1

ESTABLISHMENT AND LEADERSHIP

Establishment and headship etc.

PART 6

REVIEW OR APPEAL OF DECISIONS

CHAPTER 1

TRIBUNAL DECISIONS

Internal review

Appeal from First-tier Tribunal

Appeal from Upper Tribunal

Excluded decisions

Miscellaneous procedure

CHAPTER 2

SPECIAL JURISDICTION

PART 7

POWERS, PROCEDURE AND ADMINISTRATION

CHAPTER 1

POWERS AND ENFORCEMENT

Cases and proceedings

CHAPTER 2

PRACTICE AND PROCEDURE

Tribunal Rules

Particular matters

Issuing directions

CHAPTER 3

FEES AND ADMINISTRATION

PART 8

FINAL PROVISIONS

General and ancillary

Interpretation, commencement and short title

The Bill for this Act of the Scottish Parliament was passed by the Parliament on 11th March 2014 and received Royal Assent on 15th April 2014

An Act of the Scottish Parliament to establish the First-tier Tribunal for Scotland and the Upper Tribunal for Scotland; and for connected purposes.

CHAPTER 1

Establishment and leadership

Establishment and headship etc.

Establishment of the Tribunals

1.—(1) There are established two tribunals to be known as—   7.093
(a) the First-tier Tribunal for Scotland,
(b) the Upper Tribunal for Scotland.
(2) The Tribunals mentioned in subsection (1) are referred to in this Act—
(a) respectively as—
    (i) the First-tier Tribunal,
    (ii) the Upper Tribunal,

(b) collectively as the Scottish Tribunals.

(3) The constitution, operation and administration of the Scottish Tribunals are as provided for by or under this Act or another Act.

(4) The jurisdiction, powers and other functions of the Scottish Tribunals are as conferred by or under this Act or another Act.

GENERAL NOTE

7.094   This section establishes the Scottish Tribunals which, despite their names being the same and their structure similar, are entirely separate from the First-tier Tribunal and Upper Tribunal constituted under s.3 of the Tribunals, Courts and Enforcement Act 2007 (see Vol. III of the main work). The Lord President of the Court of Session is the Head of the Scottish Tribunals but there is also a President of Tribunals. The Lord President has assigned Lady Smith to that role.

The First-tier Tribunal for Scotland is divided into six chambers (see the First-tier Tribunal for Scotland (Chambers) Regulations 2016 (SSI 2016/341, as amended by SI 2018/349), although only five of them have been brought into operation. The social security functions of the First-tier Tribunal, which are the functions conferred on it by the Social Security (Scotland) Act 2018 and by regulations made under that Act, are allocated to the Social Security Chamber (see reg.3 of the First-tier Tribunal for Scotland (Allocation of Functions to the Social Security Chamber) Regulations 2018 (SSI 2018/350)). Currently, those functions are confined to determining appeals under ss. 46 and 61 of the 2018 Act that relate to pregnancy and baby grants and so all appeals are determined by a "legal member" sitting alone (see regs. 2(1) and 3 of the First-tier Tribunal for Scotland Social Security Chamber and Upper Tribunal for Scotland (Composition) Regulations 2018 (SSI 2018/351)). Its jurisdiction will expand as other forms of assistance under the 2018 Act are introduced and, in due course, it is expected to take over the social security functions exercised in Scotland by the First-tier Tribunal constituted under the 2007 Act.

Regulation 4 of the Allocations of Functions Regulations provides –

"The First-tier Tribunal Social Security Chamber may consider all aspects of a determination or a decision which it is called upon to consider, in exercising the functions allocated to it by regulation 3, and not only the particular aspect challenged by the party appealing against the determination or decision."

The Social Security Appeals (Expenses and Allowances) (Scotland) Regulations 2018 (SSI 2018/275) provide that the Scottish Courts and Tribunals Service may pay a party and any witness cited to attend a hearing expenses in respect of travel and subsistence and allowances for loss of remunerative time, reasonably incurred as a result of attending a hearing before either the First-tier Tribunal or the Upper Tribunal in a social security case. They are paid at such level, and under such circumstances, as the Scottish Ministers may determine.

The Upper Tribunal for Scotland hears appeals from the First-tier Tribunal, but note that there is no right of appeal to the Upper Tribunal against a decision made by the First-tier Tribunal on an appeal under s.61 of the Social Security (Scotland) Act 2018 against a process decision (see s.61(5)(b)). The Court of Session may transfer judicial review proceedings to the Upper Tribunal under s.57 of the 2014 Act but, as under the 2007 Act in relation to judicial review proceedings brought under the law of Scotland, judicial review proceedings cannot be commenced in the Upper Tribunal.

7.095   **2. to 42.** *Omitted.*

PART 6

Review or appeal of decisions

CHAPTER 1

Tribunal decisions

Internal review

Review of decisions

43.—(1) Each of the First-tier Tribunal and the Upper Tribunal may review a decision made by it in any matter in a case before it.   7.096

(2) A decision is reviewable—

(a) at the Tribunal's own instance, or

(b) at the request of a party in the case.

(3) But—

(a) there can be no review under this section of an excluded decision,

(b) Tribunal Rules may make provision—

  (i) excluding other decisions from a review under this section,

  (ii) otherwise restricting the availability of a review under this section (including by specifying grounds for a review).

(4) The exercise of discretion whether a decision should be reviewed under this section cannot give rise to a review under this section or to an appeal under section 46 or 48.

(5) A right of appeal under section 46 or 48 is not affected by the availability or otherwise of a review under this section.

General Note

This power of review is excluded in the case of appeals to the First-tier Tribunal against process decisions regarding social security (see s.61(5)(a) of the Social Security (Scotland) Act 2018) and in the case of refusals of permission to appeal to the Upper Tribunal or the Court of Session (see s.55(2)(a) of this Act). Moreover, ss. 51 and 52 have the effect that a decision cannot be reviewed twice (see also s.45) and that most decisions in reviews are not themselves reviewable because they are "excluded decisions" for the purpose of s.43(3)(a).   7.097

Actions on review

44.—(1) In a review by the First-tier Tribunal or the Upper Tribunal under section 43, the Tribunal may—   7.098

(a) take no action,

(b) set the decision aside, or

(c) correct a minor or accidental error contained in the decision.

(2) Where a decision is set aside by the First-tier Tribunal in a review, it may—

(a) re-decide the matter concerned,

(b) refer that matter to the Upper Tribunal, or

(c) make such other order as the First-tier Tribunal considers appropriate.

(3) If a decision set aside by the First-tier Tribunal in a review is referred to the Upper Tribunal, the Upper Tribunal—

(a) may re-decide the matter concerned or make such other order as it considers appropriate,

(b) in re-deciding that matter, may do anything that the First-tier Tribunal could do if re-deciding it.

(4) Where a decision is set aside by the Upper Tribunal in a review, it may—

(a) re-decide the matter concerned, or

(b) make such other order as it considers appropriate.

(5) In re-deciding a matter under this section, the First-tier or Upper Tribunal may reach such findings in fact as it considers appropriate.

Review once only

7.099 **45.**—(1) A particular decision of the First-tier Tribunal or the Upper Tribunal may not be reviewed under section 43 more than once.

(2) These are to be regarded as different decisions for the purpose of subsection (1)—

(a) a decision set aside under section 44(1)(b),

(b) a decision made by virtue of section 44(2)(a), (3)(a) or (4).

(3) Nothing in this section prevents the taking, after a review in which the decision concerned is not set aside, of administrative steps by the First-tier or Upper Tribunal to correct a minor or accidental error made in disposing of the review.

Appeal from First-tier Tribunal

Appeal from the Tribunal

7.100 **46.**—(1) A decision of the First-tier Tribunal in any matter in a case before the Tribunal may be appealed to the Upper Tribunal.

(2) An appeal under this section is to be made—

(a) by a party in the case,

(b) on a point of law only.

(3) An appeal under this section requires the permission of—

(a) the First-tier Tribunal, or

(b) if the First-tier Tribunal refuses its permission, the Upper Tribunal.

(4) Such permission may be given in relation to an appeal under this section only if the First-tier Tribunal or (as the case may be) the Upper Tribunal is satisfied that there are arguable grounds for the appeal.

(5) This section—

(a) is subject to sections 43(4) and 55(2),

(b) does not apply in relation to an excluded decision.

GENERAL NOTE

This right of appeal is excluded in the case of appeals to the First-tier Tribunal 7.101
against process decisions regarding social security (see s.61(5)(b) of the Social
Security (Scotland) Act 2018) and in the case of refusals by the First-tier
Tribunal of permission to appeal to the Upper Tribunal (see s.55(2)(b) of this
Act, in which the reference to this section is perhaps unnecessary since the
remedy for being refused permission to appeal to the Upper Tribunal by the
First-tier Tribunal is simply to apply to the Upper Tribunal for permission to
appeal against the substantive decision of the First-tier Tribunal and so one
might expect any challenge to the refusal of permission to be treated simply as a
challenge to the substantive decision). In addition, ss. 51 and 52 have the effect
that a decision that has been reviewed and most decisions in reviews are
"excluded decisions" for the purpose of s.46(5)(b) and s.43(4) provides that the
exercise of discretion whether a decision should be reviewed cannot give rise to
an appeal.

Disposal of an appeal

47.—(1) In an appeal under section 46, the Upper Tribunal may 7.102
uphold or quash the decision on the point of law in question.

(2) If the Upper Tribunal quashes the decision, it may—

(a) re-make the decision,

(b) remit the case to the First-tier Tribunal, or

(c) make such other order as the Upper Tribunal considers appropriate.

(3) In re-making the decision, the Upper Tribunal may—

(a) do anything that the First-tier Tribunal could do if re-making the
decision,

(b) reach such findings in fact as the Upper Tribunal considers
appropriate.

(4) In remitting the case, the Upper Tribunal may give directions for
the First-tier Tribunal's reconsideration of the case.

(5) Such directions may relate to—

(a) issues of law or fact (including the Upper Tribunal's opinion on
any relevant point),

(b) procedural issues (including as to the members to be chosen to
reconsider the case).

Appeal from Upper Tribunal

Appeal from the Tribunal

48.—(1) A decision of the Upper Tribunal in any matter in a case 7.103
before the Tribunal may be appealed to the Court of Session.

(2) An appeal under this section is to be made—

(a) by a party in the case,

(b) on a point of law only.

(3) An appeal under this section requires the permission of—

(a) the Upper Tribunal, or

(b) if the Upper Tribunal refuses its permission, the Court of Session.

(4) Such permission may be given in relation to an appeal under this section only if the Upper Tribunal or (as the case may be) the Court of Session is satisfied that there are arguable grounds for the appeal.

(5) This section—

(a) is subject to sections 43(4) and 55(2),

(b) does not apply in relation to an excluded decision.

GENERAL NOTE

7.103.1   This right of appeal is excluded by s.55(2)(b) in the case of refusals by the Upper Tribunal of permission to appeal from the First-tier Tribunal to itself under s.46(3)(b) and, perhaps unnecessarily, of permission to appeal from itself to the Court of Session under s.48(3)(a). In addition, ss. 51 and 52 have the effect that a decision that has been reviewed and most decisions in reviews are "excluded decisions" for the purpose of s.48(5)(b) and s.43(4) provides that the exercise of discretion whether a decision should be reviewed cannot give rise to an appeal.

Disposal of an appeal

7.104   **49.**—(1) In an appeal under section 48, the Court of Session may uphold or quash the decision on the point of law in question.

(2) If the Court quashes the decision, it may—

(a) re-make the decision,

(b) remit the case to the Upper Tribunal, or

(c) make such other order as the Court considers appropriate.

(3) In re-making the decision, the Court may—

(a) do anything that the Upper Tribunal could do if re-making the decision,

(b) reach such findings in fact as the Court considers appropriate.

(4) In remitting the case, the Court may give directions for the Upper Tribunal's reconsideration of the case.

(5) Such directions may relate to—

(a) issues of law or fact (including the Court's opinion on any relevant point),

(b) procedural issues (including as to the members to be chosen to reconsider the case).

Procedure on second appeal

7.105   **50.**—(1) Section 48(4) is subject to subsections (3) and (4) as regards a second appeal.

(2) Section 49 is subject to subsections (5) and (6) as regards a second appeal.

(3) For the purpose of subsection (1), the Upper Tribunal or (as the case may be) the Court of Session may not give its permission to the making of a second appeal unless also satisfied that subsection (4) applies.

(4) This subsection applies where, in relation to the matter in question—

(a) a second appeal would raise an important point of principle or practice, or

(b) there is some other compelling reason for allowing a second appeal to proceed.

(5) For the purpose of subsection (2), subsections (2)(b) and (3)(a) of section 49 have effect in relation to a second appeal as if the references in them to the Upper Tribunal include (as alternatives) references to the First-tier Tribunal.

(6) Where, in exercising the choice arising by virtue of subsection (5) (and instead of re-making the decision in question), the Court of Session remits the case to the Upper Tribunal rather than the First-tier Tribunal—

(a) the Upper Tribunal, instead of reconsidering the case itself, may remit the case to the First-tier Tribunal,

(b) if the Upper Tribunal does so, it must send to the First-tier Tribunal any directions accompanying the Court's remittal of the case to the Upper Tribunal.

(7) In this section, "second appeal" means appeal under section 48 against a decision in an appeal under section 46.

Excluded decisions

Excluded decisions

51.—A decision falling within any of sections 52 to 54 is an excluded decision for the purposes of—　　7.106

(a) a review under section 43,

(b) an appeal under section 46 or 48.

Decisions on review

52.—(1) Falling within this section is—　　7.107

(a) a decision set aside in a review under section 43 (see section 44(1)(b)),

(b) a decision in such a review, except a decision of the kind mentioned in subsection (2).

(2) That is, a decision made by virtue of section 44(2)(a), (3)(a) or (4) (and accordingly a decision so made is not an excluded decision).

Other appeal rights

53.—(1) Falling within this section is a decision against which there is a right of appeal under an enactment apart from this Act.　　7.108

(2) The Scottish Ministers may by regulations make provision—

(a) to which subsection (1) is subject (for example, by specifying an exception to what falls within this section),

(b) for a right of appeal under an enactment apart from this Act to cease to be exercisable in relation to a decision no longer falling within this section.

54. *Omitted.*　　7.109

Miscellaneous procedure

Process for permission

7.110   **55.**—(1) The Scottish Ministers may by regulations specify a time limit within which the permission required by section 46(3) or 48(3) must be sought.

(2) A refusal to give the permission required by section 46(3) or 48(3) is not—

(a) reviewable under section 43, or
(b) appealable under section 46 or 48.

GENERAL NOTE

7.110.1   For regulations made under subs.(1), see the Scottish Tribunals (Time Limits) Regulations 2016, below.

Participation of non-parties

7.111   **56.**—(1) Subsection (2) applies for the purposes of—

(a) a review under section 43,
(b) an appeal under section 46 or 48.

(2) The Scottish Ministers may by regulations make provision extending any reference to a party in a case so that it also includes a person falling within a specified description.

CHAPTER 2

SPECIAL JURISDICTION

7.112   **57. to 60.** *Omitted.*

PART 7

POWERS, PROCEDURE AND ADMINISTRATION

CHAPTER 1

POWERS AND ENFORCEMENT

Cases and proceedings

Venue for hearings

7.113   **61.**—(1) Each of the First-tier Tribunal and the Upper Tribunal may be convened at any time and place in Scotland to hear or decide a case or for any other purpose relating to its functions.

(2) Subsection (1) is subject to any provision made by Tribunal Rules as to the question of when and where in Scotland the Scottish Tribunals are to be convened (and such Rules may allow the President of Tribunals to determine the question).

Conduct of cases

62.—(1) In relation to the things mentioned in subsection (3), each of the First-tier Tribunal and the Upper Tribunal has such powers, rights, privileges and other authority with respect to any case before it as are provided for in Tribunal Rules.   7.114

(2) Rules making provision for the purpose of subsection (1) may (in particular) do so in relation to any kind of authority by reference to any authority of a relevant description exercisable by the sheriff or the Court of Session.

(3) The things are—

(a) the citation, attendance or examination of witnesses,

(b) the recovery, production or inspection of relevant materials,

(c) the commissioning of reports of any relevant type,

(d) other procedural, evidential or similar measures.

(4) In subsection (3)(b), "materials" means documents and other items.

Enforcement of decisions

63.—(1) A decision made by the First-tier Tribunal or the Upper Tribunal in any matter in a case before it is enforceable by the means provided for in Tribunal Rules.   7.115

(2) Subsection (1) applies to a decision—

(a) on the merits of such a case,

(b) as to—

(i) payment of a sum of money, or

(ii) expenses by virtue of section 64, or

(c) otherwise affecting the rights, obligations or interests of a party in such a case.

(3) Subsection (1) is subject to section 58(3) as respects a determination to which that section relates.

(4) Rules making provision for the purpose of subsection (1) may (in particular) do so in relation to a relevant order by reference to the means of enforcing an order of the sheriff or the Court of Session.

(5) In subsection (4), "relevant order" means order of either of the Tribunals giving effect to a decision to which subsection (1) applies.

Award of expenses

64.—(1) In connection with proceedings in a case before the First-tier Tribunal or the Upper Tribunal, the Tribunal may award expenses so far as allowed in accordance with Tribunal Rules.   7.116

(2) Where such expenses are awarded, the awarding Tribunal is to specify by and to whom they are to be paid (and to what extent).

(3) Tribunal Rules may make provision—

(a) for scales or rates of awardable expenses,

(b) for—
    (i) such expenses to be set-off against any relevant sums,
    (ii) interest at the specified rate to be chargeable on such expenses where unpaid,
(c) stating the general or particular factors to be taken into account when exercising discretion as to such expenses,
(d) about such expenses in other respects.

(4) Tribunal Rules may make provision—
(a) for disallowing any wasted expenses,
(b) for requiring a person who has given rise to such expenses to meet them.

(5) Rules making provision as described in subsection (3) or (4) may also prescribe meanings for "relevant sums", "specified rate" and "wasted expenses" as used in this section.

Supplementary provisions

Additional powers

7.117   **65.**—(1) The Scottish Ministers may by regulations confer on the First-tier Tribunal and the Upper Tribunal such additional powers as are necessary or expedient for the proper exercise of their functions.

(2) Regulations under subsection (1) may include provision—
(a) relying on the effect of an act of sederunt made by the Court of Session,
(b) causing Part 1 of the Scottish Civil Justice Council and Criminal Legal Assistance Act 2013 to apply to the making of a relevant act of sederunt as it does to the making of Tribunal Rules.

(3) Before making regulations under subsection (1), the Scottish Ministers must obtain the Lord President's approval.

Application of enactments

7.118   **66.**—(1) The Scottish Ministers may by regulations modify the application of any enactment so far as they consider to be necessary or expedient for the purposes of or in connection with the matters to which this subsection applies.

(2) Regulations under subsection (1) may include provision—
(a) relying on the effect of an act of sederunt made by the Court of Session,
(b) causing Part 1 of the Scottish Civil Justice Council and Criminal Legal Assistance Act 2013 to apply to the making of a relevant act of sederunt as it does to the making of Tribunal Rules.

(3) Subsection (1) applies to—
(a) the making of Tribunal Rules,
(b) the effect of—
    (i) this Part, or
    (ii) Tribunal Rules.

(4) Before making regulations under subsection (1), the Scottish Ministers must obtain the Lord President's approval.

Offences in relation to proceedings

67.—(1) Scottish Ministers may by regulations make provision, in relation to proceedings before the First-tier Tribunal or the Upper Tribunal—

7.119

    (a) for offences and penalties—

        (i) for making a false statement in an application in a case,

        (ii) for failure by a person to attend, or give evidence in, such proceedings when required to do so in accordance with Tribunal Rules,

        (iii) for alteration, concealment or destruction by a person of, or failure by a person to produce, something that is required to be produced in such proceedings in accordance with Tribunal Rules,

    (b) about the circumstances in which a person need not give evidence or produce something (for example, where a person could not be compelled to give evidence or produce something in proceedings in a case before the sheriff or in the Court of Session).

(2) The maximum penalties that may be provided for in regulations under subsection (1) are—

    (a) for an offence triable summarily only, imprisonment for a term not exceeding 12 months or a fine not exceeding level 5 on the standard scale (or both),

    (b) for an offence triable either summarily or on indictment—

        (i) on summary conviction, imprisonment for a term not exceeding 12 months or a fine not exceeding the statutory maximum (or both),

        (ii) on conviction on indictment, imprisonment for a term not exceeding 2 years or a fine (or both).

(3) Before making regulations under subsection (1), the Scottish Ministers must obtain the Lord President's approval.

CHAPTER 2

PRACTICE AND PROCEDURE

Tribunal Rules

Tribunal Rules

68.—(1) There are to be rules—

7.120

    (a) regulating the practice and procedure to be followed in proceedings at—

        (i) the First-tier Tribunal,

        (ii) the Upper Tribunal, and

(b) containing provision of other sorts appropriate with respect to the Scottish Tribunals (including in relation to the exercise by them of their functions).

(2) Rules of the kind mentioned in subsection (1) are to be known as Scottish Tribunal Rules (and in this Act they are referred to as Tribunal Rules).

(3) Tribunal Rules are to be made by the Court of Session by act of sederunt.

(4) Part 1 of the Scottish Civil Justice Council and Criminal Legal Assistance Act 2013 includes further provision about the making of Tribunal Rules.

Exercise of functions

7.121   **69.**—(1) Tribunal Rules may confer functions on the persons mentioned in subsection (5) or the other members of the Scottish Tribunals.

(2) Tribunal Rules may, in relation to any functions exercisable by the persons mentioned in subsection (5) or the other members of the Scottish Tribunals—

    (a) state—

        (i) how a function is to be exercised,

        (ii) who is to exercise a function,

    (b) cause something to require further authorisation,

    (c) permit something to be done on a person's behalf,

    (d) allow a specified person to make a decision about any of those matters.

(3) Tribunal Rules may make provision relying on the effect of directions issued, or to be issued, under section 74.

(4) Neither Tribunal Rules nor directions under section 74 may make provision altering the operation of section 37(1) or 39(1).

(5) For the purposes of subsections (1) and (2), the persons are—

    (a) the Lord President,

    (b) the President of Tribunals,

    (c) in the First-tier Tribunal—

        (i) a Chamber President,

        (ii) a Deputy Chamber President,

    (d) a Vice-President of the Upper Tribunal.

Extent of rule-making

7.122   **70.**—(1) Tribunal Rules may make—

    (a) provision applying—

        (i) equally to both of the First-tier Tribunal and the Upper Tribunal, or

        (ii) specifically to one of them,

    (b) particular provision for each of them about the same matter.

(2) Tribunal Rules may make particular provision for different—

    (a) chambers or divisions,

    (b) types of proceedings.

(3) Tribunal Rules may make different provision for different purposes in any other respects.

(4) The generality of section 68(1) is not limited by—

(a) sections 71 to 73, or

(b) any other provisions of this Act about the content of Tribunal Rules.

(5) As well as Chapter 1, see (for example) sections 28(5), 42(1), 43(3)(b) and 59(2).

Particular matters

Proceedings and steps

71.—(1) Tribunal Rules may make provision about proceedings in a case before the Scottish Tribunals.   7.123

(2) Rules making provision as described in subsection (1) may (in particular)—

(a) provide for the form and manner in which a case is to be brought,

(b) allow for the withdrawal of a case (with or without restrictions on subsequent proceedings as respects the same matter),

(c) set time limits for—

(i) making applications,

(ii) taking particular steps,

(d) enable two or more applications to be conjoined in certain circumstances,

(e) specify circumstances in which the Tribunals may take particular steps of their own initiative.

Hearings in cases

72.—(1) Tribunal Rules may make provision about hearings in a case before the Scottish Tribunals.   7.124

(2) Rules making provision as described in subsection (1) may (in particular)—

(a) provide for certain matters to be dealt with—

(i) without a hearing,

(ii) at a private hearing,

(iii) at a public hearing,

(b) require notice to be given of a hearing (and for the timing of such notice),

(c) specify persons who may—

(i) appear on behalf of a party in a case,

(ii) attend a hearing in order to provide support to a party or witness in a case,

(d) specify circumstances in which particular persons may appear or be represented at a hearing,

(e) specify circumstances in which a hearing may go ahead—

   (i) at the request of a party in a case despite no notice of it having been given to another party in the case,

   (ii) in the absence of a particular member chosen to exercise the function of deciding any matter in a case,

  (f) enable two or more sets of proceedings to be taken concurrently at a hearing in certain circumstances,

 (g) allow for an adjournment of a hearing for the purpose of giving the parties in a case an opportunity to use a process of negotiation, mediation, arbitration or adjudication for resolving a dispute to which the case relates,

 (h) allow for the imposition of reporting restrictions for particular reasons arising in a case.

Evidence and decisions

7.125 **73.**—(1) Tribunal Rules may, in connection with proceedings before the Scottish Tribunals—

 (a) make provision about the giving of evidence and the administering of oaths,

 (b) modify the application of any other rules relating to either of those matters so far as they would otherwise apply to such proceedings.

(2) Tribunal Rules may, in connection with proceedings before the Scottish Tribunals, provide for the payment of expenses and allowances to a person who—

 (a) gives evidence,

 (b) a document, or

 (c) attends such proceedings (or is required to do so).

(3) Tribunal Rules may, in connection with proceedings before the Scottish Tribunals, make provision by way of presumption (for example, as to the serving of something on somebody).

(4) Tribunal Rules may make provision about decisions of the Scottish Tribunals, including as to—

 (a) the manner in which such decisions are to be made,

 (b) the incorporation in such decisions of findings in fact,

 (c) the recording, issuing and publication of such decisions.

Issuing directions

Practice directions

7.126 **74.**—(1) The President of Tribunals may issue directions as to the practice and procedure to be followed in proceedings at—

 (a) the First-tier Tribunal,

 (b) the Upper Tribunal.

(2) A Chamber President in the First-tier Tribunal may issue directions as to the practice and procedure to be followed in proceedings in the chamber over which the Chamber President presides.

(3) A Vice-President of the Upper Tribunal may issue directions as to the practice and procedure to be followed in proceedings in the division over which the Vice-President presides.

(4) Directions under subsection (2) or (3) may not be issued without the approval of the President of Tribunals.

Publication and effect

75.—(1) The President of Tribunals must arrange for directions under section 74(1), (2) or (3) to be published in such manner as the President of Tribunals considers appropriate.   7.127

(2) Directions under section 74(1), (2) or (3) may—

(a) vary or revoke earlier such directions,

(b) make different provision for different purposes (in the same respects as Tribunal Rules).

(3) If (and to the extent that) any conflict arises between—

(a) directions issued under section 74(1), and

(b) directions issued under section 74(2) or (3),

those issued under section 74(1) are to prevail.

CHAPTER 3

Fees and administration

76. *Omitted.*   7.128
77. *Repealed.*
78. *Omitted.*

PART 8

Final provisions

General and ancillary

Regulation-making

79.—(1) Regulations under the preceding Parts of this Act may—   7.129

(a) make different provision for different purposes,

(b) include supplemental, incidental, consequential, transitional, transitory or saving provision.

(2) Regulations under the following provisions of those Parts are subject to the affirmative procedure—

    (a) section 20(2) or 23(2),

    (b) section 27(2) or 28(2),

    (c) section 38(1), 40(1) or 41(1),

    (d) section 65(1), 66(1) or 67(1).

(3) Regulations under any other provisions of those Parts are subject to the negative procedure.

Ancillary regulations

7.130   **80.**—(1)The Scottish Ministers may by regulations make such supplemental, incidental, consequential, transitional, transitory or saving provision as they consider necessary or expedient for the purposes of or in connection with this Act.

(2) Regulations under this section—

    (a) are subject to the affirmative procedure if they add to, replace or omit any part of the text of an Act (including this Act),

    (b) otherwise, are subject to the negative procedure.

7.131   **81.** *Omitted.*

Interpretation, commencement and short title

Interpretation

7.132   **82.**—(1) In this Act, "Lord President" means Lord President of the Court of Session.

(2) Schedule 10 is an index of expressions used in this Act together with a note of some key provisions.

Commencement

7.133   **83.**—(1) Section 82, this section and section 84 come into force on the day after Royal Assent.

(2) The other provisions of this Act come into force on such day as the Scottish Ministers may by order appoint.

(3) An order under subsection (2) may include transitional, transitory or saving provision.

Short title

7.134   **84.**—The short title of this Act is the Tribunals (Scotland) Act 2014.

7.135   **Schedules 1 to 9.** *Omitted.*

SCHEDULE 10

(introduced by section 82)

INDEX OF EXPRESSIONS

Expressions used	Relevant provisions
Lord President	Section 82(1)
Head of the Scottish Tribunals	Section 2(1)
President of Tribunals	Section 5(3)
First-tier Tribunal and Upper Tribunal	Section 1(1)
the Scottish Tribunals	Section 1(2)
Chamber President of the First-tier Tribunal (including appointment to position)	Sections 21 and 22
Vice-President of the Upper Tribunal (including assignment or appointment to position)	Sections 24 to 26
chamber of a Tribunal (First-tier)	Section 20(1)
division of a Tribunal (Upper)	Section 23(1)
members of the Scottish Tribunals	Section 13(3)
ordinary member (First-tier)	Section 15(1)
ordinary member (Upper)	Section 16(1)
legal member (First-tier)	Section 15(2)
legal member (Upper)	Section 16(2)
judicial member (First-tier)	Section 19(1)
judicial member (Upper)	Section 19(2)
extra judge (Upper)	Section 19(4)
appointment and assignment (various positions)	Section 32(1) to (4)
transfer-in to membership (various positions)	Section 29(a) and (b)
listed tribunals	Section 27(1)
Tribunal rules	Section 68(2)

The Scottish Tribunals (Time Limits) Regulations 2016

(SSI 2016/231)

Made	*17th August 2016*
Laid before the Scottish Parliament	*19th August 2016*
Coming into force	*1st December 2016*

7.137 The Scottish Ministers make the following Regulations in exercise of the powers conferred by section 55(1), 79(1)(a) and paragraph 4(2) of schedule 9 of the Tribunals (Scotland) Act 2014 and all other powers enabling them to do so.

In accordance with paragraph 4(3) of schedule 9 of that Act, the Scottish Ministers have consulted with the President of Tribunals and such other persons as they considered appropriate.

Citation, commencement and interpretation

7.138 **1.**—(1) These Regulations may be cited as the Scottish Tribunals (Time Limits) Regulations 2016.

(2) These Regulations come into force on 1st December 2016.

(3) In these Regulations—

"the 2014 Act" means the Tribunals (Scotland) Act 2014;

"appellant" means a party applying for permission to appeal; and

"hearing" means an oral hearing and includes a hearing conducted in whole or in part by video link, telephone or other means of instantaneous two-way electronic communication.

Time limits for applying to the First-tier Tribunal or Upper Tribunal for permission to appeal against its own decision

7.139 **2.**—(1) An application for permission under sections 46(3)(a) or 48(3)(a) of the Act (application for permission to appeal the Tribunal's own decision) must be received by the Tribunal whose decision is being appealed against within the period of 30 days beginning with the relevant date.

(2) The First-tier Tribunal or the Upper Tribunal, as appropriate, may on cause shown extend the period beyond 30 days if it considers such an extension to be in the interests of justice.

(3) Subject to paragraph (4), the relevant date is the later of the date on which—

(a) the decision appealed against was sent to the appellant;

(b) the statement of reasons for the decision was sent to the appellant.

(4) But where a decision is given orally at a hearing, the relevant date is either—

(a) the date on which written reasons were sent to the parties, if—

  (i) written reasons were requested at the hearing (or were requested in writing within 14 days beginning with the day after the last day of the hearing); or

  (ii) the First-tier Tribunal or the Upper Tribunal, as appropriate, undertook at the hearing to provide written reasons; or

(b) the date of the oral decision, if—

    (i) written reasons were not requested at the hearing (or were not requested in writing within 14 days beginning with the day after the last day of the hearing); or

    (ii) the First-tier Tribunal or the Upper Tribunal, as appropriate, did not undertake at the hearing to provide written reasons.

Time limits for applying to the Upper Tribunal for permission to appeal against a decision of the First-tier Tribunal

3.—(1) An application for permission under section 46(3)(b) of the 2014 Act (application for permission to appeal to the Upper Tribunal against a decision of the First-tier Tribunal) must be received by the Upper Tribunal within the period of 30 days beginning with the relevant date.   7.140

(2) The relevant date is the date on which notice of the First-tier Tribunal's refusal of permission to appeal was sent to the appellant.

(3) The Upper Tribunal may on cause shown extend the period beyond 30 days if it considers such an extension to be in the interests of justice.

The First-tier Tribunal for Scotland Social Security Chamber (Procedure) Regulations 2018

(SI 2018 No. 273)

Made	*11th September 2018*
Laid before the Scottish Parliament	*13th September 2018*
Coming into force	*22nd November 2018*

7.141 The Scottish Ministers make the following Regulations in exercise of the powers conferred by section 43(3)(b) and paragraph 4(2) of schedule 9 of the Tribunals (Scotland) Act 2014 and all other powers enabling them to do so.

In accordance with paragraph 4(3) of schedule 9 of that Act, the Scottish Ministers have consulted the President of the Scottish Tribunals and such other persons as they considered appropriate.

Citation and commencement

7.142 **1.**—(1) These Regulations may be cited as the First-tier Tribunal for Scotland Social Security Chamber (Procedure) Regulations 2018 and the Rules contained in the schedule may be cited as the First-tier Tribunal for Scotland Social Security Chamber Rules of Procedure 2018.

(2) These Regulations come into force on 22nd November 2018.

Application of the Rules set out in the schedule

7.143 **2.** The Rules in the schedule apply to any proceedings before the First-tier Tribunal for Scotland Social Security Chamber when exercising functions conferred on the Tribunal by the Social Security (Scotland) Act 2018 or by regulations made under that Act.

Regulation 2

SCHEDULE

THE FIRST-TIER TRIBUNAL FOR SCOTLAND SOCIAL SECURITY CHAMBER RULES OF PROCEDURE 2018

CONTENTS

PART 1

INTRODUCTION

PART 2

PART 3

PART 4

PART 1

INTRODUCTION

Interpretation

7.145   **1.**—(1) In these Rules—

"the 2014 Act" means the Tribunals (Scotland) Act 2014;

"the 2018 Act" means the Social Security (Scotland) Act 2018;

"the 2016 Regulations" means the Scottish Tribunals (Time Limits) Regulations 2016;

"appellant" means the person who starts proceedings (whether by notifying an appeal, or applying for permission to appeal) or a person substituted as an appellant under rule 8 (addition, substitution and removal of parties);

"chairing member" means the chairing member of the First-tier Tribunal;

"Chamber President" means the President of the First-tier Tribunal;

"the [¹Convention rights] "has the meaning given to it in section 1 of the Human Rights Act 1998;

"decision maker" means the maker of a decision or determination against which an appeal to the First-tier Tribunal is brought;

"document" means anything in which information is recorded in any form, and an obligation under these Rules to provide or allow access to a document or a copy of a document for any purpose means, unless the First-tier Tribunal directs otherwise, an obligation to provide or allow access to such document or copy in a legible form or a form which can easily be made into a legible form;

"electronic communication" has the meaning given to it by section 15(1) of the Electronic Communications Act 2000;

"excluded decision" means a decision falling under section 51 of the 2014 Act;

"the First-tier Tribunal" means the First-tier Tribunal for Scotland Social Security Chamber;

"hearing" means an oral hearing and includes a hearing conducted in whole or in part by video link, telephone or other means of instantaneous two-way electronic communication;

"legal member" means an individual holding membership of the First-tier Tribunal for Scotland in accordance with section 15(2) of the 2014 Act;

"party" means a person who is (or was at the time that the First-tier Tribunal disposed of the proceedings) an appellant or a respondent in proceedings before the First-tier Tribunal;

"practice direction" means a direction given under section 74 of the 2014 Act;

"the prescribed time period" means the period prescribed by the Scottish Ministers by virtue of section 43(5) of the 2018 Act for the re-determination by them of an individual's entitlement to a type of social security assistance described in Chapter 2 of Part 2 of the 2018 Act;

"process decision" means a decision made under section 38, 41(3) or 42 of the 2018 Act;

"representative" means a lay representative or a legal representative;

"respondent" means—

(a) the decision maker in relation to a decision or determination against which an appeal to the First-tier Tribunal is brought; or

(b) a person substituted or added as a respondent under rule 8 (addition, substitution and removal of parties);

"review" means the internal review provided for by section 43(1) of the 2014 Act; and

"the Upper Tribunal" means the Upper Tribunal for Scotland.

(2) For the purposes of these Rules, where information is sent—

(a) via the postal service to the last known address held for an individual; or

(b) by email to the last known email address held for the individual,

the individual is presumed to have received the information 48 hours after it is sent, unless the contrary is shown.

AMENDMENT

1. First-tier Tribunal for Scotland Social Security Chamber (Rules of Procedure) Amendment Regulations 2018 (SSI 2018/343) reg.2 (1) and (2) (December 21, 2018).

Overriding objective and parties' obligation to co-operate with the First-tier Tribunal

2.—(1) The overriding objective of these Rules is to enable the First-tier Tribunal to deal with cases fairly and justly.   **7.146**

(2) Dealing with a case fairly and justly includes—

(a) dealing with the case in ways which are [¹ transparent and which are] proportionate to the importance of the case, the complexity of the issues, the anticipated expenses and the resources of the parties;

(b) avoiding unnecessary formality and seeking flexibility in the proceedings;

(c) ensuring, so far as practicable, that the parties are able to participate fully in the proceedings and are treated with dignity and respect;

(d) using any special expertise of the First-tier Tribunal effectively; and

(e) avoiding delay, so far as compatible with proper consideration of the issues.

(3) The First-tier Tribunal must seek to give effect to the overriding objective when it—

(a) exercises any power under these Rules; or

(b) interprets any rule or practice direction.

(4) Parties must, insofar as reasonably possible—

(a) help the First-tier Tribunal to further the overriding objective; and

(b) co-operate with the First-tier Tribunal generally.

AMENDMENT

1. First-tier Tribunal for Scotland Social Security Chamber (Rules of Procedure) Amendment Regulations 2018 (SSI 2018/343) reg.2 (1) and (3) (December 21, 2018).

Delegation to staff

7.147   **3.**—(1) Staff of the Scottish Courts and Tribunals Service may, with the approval of the Chamber President, carry out functions of a judicial nature permitted or required to be undertaken by the First-tier Tribunal, provided the functions are of a preliminary or an incidental nature.

(2) The approval referred to in paragraph (1) may apply generally to the carrying out of specified functions by members of staff of a specified description in specified circumstances.

(3) Where the First-tier Tribunal sends notice of a decision made by a member of staff pursuant to an approval under paragraph (1) to a party, that party may, within the period of 14 days beginning with the day on which the party is presumed to have received the notice, make a written application to the First-tier Tribunal for that decision to be considered afresh by a member of the First-tier Tribunal.

PART 2

GENERAL POWERS AND PROVISIONS

Case management powers

7.148   **4.**—(1) Subject to the provisions of the 2014 Act and these Rules, the First-tier Tribunal may regulate its own procedure.

(2) The First-tier Tribunal may give an order in relation to the conduct and disposal of proceedings at any time, including an order amending, suspending or setting aside an earlier order.

(3) In particular, and without restricting the general powers in paragraphs (1) and (2), the First-tier Tribunal may—

(a) extend or shorten the time for complying with any rule, practice direction or order;

(b) conjoin or take concurrently two or more sets of proceedings or parts of proceedings raising common issues;

(c) permit or require a party to amend a document;

(d) permit or require a party or another person to provide documents, information, evidence or submissions to the First-tier Tribunal or a party;

(e) deal with an issue in the proceedings as a preliminary issue;

(f) hold a hearing to consider any matter, including a case management issue;

(g) decide the form of any hearing;

(h) adjourn or postpone a hearing;

(i) require a party to produce a file of documents for a hearing;

(j) sist proceedings;

(k) transfer proceedings to another court or tribunal if that other court or tribunal has jurisdiction in relation to the proceedings and—

    (i) because of a change of circumstances since the proceedings were started, the First-tier Tribunal no longer has jurisdiction in relation to the proceedings; or

   (ii) the First-tier Tribunal considers that the other court or tribunal is a more appropriate forum for the determination of the case;

(l) suspend the effect of its own decision pending the determination by the First-tier Tribunal or the Upper Tribunal, as the case may be, of an application for permission to appeal against, and any appeal or review of, that decision.

Procedure for applying for and giving orders

5.—(1) The First-tier Tribunal may give an order on the application of one or more of the parties or on its own initiative.   7.149

(2) An application for an order may be made—

(a) by sending or delivering a written application to the First-tier Tribunal; or

(b) orally during the course of a hearing.

(3) An application for an order must include the reasons for making that application.

(4) Unless the First-tier Tribunal considers that there is good reason not to do so, the Tribunal must send written notice of any order to each party to the case.

(5) If a party sent notice of the order under paragraph (4) wishes to challenge the order, the party may do so by applying for another order which amends, suspends or sets aside the first order.

Failure to comply with rules etc

6.—(1) An irregularity resulting from a failure to comply with any requirement in these Rules, a practice direction or an order does not of itself render void the proceedings or any step taken in the proceedings.   7.150

(2) If a party has failed to comply with a requirement in these Rules, a practice direction or an order, the First-tier Tribunal may take such action as it considers just, which may include—

    (a) waiving the requirement;

    (b) requiring the failure to be remedied; or

    (c) exercising its power under rule 7 (dismissal of a party's case).

Dismissal of a party's case

7.151   **7.**—(1) The First-tier Tribunal must dismiss the whole or a part of the proceedings if the Tribunal—

    (a) does not have jurisdiction in relation to the proceedings or that part of them; and

    (b) does not exercise its power under rule 4(3)(k) (transfer to another court or tribunal) in relation to the proceedings or that part of them.

(2) The First-tier Tribunal may dismiss the whole or a part of the proceedings if—

    (a) the appellant has failed to comply with an order which stated that failure by the appellant to comply with the order could lead to the dismissal of the proceedings or part of them;

    (b) the appellant has failed to co-operate with the First-tier Tribunal to such an extent that the First-tier Tribunal considers that it cannot deal with the proceedings fairly and justly; or

    (c) where relevant, there is no possibility of the eligibility criteria being met for the particular form of assistance to which the proceedings relate.

(3) The First-tier Tribunal may not dismiss the whole or a part of the proceedings under paragraph (1) or (2)(b) without first giving the appellant an opportunity to make representations in relation to the proposed dismissal.

(4) If the proceedings, or part of them, have been dismissed under paragraph (2)(a), the appellant may apply for the proceedings, or part of them, to be reinstated, where the appellant can satisfy the Tribunal that the appellant has good reason to apply for reinstatement.

(5) An application under paragraph (4) must be made in writing and received by the First-tier Tribunal within the period of 31 days beginning with the day on which notification of the dismissal sent to the appellant under paragraph (9) is presumed to have been received by the appellant.

(6) An application under paragraph (4) must set out the reasons on which the appellant relies in applying for reinstatement.

(7) This rule applies to a respondent as it applies to an appellant except that—

    (a) a reference to the dismissal of the proceedings is to be read as a reference to the barring of the respondent from taking further part in the proceedings; and

    (b) a reference to an application for the reinstatement of proceedings which have been dismissed is to be read as a reference to an application for the lifting of the bar on the respondent from taking further part in the proceedings.

(8) If the respondent has been barred from taking further part in proceedings under this rule and that bar has not been lifted, the First-tier Tribunal need not consider any response or other submission made by the respondent.

(9) The First-tier Tribunal must notify each party in writing that dismissal has taken place.

Addition, substitution and removal of parties

8.—(1) The First-tier Tribunal may give an order adding, substituting or removing a party if—   7.152
  (a) the wrong person has been named as a party; or
  (b) the addition, substitution or removal has become necessary because of a change in circumstances since the start of proceedings.

(2) If the First-tier Tribunal gives an order under paragraph (1) it may make such consequential orders as it considers appropriate.

(3) A person who is not a party may make a written application to the First-tier Tribunal to be added or substituted as a party under this rule.

(4) If the First-tier Tribunal refuses an application under paragraph (3) it must consider whether to permit the person who made the application to provide submissions or evidence to the First-tier Tribunal.

Representatives

9.—(1) A party may be represented in any proceedings by a representative whose details may be communicated to the First-tier Tribunal prior to any hearing.   7.153

(2) If the First-tier Tribunal receives notice that a party has appointed a representative under paragraph (1), it must send a copy of that notice to each party to the proceedings.

[¹(3) Where the First-tier Tribunal receives notice of the appointment of a representative—
  (a) it must provide to the representative—
    (i) any document which it requires under these Rules to provide to the represented party on or after the day on which it receives the notice, in addition to providing the document to the represented party, and
    (ii) any document which it required under these Rules to provide to the represented party prior to the day on which it receives the notice; and
  (b) it may assume that the representative remains appointed unless it receives written notification that this is not so from the representative or represented party.]

(4) Notwithstanding paragraphs (1) to (3), a party may be represented at a hearing by a person other than any person whose details have been communicated to the First-tier Tribunal.

(5) A party may show any document or communicate any information about the proceedings to that party's representative without contravening any prohibition or restriction on disclosure of the document or information.

(6) Where a document or information is disclosed under paragraph (5), the representative is subject to any prohibition or disclosure in the same way that the party is.

AMENDMENT

1. First-tier Tribunal for Scotland Social Security Chamber (Rules of Procedure) Amendment Regulations 2018 (SSI 2018/343) reg.2 (1) and (4) (December 21, 2018).

Supporters

7.154   **10.** A party who is an individual may be accompanied by another person, who is not a representative, to act as a supporter.

Interpreters

7.155   **11.** Where an interpreter is appointed to assist the First-tier Tribunal, the interpreter must be independent of all parties to the case and of any representatives or supporters.

Calculating time

7.156   **12.**—(1) An act required by these Rules, a practice direction or an order to be done on or by a particular day must be done before 5pm on that day.

(2) If the time specified by these Rules, a practice direction or an order for doing any act ends on a day other than a working day, the act is done in time if it is done on the next working day.

(3) In this rule "working day" means any day except a Saturday or Sunday or a bank holiday in Scotland under section 1 of the Banking and Financial Dealings Act 1971.

Sending and delivery of documents

7.157   **13.**—(1) Any document to be provided to the First-tier Tribunal under these Rules, a practice direction or an order may be sent by prepaid post, by fax or by electronic communication to the address specified for receipt by the First-tier Tribunal.

(2) Subject to paragraph (3), if a party or representative provides an email address or other details for the electronic transmission of documents to them, that party or representative must accept delivery of documents by that method.

(3) If a party informs the First-tier Tribunal that a particular form of communication (other than post) should not be used to provide documents to that party, that form of communication must not be so used by the Tribunal or any other party.

(4) If the First-tier Tribunal or a party sends a document to a party or the Tribunal by email or any other means of electronic communication,

the recipient may request that the sender provides a hard copy of the document to the recipient, and the recipient must make any such a request as soon as reasonably practicable after receiving the document electronically.

(5) The First-tier Tribunal and each party may assume that the address provided by a party or its representative is and remains the address to which documents should be sent or delivered until receiving notification to the contrary.

Disclosure of documents and information

14. The First-tier Tribunal may at any stage of the proceedings, on its own initiative or on application by one or more of the parties, make an order with a view to prohibiting or restricting the public disclosure of any aspect of those proceedings so far as it considers necessary in the interests of justice or in order to protect the Convention rights of any person.   **7.158**

Evidence and submissions

15.—(1) Without restriction on the general powers in rule 4 (case management powers), the First-tier Tribunal may give orders as to—   **7.159**
  (a) issues on which it requires evidence or submissions;
  (b) the nature of any such evidence or submissions;
  (c) whether the parties are permitted to provide expert evidence;
  (d) any limit on the number of witnesses whose evidence a party may put forward, whether in relation to a particular issue or generally;
  (e) the manner in which any evidence or submissions are to be provided, which may include an order for them to be given—
      (i) orally at a hearing; or
      (ii) by written submissions or witness statement; and
  (f) the time at which any evidence or submissions are to be provided.
(2) The First-tier Tribunal may exclude evidence that would otherwise be admissible where—
  (a) the evidence was not, without reasonable excuse, provided within the time allowed by an order or a practice direction;
  (b) the evidence was otherwise, without reasonable excuse, provided in a manner that did not comply with an order or practice direction; or
  (c) the Tribunal considers it would otherwise be unfair to admit the evidence.
(3) The First-tier Tribunal may admit evidence whether or not—
  (a) the evidence would be admissible in civil proceedings in Scotland; or
  (b) the evidence was available to a previous decision maker.
(4) The First-tier Tribunal may consent to a witness giving, or require any witness to give, evidence on oath, and may administer an oath for that purpose.

Citation of witnesses and orders to answer questions or produce documents

7.160   **16.**—(1) On the application of a party or on its own initiative, the First-tier Tribunal may—

(a) by citation require any person to attend as a witness at a hearing at the time and place specified in the citation; or

(b) order any person to answer any questions or produce any documents in that person's possession or control which relate to any issue in the proceedings.

(2) A citation under paragraph (1)(a) must—

(a) give the person required to attend at least 14 days' notice of the hearing, or such other period as the First-tier Tribunal may order;

(b) where the person is not a party, make provision for the person's necessary expenses of attendance to be paid, and state who is to pay them;

(c) state that the person on whom the requirement is imposed may apply to the First-tier Tribunal to vary or set aside the citation or order, if the person did not have an opportunity to object to it before it was made or issued; and

(d) state the consequences of failure to comply with the citation or order.

(3) No person may be compelled to give any evidence or produce any document that the person could not be compelled to give or produce in civil proceedings in a Scottish court.

Withdrawal

7.161   **17.**—(1) Subject to paragraph (2), a party may give notice of the withdrawal of the party's case, or any part of that case—

(a) by sending or delivering to the First-tier Tribunal a written notice of withdrawal; or

(b) orally at a hearing.

(2) In the circumstances described in paragraph (3), a notice of withdrawal will not take effect unless the Tribunal consents to the withdrawal.

(3) The circumstances referred to in paragraph (2) are where a party gives notice of withdrawal—

(a) in a case in which the First-tier Tribunal has directed that any notice of withdrawal will take effect only with the consent of the Tribunal; or

(b) at a hearing.

(4) An application for a withdrawn case to be reinstated may be made by—

(a) the appellant; or

(b) a respondent,

where the appellant or respondent can satisfy the First-tier Tribunal that the appellant or respondent has good reason to apply for reinstatement.

(5) An application under paragraph (4) must be received by the First-tier Tribunal within 31 days of the earlier of—

(a) the day on which the applicant for reinstatement is presumed to have received the notification sent under paragraph (7) that the withdrawal has taken effect; or

(b) if the applicant for reinstatement was present at the hearing when the case was withdrawn orally under paragraph (1)(b), the day of that hearing.

(6) An application under paragraph (5) must set out the reasons on which the applicant relies in seeking reinstatement.

(7) The First-tier Tribunal must notify each party in writing that a withdrawal has taken effect under this rule.

Chairing member and voting

18. Where a matter is to be decided by two or more members of the First-tier Tribunal, the chairing member is to be the legal member, who is to have a casting vote.   7.162

Recording of hearings

19.—(1) Subject to paragraph (2), all hearings of the First-tier Tribunal must be recorded digitally.   7.163

(2) In the event of a failure of equipment, a written record of proceedings must be produced by the legal member.

PART 3

PROCEDURE FOR CASES IN THE FIRST-TIER TRIBUNAL

Notice of appeal to the First-tier Tribunal against a determination of entitlement to assistance of a type provided for in Part 2 of the 2018 Act

20.—(1) This rule applies where an individual brings an appeal under section 46 of the 2018 Act against a determination by the Scottish Ministers of the appellant's entitlement to social security assistance of a type described in Chapter 2 of Part 2 of the 2018 Act.   7.164

(2) Where in this rule, and in rule 21 (response of the decision maker to a notice of appeal against a determination of entitlement), reference is made to a "notice of appeal", this means the form provided by the Scottish Ministers under section 44 (or as the case may be section 45) of the 2018 Act, on notifying of the outcome of re-determination of entitlement, or of a failure to re-determine entitlement within the prescribed time period.

(3) An individual must start proceedings by submitting the notice of appeal to the Scottish Ministers along with any documents which have not so far been provided to Ministers that the appellant wishes them to submit to the First-tier Tribunal in support of the appeal.

(4) Except as provided for in paragraph (10), a notice of appeal must be received by the Scottish Ministers before the end of the period of 31 days beginning with whichever is the later of the day on which the appellant—

    (a) is informed of a determination made under section 43 of the 2018 Act, following a request for re-determination; or

    (b) is informed of the appellant's right to appeal against the original determination made under section 37 of the 2018 Act, as a result of the failure of the Scottish Ministers to re-determine entitlement within the prescribed time period.

(5) The notice of appeal must state—

    (a) the name and address of the appellant;

    (b) the name and address of the appellant's representative (if any);

    (c) a postal or email address where documents for the appellant may be sent or delivered;

    (d) the determination being challenged;

    (e) the reasons for bringing the appeal;

    (f) any views of the appellant on whether the matter should be dealt with at a hearing or without a hearing; and

    (g) where the notice of appeal is received after the end of the period of 31 days beginning with the day on which the appellant is informed of the determination, but less than one year after that day, reasons why the notice of appeal was not sent or delivered to the Scottish Ministers sooner.

(6) A notice of appeal and any accompanying documents may be sent by pre-paid post, by fax, or by electronic communication to such address as may be specified for receipt by the Scottish Ministers.

(7) The Scottish Ministers must forward to the First-tier Tribunal any notice of appeal and accompanying documents submitted to them, regardless of whether the requirements set out in paragraph (5) are met, or the extent to which they are met, and inform the appellant when this has been done.

(8) At the same time as forwarding a notice and any documents under paragraph (7), the Scottish Ministers must send—

    (a) a copy of the determination issued under section 43 of the 2018 Act, following a request that entitlement be re-determined; or

    (b) a copy of the determination issued under section 37 of the 2018 Act, where there has been a failure to re-determine entitlement within the prescribed time period; and

    (c) copy of any written record of the decision under challenge.

(9) Where notice of appeal is received by the Scottish Ministers after the end of the period of 31 days beginning with the later of the days specified in paragraph (4)—

    (a) if the notice of appeal is received before the end of the period of one year beginning with the day of the determination, the First-tier Tribunal may give permission for the appeal to proceed, but only if satisfied that there was a good reason for the notice of appeal not having been sent or delivered to the Scottish Ministers sooner; or

(b) if the notice of appeal is received after the end of the period of one year beginning with the day of the determination, the First-tier Tribunal must refuse to consider the notice.

(10) The Scottish Ministers must forward a notice of appeal to the First-tier Tribunal even if one of the following situations applies—

(a) the notice is received after the end of the period of 31 days beginning with the day on which the appellant is informed of the determination, but less than one year after that day; or

(b) the notice is received one year or more after the day on which the appellant is informed of the determination.

Response of the decision maker to a notice of appeal against a determination of entitlement

21.—(1)The First-tier Tribunal must notify each party in writing when a notice of appeal submitted under rule 20 (notice of appeal against a determination of entitlement) has been accepted as containing sufficient information to be valid.   **7.165**

(2) The decision maker must send or deliver to the First-tier Tribunal a response to any notice of appeal submitted under rule 20 (notice of appeal against a determination of entitlement) before the expiry of the period of 31 days beginning with the day on which the decision maker received notification from the First-tier Tribunal that the notice of appeal had been accepted as containing sufficient information to be valid.

(3) The response must include —

(a) the name and address of the decision maker;

(b) the name and address of the decision maker's representative (if any);

(c) a postal or email address where documents for the decision maker may be sent or delivered;

(d) the position of the decision maker in relation to the appellant's case; and

(e) any views of the decision maker as to whether the matter should be dealt with at a hearing or without a hearing.

(4) Unless a practice direction states otherwise, the decision maker must provide with the response copies of any documents relevant to the case which are in the decision-maker's possession and which have not already been provided to the First-tier Tribunal.

[¹(5) The First-tier Tribunal must provide the appellant with a copy of the decision-maker's response and any documents accompanying that response which have not already been supplied to the appellant.]

(6) The appellant may make written comments to the First-tier Tribunal and supply further documents to it in reply to the decision maker's response.

(7) Any comments or further documents referred to in paragraph (5) must be provided to the First-tier Tribunal within the period of 31 days beginning with the day on which the appellant is presumed to have received the response, as sent by the decision maker, and the First-tier Tribunal must send a copy to the decision maker.

AMENDMENT

1. First-tier Tribunal for Scotland Social Security Chamber (Rules of Procedure) Amendment Regulations 2018 (SSI 2018/343) reg.2 (1) and (5) (December 21, 2018).

Notice of appeal against a process decision

7.166   **22.**—(1) This rule applies where an individual brings an appeal under section 61 of the 2018 Act against a process decision.

(2) An individual must start proceedings by sending a notice of appeal and any accompanying documents to the First-tier Tribunal.

(3) Except as provided for in paragraph (5), a notice of appeal against a process decision must be received by the First-tier Tribunal before the end of the period of 31 days beginning with the day on which the individual is informed of the decision against which the individual wishes to appeal.

(4) The notice of appeal must state—

(a) the name and address of the appellant;

(b) a postal or email address where documents for the appellant may be sent or delivered;

(d) the decision being challenged;

(e) the reasons for bringing the appeal;

(f) any views of the appellant on whether the matter should be dealt with at a hearing or without a hearing; and

(g) where the notice of appeal is received after the end of the period of 31 days beginning with the day on which the appellant is informed of the decision, but within less than one year of that day, reasons why the notice of appeal was not sent or delivered to the [¹ First-tier Tribunal] sooner.

(5) Where a notice of appeal is received after the end of the period of 31 days beginning with the day specified in paragraph (3)—

(a) if the notice of appeal is received less than one year after that day, the First-tier Tribunal may give permission for the appeal to proceed, but only if satisfied that there was a good reason for the notice of appeal not having been sent or delivered sooner; or

(b) if the notice of appeal is received one year or more after that day, the First-tier Tribunal must refuse to consider the notice.

AMENDMENTS

1. First-tier Tribunal for Scotland Social Security Chamber (Rules of Procedure) Amendment Regulations 2018 (SSI 2018/343) reg.2 (1) and (6) (December 21, 2018).

Decision with or without a hearing

7.167   **23.**—(1) Subject to the following paragraphs of this rule, the First-tier Tribunal must hold a hearing before making a decision which disposes of proceedings unless—

(a) the views of all parties have been sought and no party has objected to the matter being decided without a hearing; and

(b) the First-tier Tribunal considers that it is able to decide the matter without a hearing.

(2) This rule does not apply to decisions under Part 4 of these Rules (correcting, reviewing and appealing decisions of the First-tier Tribunal).

(3) The First-tier Tribunal may dispose of proceedings, or a part of proceedings, under rule 7 (dismissal of a party's case) without a hearing.

(4) Where the First-tier Tribunal considers that the conditions set out in paragraph (1) are met, the Tribunal must proceed to determine the case without a hearing.

(5) A case determined in accordance with paragraph (4) is to be known as a "paper case."

Entitlement to attend a hearing

24. Subject to the power to exclude persons in rule 26(4) (public and 7.168
private hearings), each party is entitled to attend any hearing together with any representative and supporter permitted by rules 9 (representatives) and 10 (supporters).

Notice of hearings

25.—(1) The First-tier Tribunal must give each party entitled to 7.169
attend a hearing reasonable notice of the time and place of any hearing (including any adjourned or postponed hearing) and any changes to the time and place of any hearing.

(2) The period of notice under paragraph (1) must be at least 14 days except that the First-tier Tribunal may give shorter notice—

(a) with the parties' consent; or

(b) in urgent or exceptional circumstances.

Public and private hearings

26.—(1) Subject to the following paragraphs of this rule, all hearings 7.170
of the First-tier Tribunal must be held in public.

(2) The First-tier Tribunal may give an order that a hearing, or part of it, is to be held in private if the First-tier Tribunal considers that restricting access to the hearing is justified—

(a) in the interests of public order;

(b) in order to protect a person's right to respect for their private and family life;

(c) in order to maintain the confidentiality of sensitive information;

(d) in order to avoid serious harm to the public interest; or

(e) because not to do so would prejudice the interests of justice.

(3) Where a hearing, or any part of it, is to be held in private, the First-tier Tribunal may determine who is permitted to attend the hearing or part of it.

(4) The First-tier Tribunal may give an order excluding from any hearing, or part of it—

(a) any person whose conduct the First-tier Tribunal considers is disrupting or is likely to disrupt the hearing;

(b) any person whose presence the First-tier Tribunal considers is likely to prevent another person from giving evidence or making submissions freely; or

(c) any person where the purpose of the hearing would be defeated by the attendance of that person.

(5) The First-tier Tribunal may give an order excluding a witness from a hearing until that witness gives evidence.

(6) When publishing a decision notice referred to in rule 28(2) (notice of decisions) resulting from a hearing which was held wholly or partly in private, the First-tier Tribunal must, so far as practicable, ensure that the decision notice does not disclose information which was referred to only in a part of the hearing that was held in private (including such information which enables the identification of any person whose affairs were dealt with in the part of the hearing that was held in private) if to do so would undermine the purpose of holding the hearing in private.

Hearings in a party's absence

7.171　**27.** If a party fails to attend a hearing the First-tier Tribunal may proceed with the hearing if the Tribunal—

(a) is satisfied that the party has been notified of the hearing or that reasonable steps have been taken to notify the party of the hearing; and

(b) considers that it is in the interests of justice to proceed with the hearing.

Notice of decisions

7.172　**28.**—(1) The First-tier Tribunal may give a decision orally at a hearing.

(2) The First-tier Tribunal must provide a decision notice to each party as soon as reasonably practicable after making a decision which finally disposes of all issues in the proceedings or of a preliminary issue dealt with following an order under rule 4(3)(e) (dealing with an issue as a preliminary issue).

(3) A decision notice must—

(a) state the First-tier Tribunal's decision;

(b) where appropriate, notify each party of the right to apply for a full written statement of reasons under rule 29(2) (reasons for decisions); and

(c) once a written summary of a decision or a full statement of reasons has been issued, notify each party of the right to apply for permission to appeal to the Upper Tribunal against the decision, and the time within which, and the method by which, such an application must be made.

(4) This rule does not apply to a decision under Part 4 of these Rules (correcting, reviewing and appealing decisions of the First-tier Tribunal).

Reasons for decisions

29.—(1) The First-tier Tribunal may give reasons for a decision which   7.173
disposes of proceedings—

(a) orally at a hearing; or

(b) in a full written statement of reasons [¹ or a written summary of a
decision, which is to be issued] to each party.

(2) Unless the First-tier Tribunal has already provided a full written
statement of reasons under paragraph (1)(b), a party may make a written
application to the Tribunal for such statement following a decision which
finally disposes of—

(a) all issues in the proceedings; or

(b) a preliminary issue dealt with following an order under rule
4(3)(e) (dealing with an issue as a preliminary issue).

(3) An application under paragraph (2) must be received within the
period of 31 days beginning with the day on which the decision notice
relating to the decision provided to the appellant by the First-tier Tribunal under rule 28 (notice of decisions) is presumed to have been received
by the appellant.

(4) If a party makes an application in accordance with paragraphs (2)
and (3), the First-tier Tribunal must, subject to rule 14 (disclosure of
documents and information), send a full written statement of reasons to
each party within the period of 31 days beginning with the day on which
the Tribunal received the application or as soon as reasonably practicable
after the end of that period.

(5) This rule does not apply to a decision under Part 4 of these Rules
(correcting, reviewing and appealing decisions of the First-tier Tribunal).

AMENDMENT

1. First-tier Tribunal for Scotland Social Security Chamber (Rules of
Procedure) Amendment Regulations 2018 (SSI 2018/343) reg.2 (1)
and (7) (December 21, 2018).

Publication of decisions

30.—(1) The Chamber President must make such arrangements as   7.174
the Chamber President considers appropriate for the publication of
decisions of the First-tier Tribunal.

(2) Decisions may be published electronically.

(3) A decision may be published in an edited form, or subject to any
deletions, where the Chamber President or a legal member considers
that to be appropriate bearing in mind—

(a) the need to safeguard the welfare, wellbeing and interests of the
appellant or any other person;

(b) the need to protect the private life of any person;

(c) any representations on the matter which any person has provided
in writing to the First-tier Tribunal at any time prior to publication under the arrangements made under paragraph (1).

(4) A decision of the First-tier Tribunal must be published in such a manner as to protect the anonymity of the appellant.

PART 4

CORRECTING, REVIEWING AND APPEALING DECISIONS OF THE FIRST-TIER TRIBUNAL

Interpretation

7.175   **31.** In this Part—
"appeal" means the exercise of a right of appeal on a point of law under section 46(1) of the 2014 Act; and
"review" means the internal review provided for by section 43(1) of the 2014 Act.

Correction of clerical mistakes or accidental slips or omissions

7.176   **32.** The First-tier Tribunal may at any time correct any clerical mistake or other accidental slip or omission contained in a decision, order or any document produced by it, by—
(a) sending notification of the amended decision or order, or a copy of the amended document, to all parties; and
(b) making any necessary amendment to any information published in relation to the decision, order or document.

Application for permission to appeal against a decision of the First-tier Tribunal

7.177   **33.**—(1) A person seeking permission to appeal against a decision of the First-tier Tribunal must make a written application to the First-tier Tribunal for permission to appeal.
(2) An application under paragraph (1) must—
(a) identify the decision of the First-tier Tribunal to which it relates;
(b) identify the alleged point or points of law on which the person making the application wishes to appeal; and
(c) state the result that the [¹ person] making the application is seeking.
(3) Where an application under paragraph (1) has been submitted after the expiry of the 30 day period referred to in regulation 2(1) of the 2016 Regulations—
(a) the application must include a request for an extension of time and state the reasons why the application was not submitted in time; and
(b) unless the First-tier Tribunal extends the time period, the Tribunal must not admit the application.

AMENDMENT

1. First-tier Tribunal for Scotland Social Security Chamber (Rules of Procedure) Amendment Regulations 2018 (SSI 2018/343) reg.2 (1) and (8) (December 21, 2018).

First-tier Tribunal's consideration of application for permission to appeal against its decision

34.—(1) On receiving an application for permission to appeal, the First-tier Tribunal must decide whether to give permission to appeal on any point of law.   7.178

(2) The First-tier Tribunal must provide a notice of its decision to the parties as soon as reasonably practicable.

(3) If the First-tier Tribunal refuses permission to appeal it must send with the notice of its decision—

(a) a statement of its reasons for such a refusal; and

(b) notification of the right to make an application to the Upper Tribunal for permission to appeal and the time within which, and the method by which, such an application must be made.

Review of a decision

35.—(1) A party may request a review of a decision [¹ . . .] of the First-tier Tribunal on the basis of a point of law [¹ (unless it is an excluded decision or a process decision)].   7.179

(2) An application for a review must—

(a) be made in writing;

(b) be made within the period of 14 days beginning with the day on which the decision was made or the day that the written reasons were sent to the parties (if later); and

(c) identify the alleged point or points of law on the basis of which a review is being sought.

(3) If the First-tier Tribunal considers that the application is without merit, the First-tier Tribunal must refuse the application and inform the parties of the reasons for the refusal.

(4) Except where the application is rejected under paragraph (3), the First-tier Tribunal must send a notice to the parties—

(a) setting a time limit for any response to the application by the other parties and seeking the views of the parties on whether the application can be determined without a hearing; and

(b) if the First-tier Tribunal considers it appropriate to do so, setting out its provisional views on the application.

(5) Except where the application is rejected under paragraph (3), the decision is to be reviewed at a hearing unless the First-tier Tribunal considers, having regard to all of the responses to the notice provided under paragraph [¹ (4)], that a hearing is not necessary in the interests of justice.

(6) Where practicable, the review is to be undertaken by one or more of the members of the First-tier Tribunal who made the decision to which it relates.

(7) A notice of the decision on a review under paragraph (4) must as soon as reasonably practicable be sent by the First-tier Tribunal to each party.

(8) [¹ An application for a review] by the First-tier Tribunal in terms of paragraph (1) does not affect the time limit of 30 days in regulation 2(1) of the 2016 Regulations for making an application for permission to appeal.

AMENDMENT

1. First-tier Tribunal for Scotland Social Security Chamber (Rules of Procedure) Amendment Regulations 2018 (SSI 2018/343) reg.2 (1) and (9) (December 21, 2018).

Duty to treat a request for a review as an application for permission to appeal

7.180   **36.**—(1) The First-tier Tribunal must treat a request for a review under rule 35 (review of a decision) as also being an application for permission to appeal under rule 33 (application for permission to appeal against a decision of the First-tier Tribunal), unless the appellant states expressly that they do not wish it to be so treated.

(2) Where an appellant is given notice of a review decision under rule 35(7) (notice of decision on a review to be sent as soon as reasonably practicable), the appellant is to be given the opportunity to state whether or not the appellant wishes to proceed with an appeal.

The Upper Tribunal for Scotland (Social Security Rules of Procedure) Regulations 2018

SSI 2018 No. 274

Made	*11th September 2018*
Laid before the Scottish Parliament	*13th September 2018*
Coming into force	*22nd November 2018*

The Scottish Ministers make the following Regulations in exercise of the powers conferred by paragraph 4(2) of schedule 9 of the Tribunals (Scotland) Act 2014 and all other powers enabling them to do so.   7.181

In accordance with paragraph 4(3) of schedule 9 of that Act, the Scottish Ministers have consulted the President of the Scottish Tribunals and such other persons as they considered appropriate.

Citation, commencement and interpretation

1.—(1) These Regulations may be cited as the Upper Tribunal for   7.182
Scotland (Social Security Rules of Procedure) Regulations 2018 and the Rules contained in the schedule may be cited as the Upper Tribunal for Scotland Social Security Rules of Procedure 2018.

(2) These Regulations come into force on 22nd November 2018.

(3) In these Regulations, "the 2018 Act" means the Social Security (Scotland) Act 2018.

Disapplication of the Upper Tribunal for Scotland Rules 2016

2. The Upper Tribunal for Scotland Rules of Procedure 2016 do not   7.183
apply to proceedings before the Upper Tribunal relating to the exercise by the Scottish Ministers of functions conferred on them by the 2018 Act or by regulations made under that Act.

Application of Rules in schedule

3. The Rules in the schedule of these Regulations apply to all proceed-   7.184
ings before the Upper Tribunal relating to the exercise by the Scottish Ministers of functions conferred on them by the 2018 Act or by regulations made under that Act.

Regulation 3

SCHEDULE

THE UPPER TRIBUNAL FOR SCOTLAND SOCIAL SECURITY RULES OF
PROCEDURE 2018

PART 1

INTERPRETATION

1. Interpretation   **7.185**

PART 2

ROLE OF THE UPPER TRIBUNAL

2. Purpose of the Upper Tribunal and overriding objective

PART 3

PROCEDURE FOR CASES IN THE UPPER TRIBUNAL

3. Application for permission to appeal against a decision of the First-tier Tribunal
4. Notice of appeal against a decision of the First-tier Tribunal
5. Response to the notice of appeal
6. Appellant's reply

PART 4

GENERAL POWERS AND PROVISIONS

7. Delegation to staff
8. Case management
9. Procedure for applying for and giving orders
10. Failure to comply with rulesetc.
11. Dismissal of a party's case
12. Addition, substitution and removal of parties
13. Representatives
14. Supporters
15. Calculating time
16. Sending and delivery of documents
17. Disclosure of documents and information
18. Evidence and submissions
19. Citation of witnesses and orders to answer questions or produce documents
20. Withdrawal
21. Chairing member

PART 5

HEARINGS

22. Decision with or without a hearing
23. Entitlement to attend a hearing
24. Notice of hearings

PART 6

Decisions

PART 7

Appealing Decisions of the Upper Tribunal

PART 8

Legal Aid

PART 1

Interpretation

Interpretation

1.—(1) In these Rules—
"the 2014 Act" means the Tribunals (Scotland) Act 2014;
"the 2018 Act" means the Social Security (Scotland) Act 2018;
"the 2016 Regulations" means the Scottish Tribunals (Time Limits) Regulations 2016;

7.186

"Appeal Appendix" means all the documents and authorities to be relied on for the purpose of the appeal along with an inventory of those documents and authorities;

"appellant" means—

    (a) a person who makes an appeal to the Upper Tribunal; or

    (b) a person substituted as an appellant under rule 12 (addition, substitution and removal of parties);

"the Convention rights" has the meaning given to it in section 1 of the Human Rights Act 1998;

"document" means anything in which information is recorded in any form;

"electronic communication" has the meaning given to it by section 15(1) of the Electronic Communications Act 2000;

"excluded decision" means a decision falling under section 51 of the 2014 Act;

"the First-tier Tribunal" means the First-tier Tribunal for Scotland Social Security Chamber;

"hearing" means an oral hearing and includes a hearing conducted in whole or in part by video link, telephone or other means of instantaneous two-way electronic communication;

"party" means a person who is (or was at the time that the Upper Tribunal disposed of the proceedings) an appellant or respondent in proceedings before the Upper Tribunal;

"practice direction" means a practice direction issued in terms of section 74 of the 2014 Act;

"President" means the President of the Scottish Tribunals;

"proceedings" includes a part of the proceedings;

"representative" means a lay representative or a legal representative;

"respondent" means—

    (a) in an appeal against a decision of the First-tier Tribunal, that Tribunal and any person other than the appellant who was a party before the First-tier Tribunal; or

    (b) a person substituted or added as a respondent under rule 12 (addition, substitution and removal of parties);

"review period" means the time period between the day of an application by a party for a review under rule 28(1) or, as the case may be, the Upper Tribunal's decision to review a decision under that rule, and the receipt by each party of a notice sent under rule 28(5);

"the Upper Tribunal" means the Upper Tribunal for Scotland; and

"witness statement" means a written statement of a witness ordered by the Upper Tribunal to stand for the evidence-in-chief of the witness.

(2) For the purposes of these Rules, where information is sent—

    (a) via the postal service to the last known address held for an individual; or

    (b) by email to the last known email address held for the individual,

the individual is presumed to have received the information 48 hours after it is sent, unless the contrary is shown.

PART 2

Role of the Upper Tribunal

Purpose of the Upper Tribunal and overriding objective

2.—(1) The Upper Tribunal hears and decides cases referred to it   7.187
from the First-tier Tribunal for Scotland and hears and decides appeals
from the First-tier Tribunal.

(2) The overriding objective of these Rules is to secure that proceedings before the Upper Tribunal to which the Rules apply are handled
fairly and justly.

(3) Dealing with a case fairly and justly includes—

(a) dealing with the case in ways which are transparent, proportionate
to the importance of the case, the complexity of the issues, the
anticipated expenses and the resources of the parties;

(b) avoiding unnecessary formality and seeking flexibility in the
proceedings;

(c) ensuring, so far as practicable, that the parties are able to participate fully in the proceedings and are treated with dignity and
respect;

(d) using any special expertise of the Upper Tribunal effectively;
and

(e) avoiding delay, so far as compatible with proper consideration of
the issues.

(4) The Upper Tribunal must seek to give effect to the overriding
objective when it—

(a) exercises any power under these Rules; or

(b) interprets any rule or practice direction.

(5) Parties must, insofar as reasonably possible—

(a) help the Upper Tribunal to further the overriding objective; and

(b) co-operate with the Upper Tribunal generally.

PART 3

Procedure for Cases in the Upper Tribunal

Application for permission to appeal against a decision of the First-tier Tribunal

3.—(1) A person may lodge with the Upper Tribunal an application   7.188
for permission to appeal against a decision of the First-tier Tribunal,
where the First-tier Tribunal has refused permission to appeal in whole
or in part.

(2) An application for permission to appeal must—

(a) identify the decision of the First-tier Tribunal to which it relates;
and

    (b) identify the alleged point or points of law in relation to the decision.

(3) The appellant must provide with the application for permission a copy of—

    (a) any written record of the decision being challenged;

    (b) any separate written statement of reasons for that decision; and

    (c) the notice of refusal of permission to appeal from the First-tier Tribunal.

(4) If the appellant lodges the application for permission to appeal with the Upper Tribunal after the expiry of the 30 day period referred to in regulation 3(1) of the 2016 Regulations—

    (a) the application for permission to appeal must—

        (i) include a request for an extension of time;

        (ii) explain why the application for permission to appeal was not made in time; and

        (iii) state why it is said to be in the interests of justice that the time be extended.

    (b) unless the Upper Tribunal extends the time for lodging an application for permission to appeal the Upper Tribunal must not admit the application for permission to appeal.

(5) The Upper Tribunal may, where the First-tier Tribunal has refused permission to appeal—

    (a) refuse permission to appeal;

    (b) give permission to appeal; or

    (c) give permission to appeal on limited grounds or subject to conditions,

and must send a notice of its decision to each party including reasons for a refusal of permission or for limitations or conditions on any grant of permission.

(6) Where the Upper Tribunal, without a hearing—

    (a) refuses permission to appeal; or

    (b) gives permission to appeal on limited grounds or subject to conditions,

the appellant may make a written application (within the period of 14 days beginning with the day on which the appellant is presumed to have received notice of refusal of permission, sent under paragraph (5)) to the Upper Tribunal for the decision to be reconsidered at a hearing.

(7) An application under paragraph (6) must be heard and decided by a member or members of the Upper Tribunal different from the member or members who refused permission without a hearing.

(8) Where the Upper Tribunal gives permission to appeal against a decision of the First-tier Tribunal, a valid notice of appeal will be deemed to have been provided to the Upper Tribunal, for the purposes of rule 4 (notice of appeal against a decision of the First-tier Tribunal).

Notice of appeal against a decision of the First-tier Tribunal

7.189   **4.**—(1) Where the First-tier Tribunal sends a notice of permission to appeal to a party who has sought permission to appeal, that party, if intending to appeal, must provide a notice of appeal to the Upper Tribunal within the period of 30 days beginning with the day on which the party is presumed to have received the notice of permission.

(2) A notice of appeal must —

(a) identify the decision of the First-tier Tribunal to which it relates;

(b) identify the alleged point or points of law in relation to the decision; and

(c) include any views of the appellant on whether the matter should be dealt with at a hearing or without a hearing.

(3) The appellant must provide with the notice of appeal a copy of—

(a) any written record of the decision being challenged;

(b) any separate written statement of reasons for that decision; and

(c) the notice of permission to appeal.

(4) When the Upper Tribunal receives a notice of appeal it must send a copy of the notice and any accompanying documents to each respondent.

(5) If the appellant lodges the notice of appeal with the Upper Tribunal after the end of the period mentioned in paragraph (1)—

(a) the notice of appeal must—

(i) include a request for an extension of time;

(ii) explain why the notice of appeal was not provided in time; and

(iii) state why it is said to be in the interests of justice that the time be extended; and

(b) unless the Upper Tribunal extends the time for lodging a notice of appeal the Upper Tribunal must not admit the notice of appeal.

Response to the notice of appeal

5.—(1) Subject to any order given by the Upper Tribunal, a respondent may provide a written response to a notice of appeal.   7.190

(2) Any response provided under paragraph (1) must be sent or delivered to the Upper Tribunal so that it is received before the end of the period of 30 days beginning with the day on which the respondent is presumed to have received the copy of the notice of appeal as sent by the Upper Tribunal.

(3) The response must state—

(a) the name and address of the respondent;

(b) the name and address of the representative (if any) of the respondent;

(c) an address where documents for the respondent may be sent or delivered;

(d) whether the respondent opposes the appeal;

(e) the grounds on which the respondent relies, including any grounds on which the respondent was unsuccessful in the proceedings which are the subject of the appeal, but intends to rely on in the appeal.

(4) The response may include a request that the case be dealt with at a hearing or without a hearing.

(5) If the respondent provides the response to the Upper Tribunal later than the time required by paragraph (2) or by an extension of time allowed under rule 8(3)(a) (power to extend time), the response must include a request for an extension of time and the reason why the response was not provided in time.

(6) When the Upper Tribunal receives the response it must send a copy of the response and any accompanying documents to the appellant.

Appellant's reply

7.191   **6.**—(1) Subject to any order given by the Upper Tribunal, the appellant may provide a written reply to any response provided under rule 5 (response to the notice of appeal).

(2) Any reply provided under paragraph (1) must be sent or delivered to the Upper Tribunal so that it is received within the period of 30 days beginning with the day on which the appellant is presumed to have received a copy of the response as sent by the Upper Tribunal.

(3) If the appellant provides the reply to the Upper Tribunal later than the time required by paragraph (2) or by an extension of time allowed under rule 8(3)(a) (power to extend time), the reply must include a request for an extension of time and the reason why the reply was not provided in time.

(4) When the Upper Tribunal receives the reply it must send a copy of the reply and any accompanying documents to each respondent.

PART 4

GENERAL POWERS AND PROVISIONS

Delegation to staff

7.192   **7.**—(1) Staff of the Scottish Courts and Tribunals Service may, with the approval of the President, carry out functions of a judicial nature permitted or required to be undertaken by the Upper Tribunal, provided that they are of a preliminary or an incidental nature.

(2) The approval referred to in paragraph (1) may apply generally to the carrying out of specified functions by members of staff of a specified description in specified circumstances.

(3) Where the Upper Tribunal sends notice of a decision made by a member of staff pursuant to an approval under paragraph (1) to a party, that party may, within the period of 14 days beginning with the day on which the party is presumed to have received the notice, make a written application to the Upper Tribunal for that decision to be considered afresh by a member of the Upper Tribunal.

Case management

8.—(1) Subject to the provisions of the 2014 Act and these Rules, the   7.193
Upper Tribunal may regulate its own procedure.

(2) The Upper Tribunal may give an order in relation to the conduct
of proceedings before it at any time, including an order amending,
suspending or setting aside an earlier order.

(3) In particular, and without restricting the general powers in paragraphs (1) and (2), the Upper Tribunal may—

(a) extend or shorten the time for complying with any rule or
order;

(b) conjoin or take concurrently two or more sets of proceedings or
parts of proceedings raising common issues;

(c) specify one or more cases as a lead case or lead cases where—
(i) two or more cases are before the Upper Tribunal;
(ii) in each such case the proceedings have not been finally
determined; and
(iii) the cases give rise to common or related issues of fact or
law,
and sist the other cases until the common or related issues
have been determined;

(d) permit or require a party to amend a document;

(e) permit or require a party or another person to provide documents,
information, evidence or submissions to the Upper Tribunal or a
party;

(f) deal with an issue in the proceedings as a preliminary issue;

(g) hold a hearing to consider any matter, including a case management issue;

(h) decide the form of any hearing;

(i) adjourn or postpone a hearing;

(j) require a party to produce or lodge documents including but not
confined to a note of argument and the Appeal Appendix;

(k) sist proceedings;

(l) transfer proceedings to another court or tribunal if that other
court or tribunal has jurisdiction in relation to the proceedings
and—
(i) because of a change of circumstances since the proceedings
were started, the Upper Tribunal no longer has jurisdiction
in relation to the proceedings; or
(ii) the Upper Tribunal considers that the other court or tribunal
is a more appropriate forum for the determination of the
case;

(m) suspend the effect of its own decision pending an appeal of that
decision;

(n) in an appeal against the decision of the First-tier Tribunal, suspend the effect of that decision pending the determination of any
permission to appeal or any appeal;

(o) require the First-tier Tribunal to provide reasons for the decision,
or other information or documents in relation to the decision or
any proceedings before the First-tier Tribunal.

Procedure for applying for and giving orders

7.194   **9.**—(1) The Upper Tribunal may give an order on the application of one or more of the parties or on its own initiative.

(2) An application for an order may be made—

(a) by sending or delivering a written application to the Upper Tribunal; or

(b) orally during the course of a hearing.

(3) An application for an order must include the reasons for making that application.

(4) The Tribunal must send written notice of any order to each party to the case.

(5) If a party sent a notice of the order under paragraph (4) wishes to challenge the order, the party may do so by applying for another order which amends, suspends or sets aside the first order.

Failure to comply with rules etc.

7.195   **10.**—(1) An irregularity resulting from a failure to comply with any requirement in these Rules, a practice direction or an order, does not of itself render void the proceedings or any step taken in the proceedings.

(2) If a party has failed to comply with a requirement in these Rules, a practice direction or an order, the Upper Tribunal may take such action as it considers just, which may include—

(a) waiving the requirement;

(b) requiring the failure to be remedied; or

(c) exercising its power under rule 11 (dismissal of a party's case).

Dismissal of a party's case

7.196   **11.**—(1) The Upper Tribunal must dismiss the whole or a part of the proceedings if the Upper Tribunal—

(a) does not have jurisdiction in relation to the proceedings or that part of them; and

(b) does not exercise its power under rule 8(3)(l) (transfer to another court or tribunal) in relation to the proceedings or that part of them.

(2) The Upper Tribunal may dismiss the whole or a part of the proceedings if—

(a) the appellant has failed to comply with an order which stated that failure by the appellant to comply with the order could lead to the dismissal of the proceedings or part of them; or

(b) the appellant has failed to co-operate with the Upper Tribunal to such an extent that the Upper Tribunal considers that it cannot deal with the proceedings fairly.

(3) The Upper Tribunal may not dismiss the whole or a part of the proceedings under paragraph (1) or (2)(b) without first giving the appellant an opportunity to make representations in relation to the proposed dismissal.

(4) If the proceedings, or part of them, have been dismissed under paragraph (2)(a), the appellant may apply for the proceedings, or part of

them, to be reinstated, where the appellant can satisfy the Upper Tribunal that the appellant has good reason to apply for reinstatement.

(5) An application under paragraph (4) must be made in writing and received by the Upper Tribunal within the period of 31 days beginning with the day on which the notification sent to the appellant under paragraph (8) is presumed to have been received.

(6) An application under paragraph (4) must set out the reasons on which the appellant relies in applying for reinstatement.

(7) This rule applies to a respondent as it does to an appellant except that—

(a) a reference to the dismissal of the proceedings is to be read as a reference to the barring of the respondent from taking further part in the proceedings; and

(b) a reference to an application for the reinstatement of proceedings which have been dismissed is to be read as a reference to an application for the lifting of the bar on the respondent taking further part in the proceedings.

(8) The Upper Tribunal must notify each party in writing that dismissal has taken place.

Addition, substitution and removal of parties

12.—(1) The Upper Tribunal may give an order adding, substituting   7.197
or removing a party as an appellant or a respondent including where—

(a) the wrong person has been named as a party; or

(b) the addition, substitution or removal has become necessary because of a change in circumstances since the start of proceedings.

(2) If the Upper Tribunal gives an order under paragraph (1) it may give such consequential orders as it considers appropriate.

(3) A person who is not a party may make a written application to the Upper Tribunal to be added or substituted as a party under this rule.

(4) If the Upper Tribunal refuses an application under paragraph (3) it must consider whether to permit the person who made the application to provide submissions or evidence to the Upper Tribunal.

Representatives

13.—(1) A party may be represented in any proceedings by a repre-   7.198
sentative whose details may be communicated to the Upper Tribunal prior to any hearing.

(2) A party may show any document or communicate any information about the proceedings to that party's representative without contravening any prohibition or restriction on disclosure of the document or information.

(3) Where a document or information is disclosed under paragraph (2), the representative is subject to any prohibition or restriction on disclosure in the same way that the party is.

(4) For the avoidance of doubt, a party may be represented at a hearing by a person other than any person whose details have been communicated to the Upper Tribunal under paragraph (1).

Supporters

7.199   **14.** A party who is an individual may be accompanied by another person, who is not a representative, to act as a supporter.

Calculating time

7.200   **15.**—(1) An act required by these Rules, a practice direction or an order to be done on or by a particular day must be done by 5 pm on that day.

(2) If the time specified by these Rules, a practice direction or an order for doing any act ends on a day other than a working day, the act is done in time if it is done on the next working day.

(3) In this rule and in rule 28 (reviews), "working day" means any day except a Saturday, a Sunday, or a bank holiday in Scotland under section 1 of the Banking and Financial Dealings Act 1971.

Sending and delivery of documents

7.201   **16.**—(1)Any document to be provided to the Upper Tribunal under these Rules, a practice direction or an order must be—

(a) sent by pre-paid post or by document exchange, or delivered to, the address of the Upper Tribunal; or

(b) sent or delivered by such other method as the Upper Tribunal may permit or direct.

(2) Subject to paragraph (3), if a party provides a fax number, email address or other details for the electronic transmission of documents to them, that party must accept delivery of documents by that method.

(3) If a party informs the Upper Tribunal and all other parties that a particular form of communication, other than post, should not be used to provide documents to that party, that form of communication must not be so used.

(4) If the Upper Tribunal or a party sends a document to a party or the Upper Tribunal by email or any other electronic means of communication, the recipient may request that the sender provides a hard copy of the document to the recipient, and the recipient must make any such a request as soon as reasonably practicable after receiving the document electronically.

(5) The Upper Tribunal and each party may assume that the address provided by a party or its representative is and remains the address to which documents should be sent or delivered until receiving written notification to the contrary.

Disclosure of documents and information

7.202   **17.** The Upper Tribunal may at any stage of the proceedings, on its own initiative or on application by one or more of the parties, make an order with a view to preventing or restricting the public disclosure of any aspect of those proceedings so far as it considers necessary in the interests of justice or in order to protect the Convention rights of any person.

Evidence and submissions

18.—(1) Without restriction on the general powers in rule 8(1) and (2) (case management powers), the Upper Tribunal may give orders as to—

    7.203

(a) issues on which parties may lead fresh evidence or make submissions;

(b) the nature of any such evidence;

(c) whether the parties are permitted to provide expert evidence, and if so whether the parties must jointly appoint a single expert to provide such evidence;

(d) any limit on the number of witnesses whose evidence a party may put forward, whether in relation to a particular issue or generally;

(e) the manner in which any evidence or submissions are to be provided, which may include an order for them to be given—

    (i) orally at a hearing; or

    (ii) by written submissions or witness statement; and

(f) the time at which any evidence or submissions are to be provided.

(2) The Upper Tribunal may exclude evidence that would otherwise be admissible where—

(a) the evidence was not, without reasonable excuse, provided within the time allowed by an order or a practice direction;

(b) the evidence was otherwise, without reasonable excuse, provided in a manner that did not comply with an order or a practice direction; or

(c) it would otherwise be unfair to admit the evidence.

(3) The Upper Tribunal may consent to a witness giving, or require any witness to give, evidence on oath or affirmation, and may administer an oath or affirmation for that purpose.

Citation of witnesses and orders to answer questions or produce documents

19.—(1) On the application of a party or on its own initiative, the Upper Tribunal may—

    7.204

(a) by citation require any person to attend as a witness at a hearing at the time and place specified in the citation; or

(b) order any person to answer any questions or produce any documents in that person's possession or control which relate to any issue in the proceedings.

(2) A citation under paragraph (1)(a) must—

(a) give the person required to attend 14 days' notice prior to the day of the hearing or such other period as the Upper Tribunal may order;

(b) where the person is not a party, state how expenses of attendance necessarily incurred may be recovered;

(c) state that the person on whom the requirement is imposed may apply to the Upper Tribunal to vary or set aside the citation or order, if the person did not have an opportunity to object to it before it was made or issued; and

(d) state the consequences of failure to comply with the citation or order.

(3) A person making an application referred to in sub-paragraph (2)(c) must do so as soon as reasonably practicable after receiving notice of the citation or order.

(4) No person may be compelled to give any evidence or produce any document that the person could not be compelled to give or produce at a civil trial of an action in a court of law in Scotland.

Withdrawal

7.205   **20.**—(1) Subject to paragraph (2), a party may give notice to the Upper Tribunal of the withdrawal of the party's case, or any part of that case—

(a) by sending or delivering to the Upper Tribunal a notice of withdrawal; or

(b) orally at a hearing.

(2) Notice of withdrawal will not take effect unless the Upper Tribunal consents to the withdrawal except in relation to an application for permission to appeal.

(3) Unless satisfied that a party has already been notified, the Upper Tribunal must notify each party in writing that a withdrawal has taken effect under this rule.

(4) Where a case has been withdrawn in accordance with paragraphs (1) and (2), the party which has withdrawn its case may apply to the Upper Tribunal for the case to be reinstated, where the party can satisfy the Tribunal that the party has good reason to apply for reinstatement.

(5) An application under paragraph (4) must be made in writing and be received by the Upper Tribunal within the period of 31 days beginning with the earlier of—

(a) the day on which the party which has withdrawn its case is presumed to have received the notification sent under paragraph (3) that the withdrawal has taken effect; or

(b) if the party which has withdrawn its case was present at the hearing when the case was withdrawn orally under paragraph (1)(b), the day of that hearing.

(6) An application under paragraph (4) must set out the reasons on which the applicant relies in applying for reinstatement of the case.

Chairing member

7.206   **21.** Where a matter is to be decided by two or more members of the Upper Tribunal, the President must determine the chairing member.

PART 5

HEARINGS

Decision with or without a hearing

22.—(1) Subject to paragraph (2), the Upper Tribunal may make any   7.207
decision without a hearing.

(2) The Upper Tribunal must have regard to any view expressed by
any party when deciding whether to hold a hearing to consider any
matter, and the form of any such hearing.

Entitlement to attend a hearing

23. Subject to the power to exclude persons in rule 25(4) (public and   7.208
private hearings), each party is entitled to participate at a hearing
together with any representatives and supporters permitted by rules 13
(representatives) and 14 (supporters).

Notice of hearings

24.—(1) The Upper Tribunal must give each party entitled to attend   7.209
a hearing reasonable notice of the time and place of the hearing (including any adjourned or postponed hearing) and any change to the time and
place of the hearing.

(2) The period of notice under paragraph (1) must be at least 14 days
prior to the day of the hearing except that the Upper Tribunal may give
shorter notice—

(a) with the consent of the parties; or

(b) in urgent or exceptional circumstances.

Public and private hearings

25.—(1) Subject to the following paragraphs, all hearings must be   7.210
held in public.

(2) The Upper Tribunal may give an order that a hearing, or part of
it, is to be held in private if the Upper Tribunal considers that restricting
access to the hearing is justified—

(a) in the interests of public order;

(b) in order to protect a person's right to respect for their private and
    family life;

(c) in order to maintain the confidentiality of sensitive information;

(d) in order to avoid serious harm to the public interest; or

(e) because to hold it in public would prejudice the interests of jus-
    tice.

(3) Where a hearing, or any part of it, is to be held in private, the
Upper Tribunal may determine who is entitled to attend the hearing or
part of it.

(4) The Upper Tribunal may give an order excluding from any hearing, or part of it—

    (a) any person whose conduct the Upper Tribunal considers is disrupting or is likely to disrupt the hearing;

    (b) any person whose presence the Upper Tribunal considers is likely to prevent another person from giving evidence or making submissions freely; or

    (c) any person where the purpose of the hearing would be defeated by the attendance of that person.

(5) The Upper Tribunal may give a direction excluding a witness from a hearing until that witness gives evidence.

(6) When publishing a decision in terms of rule 27(4) (notice of decisions and reasons) following a hearing which was held wholly or partly in private, the Upper Tribunal must, so far as practicable, ensure that the decision does not disclose information which was referred to in a part of the hearing that was held in private.

Hearings in a party's absence

7.211   **26.** If a party fails to attend a hearing, the Upper Tribunal may proceed with the hearing if the Upper Tribunal—

    (a) is satisfied that the party has been notified of the hearing or that reasonable steps have been taken to notify the party of the hearing; and

    (b) considers that it is in the interests of justice to proceed with the hearing.

PART 6

DECISIONS

Notice of decisions and reasons

7.212   **27.**—(1) Subject to the remainder of this rule, the Upper Tribunal may give a decision orally at a hearing.

(2) The Upper Tribunal must provide to each party as soon as reasonably practicable after making a decision (other than a decision under Part 7 (appealing decisions of the Upper Tribunal)) which finally disposes of all issues in the proceedings or on a preliminary issue dealt with following an order under rule 8(3)(f) (dealing with an issue as a preliminary issue)—

    (a) a decision notice stating the Upper Tribunal's decision; and

    (b) notification of any rights of appeal against the decision and the time and manner in which such rights of appeal may be exercised.

(3) If the Upper Tribunal does not provide written reasons for a decision, a party may request written reasons, within the period of 14 days beginning with the day of the decision.

(4) The Upper Tribunal may publish any of its decisions if it considers it in the public interest so to do, with the manner of publication also at the discretion of the Upper Tribunal.

Reviews

28.—(1) The Upper Tribunal may at its own instance or at the request   7.213
of a party review a decision (except an excluded decision) made by it if
it considers it necessary in the interests of justice to do so and on review
it may confirm, set aside, or set aside and re-decide the decision.

(2) An application under paragraph (1) must be made in writing
within the period of 14 days beginning with the day of the decision and
must state the reasons for making the application.

(3) The Upper Tribunal must send a copy of the application to any
other party involved in the proceedings within the period of 10 working
days beginning with the day of receipt of the application.

(4) The review must be decided as soon as reasonably practicable by
the Upper Tribunal, with insofar as practicable the same members that
decided the case, or where this is not practicable with members selected
by the President.

(5) A notice of the decision on a review under paragraph (1) must as
soon as reasonably practicable be sent by the Upper Tribunal to each
party.

(6) The 30 days referred to in regulation 3(1) of the 2016 Regulations
in respect of an application to the Upper Tribunal is extended by any
review period.

PART 7

APPEALING DECISIONS OF THE UPPER TRIBUNAL

Interpretation

29. In this Part, "appeal" means the exercise of a right of appeal under   7.214
section 48(1) of the 2014 Act.

Application for permission to appeal a decision of the Upper Tribunal

30.—(1) A party seeking permission to appeal must make a written   7.215
application to the Upper Tribunal.

(2) An application under paragraph (1) must—

(a) identify the decision of the Upper Tribunal to which it relates;

(b) identify the alleged point or points of law raised in relation to the
decision; and

(c) state in terms of section 50(4) of the 2014 Act what important
point of principle or practice would be raised by a second appeal
or what other compelling reason there is that shows the appeal
should be allowed to proceed.

Upper Tribunal's consideration of application for permission to appeal

31.—(1) The Upper Tribunal must consider whether to give permis-   7.216
sion to appeal in relation to the decision or part of it.

(2) The Upper Tribunal must provide a record of its decision to the parties as soon as practicable.

(3) If the Upper Tribunal refuses permission to appeal it must provide with the record of its decision—

    (a) a statement of its reasons for such a refusal; and

    (b) notification of the right to make an application to the Court of Session for permission to appeal and the time within which, and the method by which, such application must be made.

(4) The Upper Tribunal may give permission to appeal on limited grounds, but must comply with paragraph (3) in relation to any grounds on which it has refused permission.

PART 8

Legal Aid

Legal aid

7.217   **32.** If a party is granted legal aid by the Scottish Legal Aid Board in respect of a case before the Upper Tribunal that party must as soon as practicable send a copy of the legal aid certificate to the Upper Tribunal.

PART VIII

FORTHCOMING CHANGES AND UP-RATINGS OF BENEFITS

FORTHCOMING CHANGES

Universal Credit

The Universal Credit (Transitional Provisions) (SDP Gateway) **8.001** Amendment Regulations 2019 (SI 2019/10), in force as from January 16, 2019, amend the Universal Credit (Transitional Provisions) Regulations 2014 and make amendments to Orders commencing provisions in the Welfare Reform Act 2012. The amendments introduce a 'Gateway Condition' so that claimants who are receiving income-related ESA, income-based JSA or income support (or housing benefit) with a severe disability premium (SDP) included in their award will not claim universal credit if they need to make a new claim for support. Instead they will remain on existing legacy benefits until they are moved to universal credit as part of the Department's managed migration process. There is, of course, no equivalent to the SDP in the universal credit scheme.

The Universal Credit (Restriction on Amounts for Children and Qualifying Young Persons) (Transitional Provisions) Amendment Regulations 2019 (SI 2019/27) amend the so-called "two children rule". They amend both the Universal Credit Regulations 2013 and the Universal Credit (Transitional Provisions) Regulations 2014 so as to continue to make provision for the payment of child element in new claims to universal credit for all children born before April 6, 2017 (where entitlement exists). This reform was announced by the Minister of State for Employment in a written statement on January 11, 2019.

On February 5, 2019 it was announced that the Secretary of State had determined that the "termporary de minimis amount" under reg.54A(6) of the Universal Credit Regulations 2013 is not to revert to £300 from £2,500 on April 1, 2019 and that the operation of the higher amount is extended until March 31, 2020 at least."

State pension credit

As from May 15, 2019, so-called "mixed age couples" will be excluded **8.002** from entitlement to state pension credit. Under the previous rules couples were able to transition from working age to pension age benefits as soon as the oldest partner reached state pension age. However, as a result of this change the couple will only be able to transition once the youngest member of the pair reaches state pension age. This is because of s.4(1A) of the State Pension Credit Act 2002 as amended by paragraph 64 of Schedule 2 to the Welfare Reform Act, brought into effect by the Welfare Reform Act 2012 (Commencement No. 31 and Savings and Transitional Provisions and Commencement No. 21 and 23 and Transitional and Transitory Provisions (Amendment)) Order 2019 (SI 2019/37). This exclusionary rule is subject to certain savings provisions.

NEW BENEFIT RATES FROM APRIL 2019

NEW BENEFIT RATES FROM APRIL 2019

(Benefits covered in Volume I)

	April 2018	April 2019
	£ pw	£ pw
Disability benefits		
Attendance allowance		
higher rate	85.60	87.65
lower rate	57.30	58.70
Disability living allowance		
care component		
highest rate	85.60	87.65
middle rate	57.30	58.70
lowest rate	22.65	23.20
mobility component		
higher rate	59.75	61.20
lower rate	22.65	23.20
Personal independence payment		
daily living component		
enhanced rate	85.60	87.65
standard rate	57.30	58.70
mobility component		
enhanced rate	59.75	61.20
standard rate	22.65	23.20
Carer's allowance	64.60	66.15
Severe disablement allowance		
basic rate	77.65	79.50
age related addition—higher rate	11.60	11.90
age related addition—middle rate	6.45	6.60
age related addition—lower rate	6.45	6.60

	April 2018 £ pw	April 2019 £ pw
Maternity benefits		
Maternity allowance		
standard rate	145.18	148.68
Bereavement benefits and retirement pensions		
Widowed parent's allowance or widowed mother's allowance	117.10	119.90
Bereavement allowance or widow's pension		
standard rate	117.10	119.90
Retirement pension		
Category A	125.95	129.20
Category B (higher)	125.95	129.20
Category B (lower)	75.50	77.45
Category C	75.50	77.45
Category D	75.50	77.45
New state pension	164.35	168.60
Incapacity benefit		
Long-term incapacity benefit		
basic rate	109.60	112.25
increase for age—higher rate	11.60	11.90
increase for age—lower rate	6.45	6.60
invalidity allowance—higher rate	11.60	11.90
invalidity allowance—middle rate	6.45	6.60
invalidity allowance—lower rate	6.45	6.60
Short-term incapacity benefit		
under pension age—higher rate	97.85	100.20
under pension age—lower rate	82.65	84.65
over pension age—higher rate	109.60	112.25
over pension age—lower rate	105.15	107.65
Dependency increases		
Adult		
carer's allowance	38.00	38.90
severe disablement allowance	38.20	39.10
retirement pension (Category A)	68.35	70.00
retirement pension (Category C)	40.90	41.90
long-term incapacity benefit	63.65	65.20
short-term incapacity benefit under pension age	49.60	50.80
short-term incapacity benefit over pension age	61.30	62.75
Child	11.35[1]	11.35[1]

	April 2018	April 2019
	£ pw	£ pw

Industrial injuries benefits

Disablement benefit

100%	174.80	179.00
90%	157.32	161.10
80%	139.84	143.20
70%	122.36	125.30
60%	104.88	107.40
50%	87.40	89.50
40%	69.92	71.60
30%	52.44	53.70
20%	34.96	35.80

unemployability supplement

basic rate	108.05	110.65
increase for adult dependant	64.60	66.15
increase for child dependant	11.35[1]	11.35[1]
increase for early incapacity—higher rate	22.35	22.90
increase for early incapacity—middle rate	14.40	14.70
increase for early incapacity—lower rate	7.20	7.35

constant attendance allowance

exceptional rate	139.80	143.20
intermediate rate	104.85	107.40
normal maximum rate	69.90	71.60
part-time rate	34.95	35.80

exceptionally severe disablement allowance	69.90	71.60

Reduced earnings allowance

maximum rate	69.90	71.60

Death benefit
widow's pension

higher rate	125.95	129.20
lower rate	37.79	38.76
widower's pension	125.95	129.20

Notes
1. These sums payable in respect of children are reduced if payable in respect of the only, elder or eldest child for whom child benefit is being paid (see reg.8 of the Social Security (Overlapping Benefits) Regulations 1979 on p.619 of Vol.1 of the main work).

New Benefit Rates from April 2019

	April 2018	April 2019
	£ pw	£ pw

Employment and support allowance

Contribution-based personal rates

assessment phase—*aged under 25*	57.90	57.90
aged 25 or over	73.10	73.10
main phase	73.10	73.10

Components

work-related activity	29.05	29.05
support	37.65	38.55

Income-based personal allowances

single person—*aged under 25*	57.90	57.90
aged 25 or over	73.10	73.10
lone parent—*aged under 18*	57.90	57.90
aged 18 or over	73.10	73.10
couple—*both aged under 18*	57.90	57.90
both aged under 18, with a child	87.50	87.50
both aged under 18, (main phase)	73.10	73.10
both aged under 18, with a child (main phase)	114.85	114.85
one aged under 18, one aged 18 or over	114.85	114.85
both aged 18 or over	114.85	114.85

Premiums

pensioner—*single person with no component*	89.90	94.15
couple with no component	133.95	140.40
enhanced disability—*single person*	16.40	16.80
couple	23.55	24.10
severe disability—*single person*	64.30	65.85
couple (one qualifies)	64.30	65.85
couple (both qualify)	128.60	131.70
carer	36.00	36.85

NEW BENEFIT RATES FROM APRIL 2019

(Benefits covered in Volume II)

	April 2018 £ pw	April 2019 £ pw
Contribution-based jobseeker's allowance		
personal rates—*aged under 25*	57.90	57.90
aged 25 or over	73.10	73.10
Income support and income-based jobseeker's allowance		
personal allowances		
single person—*aged under 25*	57.90	57.90
aged 25 or over	73.10	73.10
lone parent—*aged under 18*	57.90	57.90
aged 18 or over	73.10	73.10
couple—*both aged under 18*	57.90	57.90
both aged under 18, with a child	87.50	87.50
one aged under 18, one aged under 25	57.90	57.90
one aged under 18, one aged 25 or over	73.10	73.10
both aged 18 or over	114.85	114.85
child	66.90	66.90
premiums		
family—*ordinary*	17.45	17.45
lone parent	17.45	17.45
pensioner—*single person (JSA only)*	89.90	94.15
couple	133.95	140.40
disability—*single person*	33.55	34.35
couple	47.80	48.95
enhanced disability—*single person*	16.40	16.80
couple	23.55	24.10
disabled child	25.48	26.04
severe disability—*single person*	64.30	65.85
couple (one qualifies)	64.30	65.85
couple (both qualify)	128.60	131.70
disabled child	62.86	64.19
carer	36.00	36.85
Pension credit		
Standard minimum guarantee		
single person	163.00	167.25
couple	248.80	255.25

New Benefit Rates from April 2019

	April 2018 £ pw	April 2019 £ pw
Additional amount for severe disability		
single person	64.30	65.85
couple (one qualifies)	64.30	65.85
couple (both qualify)	128.60	131.70
Additional amount for carers	36.00	36.85
Savings credit threshold		
single person	140.67	144.38
couple	223.82	229.67
Maximum savings credit		
single person	13.40	13.72
couple	14.99	15.35

NEW TAX CREDIT AND BENEFIT RATES 2019–2020

(Benefits covered in Volume IV)

	2018–19	2019–20
	£ pw	£ pw
Benefits in respect of children		
Child benefit		
only, elder or eldest child (couple)	20.70	20.70
each subsequent child	13.70	13.70
Guardian's allowance	17.20	17.60
Employer-paid benefits		
Standard rates		
Statutory sick pay	92.05	94.25
Statutory maternity pay, Statutory paternity pay	145.18	148.68
Statutory shared parental pay	145.18	148.68
Statutory adoption pay	145.18	148.68
Income threshold	116.00	118.00

	2018–19	2019–20
	£ pa	£ pa
Working tax credit		
Basic element	1,960	1,960
Couple and lone parent element	2,010	2,010
30 hour element	810	810
Disabled worker element	3,090	3,165
Severe disability element	1,330	1,365
Child care element		
maximum eligible cost for one child	*175 pw*	*175 pw*
maximum eligible cost for two or more		
children	*300 pw*	*300 pw*
per cent of eligible costs covered	*70%*	*70%*
Child tax credit		
Family element	545	545
Child element	2,780	2,780
Disabled child element	3,275	3,355
Severely disabled child element	4,600	4,715
Tax credit income thresholds		
Income rise disregard	2,500	2,500
Income fall disregard	2,500	2,500
Income threshold	6,420	6,420
Income threshold for those entitled to child tax		
credit only	16,105	16,105
Withdrawal rate	*41%*	*41%*

NEW UNIVERSAL CREDIT RATES FROM APRIL 2019

(Benefits covered in Volume V)

	April 2018	April 2019
	£ pm	£ pm
Standard allowances		
Single claimant—*aged under 25*	251.77	251.77
aged 25 or over	317.82	317.82
Joint claimant—*both aged under 25*	395.20	395.20
one or both aged 25 or over	498.89	498.89
Child element—*first child*	277.08	277.08
second/ subsequent child	231.67	231.67
Disabled child addition—*lower rate*	126.11	126.11
higher rate	383.86	392.08
Limited Capability for Work element	126.11	126.11
Limited Capability for Work and Work-Related Activity element	328.32	336.20
Carer element	156.45	160.20
Childcare element—*maximum for one child*	646.35	646.35
maximum for two or more children	1,108.04	1,108.04
Non-dependants' housing cost contributions	72.16	73.89
Work allowances		
Higher work allowance (no housing element)		
one or more children	409.00	503.00
limited capability for work	409.00	503.00
Lower work allowance		
one or more children	198.00	287.00
limited capability for work	198.00	287.00